Jewish on Their Own Terms

Jewish on Their Own Terms

How Intermarried Couples Are Changing American Judaism

JENNIFER A. THOMPSON

RUTGERS UNIVERSITY PRESS

NEW BRUNSWICK, NEW JERSEY, AND LONDON

Library of Congress Cataloging-in-Publication Data
Thompson, Jennifer A. 1976–
    Jewish on their own terms : how intermarried couples are changing American
Judaism / Jennifer Thompson
        pages cm
    Includes bibliographical references and index.
    ISBN 978–0-8135–6282–7 (hardcover : alk. paper)—ISBN 978–0-8135–6281–0
(pbk. : alk. paper)—ISBN 978–0-8135–6283–4
    1. Interfaith marriage—United States. 2. Intermarriage—United States. 3. Jews—
United States—Identity. 4. Marriage—Religious aspects—Judaism. 5. Jews—United
States—Cultural assimilation. 6. Judaism—United States—21st century. I. Title
    HQ1031.T46 2014
    305.892'4073—dc23

                                                                    2013010366

            A British Cataloging-in-Publication record for this book is available
                            from the British Library.

                Visit our website: http://rutgerspress.rutgers.edu

                    Manufactured in the United States of America

For Suzette Cohen, to whom so many Jewish families are grateful

CONTENTS

ACKNOWLEDGMENTS

During the nine years I spent working on the research and writing of this book, I received help from many sources. I want to express my sincere gratitude to the many people who made this project possible.

My work has been shaped in important ways by the mentoring and guidance of Don Seeman, Eric Goldstein, Gary Laderman, Bradd Shore, Steve Tipton, Nancy Eiesland, and Bruce Phillips. Other colleagues and friends who offered suggestions and encouragement include Wesley Barker, Michael Berger, Kent Brintnall, Brad Crowell, Steve Edelman-Blank, Bob Fallon, Rokhl Kafrissen, Leah Kalmanson, Keren McGinity, Samira Mehta, Laurie Patton, Marina Rustow, Heidi Tauscher, Lawrence Weinberg, Kate Wilkinson, Niki Whiting, and Leah Wolfson. Arnold Dashefsky introduced me to the sociological study of intermarriage. Jennifer Harvey and Jennifer McCrickerd helped me develop the experientially focused pedagogy that informs the afterword of this book. The courage and creativity of my colleagues in the 2012 Seminar on Debates about Religion and Sexuality at Harvard Divinity School—Jeff Chu, Zach Corleissen, Hannah Hofheinz, Mark Jordan, A. J. Lewis, E. L. Kornegay, Jr., Jennifer Leath, Darnell Moore, Daniel Sander, Evren Savci, Zachary Rodriguez, and Farah Zeb—provided just the inspiration I needed to finish the book. I am grateful to them all.

I also appreciate the always-prompt helpfulness of Peter Mickulas, my editor at Rutgers University Press, and the incisive and thoughtful comments on the manuscript that he offered, along with those of Deborah Dash Moore and an anonymous reviewer. Ulrike Guthrie also offered keen editorial insight as I completed the manuscript, and copy editors Dawn Potter and Rebecca Vogan provided fine tuning. Thanks also to the Association for Jewish Studies, along with Emory University's Tam Institute for Jewish Studies and Center for Myth and Ritual in American Life (a Sloan Center on Working Families), which have enabled me to present my work to other scholars and learn from them.

Generous financial support from a number of sources made my research and writing possible. At Emory University, the Laney Graduate School, the Graduate Division of Religion, the Tam Institute for Jewish Studies, and the Center for Myth and Ritual in American Life supported me as I conducted the majority of the research for this book. Travel grants from the Association for Jewish Studies helped me to attend several annual meetings. The support of the Maurice Amado Foundation and California State University, Northridge, enabled me to complete the book.

I also deeply appreciate the personal support I have received in completing this project. Without Bernadette Brooten's practical and imaginative mentoring, I would not have attempted this project in the first place. Jody Myers, Rick Talbott, Cheryl Spector, Amanda Baugh, and Claire White, my colleagues at California State University, Northridge, have also provided encouragement. My friends Heidi Tauscher, Wylin Dassie, and Andrea Greco provided moral support as well as fantastic home-cooked dinners as I labored over the dissertation version of this book. My parents, Ralph and Rita Thompson, and my sisters, Liz Thompson and Valerie Thompson, made sure that I persevered. My husband, Jeff Carr, single-handedly kept our house from falling down, and our son, Sam Thompson-Carr, was the best infant research assistant I have ever encountered. Thanks to all of them.

Lastly, I owe especially heartfelt thanks to the many men and women who shared their experiences with me. I regret that I cannot name each of them here, but I hope that I have done justice to them.

Jewish on Their Own Terms

Introduction

It's not enough," said Abe in a pained voice. His daughter had married a non-Jew. While Abe, an active member of a Conservative synagogue, hoped that she and her husband would become actively involved in organized Jewish activities, he did not have a great deal of hope that his descendants would carry on Jewishness. He asserted that the number of intermarried couples raising Jewish children was insufficient to prevent Judaism from dying out entirely. Abe participates in religious services and also serves on committees that perform the work of the synagogue—teaching, organizing, brainstorming, managing its financial affairs. He has made clear his commitment to Judaism with both time and treasure. But Abe believes that intermarriage will ultimately lead to the decline of Judaism. His conversations with other Jews and the Jewish books, magazines, newspapers, and websites that he reads reflect this view; it is common wisdom among many American Jews.

Yet as I learned from eight years of ethnographic fieldwork, common wisdom about intermarriage does not correspond to the lived experiences of intermarried Jews and their families, many of whom value the same traditions and ideas that Abe and other in-married (endogamous) Jews do. Why, then, is this (incorrect) common wisdom about intermarriage such a prominent part of American Jews' conversation in public media, between pulpit and congregation, and among individual Jews? This book answers that question.

Intermarriage in Public Discourse

The July 2010 wedding of former First Daughter Chelsea Clinton, a Methodist, to Marc Mezvinsky, a Jew, elicited a great deal of commentary in both the Jewish press and American media outlets more generally that reflected common

wisdom about intermarriage. Few, if any, of these news items relied upon interviews with Clinton or her husband, but their individual views would have made
little difference in the Jewish public discourse surrounding their marriage. Various authors and interviewees complained that the wedding had been held on
a Saturday, the Jewish sabbath, which is contrary to Jewish law; that a Reform
rabbi had co-officiated the wedding with a Methodist minister, a practice with
which many rabbis disagree; and that the couple's home and children were
unlikely to be Jewish, a prediction based upon statistics about American Jewry.
For sociologists Steven M. Cohen and Leonard Saxe and Reform movement president Eric Yoffie, the Clinton-Mezvinsky marriage demonstrated the degree to
which American Jews have achieved acceptance and integration into American
society. For Cohen, it also pointed to the steep price of such acceptance—the
prospect that Jewish men who marry Christian women may not raise their children as Jews, thus ending their families' Jewish lineage. Yoffie underscored that
raising children in only one religion, preferably Judaism, was vital. Other commentators suggested welcoming the couple into Judaism without hesitation and
viewed the Jewish elements of their wedding as signs that they wished to identify with Judaism (Berkman 2010). Jewish media had hosted such discussions
well before the Clinton-Mezvinsky wedding. This particular instance was simply
a novel occasion on which to rehash the same points of view that had already
been aired many times.

These viewpoints reflect a long history of sociological study of intermarriage
that began in the late nineteenth century and became part of public conversation among Jews in the mid-twentieth century. Such sociological study took
up questions about Jews' assimilation into the broader societies in which they
lived. Enormous political, social, and religious changes had been taking place,
raising deep and unsettling questions about how and why Jews could remain
different from non-Jews while also being integrated into non-Jewish society. A
2010 study found that Jews were the most broadly popular group in America
(Putnam and Campbell 2010), suggesting that they no longer needed to band
together as strongly against antisemitism as they had in the past. But what distinguished Jews from non-Jews if not external constraints such as antisemitism?

Conversation about intermarriage in American Judaism is a way of working out these questions. Common wisdom, as exemplified by Abe's comments,
equates intermarriage with individualism and assimilation. This presumed
equivalence relies on a narrative that portrays intermarrying Jews as disloyal to
the Jewish people, ignorant of their Jewish heritage, rebellious against their parents, and often choosing to break their ties to other Jews as well as to monolithic
concepts of Jewish tradition and Jewish community. This portrayal attributes
individualism specifically to intermarried couples as if endogamous Jews were
immune from it. Often, it depicts intermarried couples as clearly distinct from

in-married Jews, with divided loyalties and ineffectual transmission of Jewishness to their children. Each day, a Google News alert delivers to my email inbox articles from the United States and Israel in which intermarriage is invoked as shorthand for assimilation and Jewish communal dissolution. As chapter 1 discusses, such images have been recycled for decades, even though they bear little relationship to the lives of actual intermarried couples.

My ethnographic research shows that many intermarried couples experience Jewishness in nearly the same ways that endogamous, or in-married, couples do. Yet discourse about intermarriage typically constructs opposing categories of in-married and intermarried. The experiences of intermarried Jews and their families are not necessarily reflected in such categories. Rather, American Jews are using intermarriage to "think with," a concept that anthropologist Claude Lévi-Strauss (1968) advanced in the context of his study of totemism.

"Thinking with" Intermarriage

Given the frequency with which comments like Abe's are repeated in American Jewish media and in many American Jewish communities, one might expect to find significant differences between his perspective on Judaism and intermarriage and that of intermarried Jewish-Christian couples themselves. But the intermarried couples I interviewed and with whom I spent time as a participant-observer (and to whom I refer in this book as my informants, following anthropological convention) cared deeply about carrying on Jewishness in their families and through their descendants, just as Abe does. One Jewish man told me that he simply could not raise his child in his wife's Catholicism: "I felt like I would be forever alienated from my kid if he was in the Savior mode and I wasn't." Both Christian and Jewish spouses wanted their children to feel Jewish, out of respect for Jewish worries about population decline, reverence for those lost in the Holocaust, and love for what some of them called "strong traditions." The ways in which these couples understand their religious lives and their relationships to Judaism and Jewish communities reveal much about the paradoxes of modern American Jewishness for intermarried as well as endogamous Jews.

But even as similarities between intermarried and endogamous Jews exist, and even though scholars have created a much more complex picture of intermarriage than Abe imagines, common-wisdom portrayals of intermarriage as an assimilationist threat persist in American Jewish conversations. Why do these portrayals have such staying power? What are the realities that they obscure? And what are the consequences of ignoring the realities in favor of preserving the common wisdom?

With more than half of all Jewish children being raised in households with one Jewish and one non-Jewish parent, we can expect intermarried couples and their families to have a tremendous impact on American Judaism as it is lived and practiced by average American Jews.[1] The title of this book, *Jewish on Their Own Terms: How Intermarried Couples Are Changing American Judaism*, recognizes that American Jews are thinking about issues of assimilation and the nature of Jewishness itself through the topic of intermarriage. One result of "thinking with" intermarriage has been the broadening of Jewish institutions' efforts to do "outreach," which I discuss later, from an initially narrow focus on intermarried couples to a broader one that includes converts to Judaism (often called "Jews by Choice") and people of color. Such institutions are acknowledging a more diverse Jewish population than dominant cultural narratives about assimilation have generally recognized. By forcing the Jewish community to think about inclusion more broadly, intermarried Jews are gradually changing American Judaism.

Instead of focusing on narrow and overdetermined questions such as "what's good for the Jews?" I have turned to ethnography, or cultural analysis built on participant-observation, to describe the compelling concerns of contemporary intermarried couples themselves. This approach also lifts debates concerning intermarriage out of the narrow context of American Jewish continuity (a concept that I examine throughout the book) and into the sphere of American religion more generally. Lived experience comprises the conflicts and contradictions that intermarried Jews and their families, along with Jewish educators and rabbis, face on a daily basis. They respond to reified discourses about intermarriage and what it means to be a good Jew from their larger contexts of American religious culture and morality. By focusing on these individuals' choices as well as the constraints of institutions and discourses, we arrive at a more nuanced picture, revealing that people's actions are rarely motivated by a single belief or desire but often take place amid contradictory views and mixed motives.

Focusing on lived experience calls into question not just the opposing categories of in-married and intermarried but also the predominant scholarly focus on ethnicity as the most salient analytic category for the study of intermarriage. Sociology understands intermarriage to be a key part of the assimilation process as ethnic immigrants become integrated into their new societies. This theoretical approach has dominated much of American Jews' conversation about intermarriage on both scholarly and popular levels. Understanding American Jews primarily through the lens of ethnicity supports the "decline" narrative. Steven M. Cohen (2006) argues in *A Tale of Two Jewries: The "Inconvenient Truth" for American Jews* that ethnicity is precisely "the social tissue that ties Jews together." As he defines it, ethnicity includes Jews' feelings of a shared destiny and of special responsibility for one another and Israel, along with their participation in Jewish institutions and contributions to Jewish causes. Based on responses to survey questions about these matters and membership in ethnic organizations such as Hadassah, Cohen found a decline in ethnic cohesion among Jews and predicted further decline in years to come. He acknowledges that religious activities, including synagogue membership and engagement in Jewish education, have continued apace; but he undercuts the importance of such activity by pointing out that, while the Bible refers to Jews as a people and a nation, it never uses the term religion (5–7).

The notion of Judaism as a religion is modern, a product of the Enlightenment and Protestant Christianity (Batnitzky 2011), as I will detail later. But it is a notion with which contemporary American Jews have grown up. While sociologists may view religion and ethnicity as distinct categories, and a distinct set of sociological theory has accumulated around each category, my informants did not experience them as separate. Rather, they saw religion and ethnicity as part of the same continuum. The lack of a sociological concept that captures or expresses the wholeness of this continuum points to the paucity of our contemporary language, not to deficiencies in American Jews' lived experiences.

Sociologist Emile Durkheim's ([1912] 1995) definition of religion in *The Elementary Forms of Religious Life* brings into focus elements of what we now consider to be ethnicity as well as what we might typically call religion. He includes under the umbrella of religion "beliefs and practices which unite into one single moral community called a Church, all those who adhere to them" (xxxiv). This definition encompasses a continuum of lived experience under the framework of what we might call a "People" instead of the Christian-centric "Church."

I draw on Durkheim's understanding of religion as a broad continuum of moral and social experience, and the ethnography I present here aligns well with this understanding. At the same time, this book also builds on narrower sociological theories about religion, such as secularization theory's thesis of the transformation of religious authority in the modern world. Intermarriage is an excellent lens through which to explore this transformation because it has been at the heart of questions about Jewish adaptation to secular social settings since the late 1700s, when the United States and western European countries began to grant Jews citizenship. The fact that intermarriage and assimilation remain deeply controversial in American Jewish discourses shows that these questions of adaptation have not been resolved, even though Jews face no legal and few social obstacles to full participation in American society. In that sense, the lack of change in intermarriage discourse, despite Jewish integration into society, helps us to extend our understanding of religious change under secularization: even as change happens on the ground, dominant cultural narratives help to preserve religious norms and demand conformity to them. At the same time, people find creative ways to conform. Ethnography of lived religion provides the depth needed to discern how creativity, individuality, and conformity interact as religion changes through secularization.

By investigating how American Jews are ultimately concerned with religious authority, I step back from some of the matters that dominate many studies of Jewish intermarriage, such as demographic projections about the makeup of the Jewish community, ways in which intermarriage harms traditional conceptions of Jewish unity, and intermarrying Jews' connection, or lack thereof, to Jewish communities. Instead, I argue that intermarried Jews serve a symbolic function, allowing American Jews to discuss their anxieties about a perceived loss of Jewish distinctiveness amid their success in assimilating into American culture. By projecting these anxieties onto intermarried Jews, other American Jews can express them without having to recognize that they face the same challenges themselves.

In providing ethnographic description of the complex ways in which individual and social experiences intertwine and conflict, this book also contributes to Jewish policy-oriented literature by departing from the quantitative studies that dominate the field. While surveys can include a much larger number of participants than ethnography can, ethnography allows dialogue and can encourage informants' concerns and interests to emerge more holistically and organically. Some intermarried couples themselves have said that they do not feel that existing studies accurately represent them. "I think that researchers who have looked at intermarriage have often framed their studies and interpretations based on their own preconceived ideas," said one woman. "I think it is usually clear that the researchers did not start with a positive view of intermarriage, so it is not surprising that their conclusions support the negative views they started with."[2] I do not mean to suggest that ethnographers are exempt from constraints on their research. They simply face different ones, as I will explain later.

My informants often see these debates among policymakers and scholars as largely irrelevant to their daily lives even though they are troubled by the judgments that they perceive in them. Noticing this gap between discourse and lived experience was what led me to study intermarriage in American Judaism. From 2003 to 2005, I worked in Atlanta, the eleventh-largest Jewish community in the United States, as an interviewer for a sociological study on intermarriage sponsored by the Susan and David Wilstein Institute of Jewish Policy Studies (now the National Center for Jewish Policy Studies). The study sought to understand the communication between intermarried couples and American Jewish community organizations. Using a series of questions given to me by the principal investigators, I conducted thirty-six individual interviews, each lasting between forty-five minutes and an hour and a half, with intermarried Jews and their spouses. In these interviews, informants described the religious aspects of their upbringing, their experiences with rabbis and synagogues, how they raised or would raise their children, sources of tension in their marriages, and their ways of resolving it. Informants, particularly the non-Jewish women, often told me that they were happy that this study was being done and that they felt that they had much to contribute to the Jewish community if it would accept them.

But even though the informants appreciated the study, they found some of the interview questions strange. Responding to a question about their needs as intermarried couples, many said only that they wanted to feel welcome in Jewish organizations. They hoped for educational opportunities that were free of judgment and that did not pressure the non-Jewish partner to convert to Judaism. Others saw this question as odd: why would their needs differ from anyone else's? Some of the men answered the question in a sarcastically literal way, saying that their needs were food, water, shelter, and clothing.

In order to understand intermarried couples' experiences, particularly their relationship to debates about intermarriage and Jewish communities, I conducted open-ended interviews and participant-observation from 2004 to 2010. I interviewed more than fifty Jews and non-Jews affected by intermarriage, including members of intermarried and endogamous couples, rabbis, and Jewish educators. This work took place primarily in the Atlanta area, which is an especially robust setting in which to study intermarriage. Nearly 70 percent of Atlanta Jews' marriages since 1990 have been intermarriages (Ukeles Associates 2007), though the national average lies between 40 and 50 percent. My intermarried informants were in the majority among their cohort, even though they are regarded as outsiders because of their intermarriage.

With so many intermarried couples in Atlanta, an infrastructure of community organizations has arisen to support them. I became well acquainted with a specific one: the Mothers Circle. Between March 2006 and April 2008, I spent many Sunday mornings and some Friday and Saturday nights with its members. An educational support group for non-Jewish women raising Jewish children, the Mothers Circle began as a pilot program in the Atlanta Jewish community in the early 2000s. Through the work of the Jewish Outreach Institute, it later spread to many more U.S. cities, each of which uses its own local funding sources to pay Mothers Circle facilitators and coordinators. I also attended events sponsored by Pathways, an Atlanta Jewish community organization that does outreach to intermarried couples with free classes about Judaism and celebrations of Jewish holidays. I met many intermarried couples through these groups and events and also spent time with them informally in their homes. In these contexts, I participated along with my informants in both planned activities and informal conversation, brought my non-Jewish husband and Jewish son along to family events, and shared my experiences (which I will explain later) with informants as they shared theirs with me.

In addition to the strong non-rabbinic organizations focused on intermarriage in Atlanta, I learned that rabbis in the area interacted with intermarried couples on an individual basis. Some rabbis participated in Pathways events. But one rabbi told me that, even on a matter as basic as identifying which local rabbis officiate at interfaith weddings, the only information available came "through the grapevine." Between August 2005 and June 2008, I conducted interviews, each of which lasted between thirty minutes and an hour and a half, with thirteen Atlanta Orthodox, Reform, Reconstructionist, and Conservative rabbis and Jewish educators.

Along with my work in Atlanta, I ventured to Washington, D.C., to participate in and observe two conferences. In January 2006, I spent three days at a conference sponsored by the Dovetail Institute for Interfaith Family Resources in Bethesda, Maryland, to learn about one influential approach to intermarried family life. This organization emphasizes that "there are no definitive answers to the questions facing interfaith families," as its publication, *Dovetail: A Journal by and for Jewish/Christian Families*, explains. In October 2007, I spent two days at the Jewish Outreach Institute conference for Jewish educators from all over the United States who hope to reach intermarried couples through educational programs.

In 2010, I moved with my family to Des Moines, Iowa, where I continued to talk about intermarriage and Jewishness with local rabbis, intermarried Jews, and endogamous Jews. Des Moines is a setting quite different from the others in that its Jewish community is much smaller and offers a less extensive infrastructure of Jewish organizations. Focusing on cities such as Atlanta and Des Moines, with scattered Jewish populations and cultural contexts quite different from the more concentrated Jewish populations in the Northeast and the large cities of the West Coast, allowed me to talk with intermarried couples who could not depend on a heavily Jewish environment to shape their family's Jewish choices. Taken together, these field settings both overlap with and diverge from the settings of other research on intermarriage.

While the small and nonrandom sample that I analyze in this study does not allow me to generalize to say that all (or *n* percent of) intermarried couples understand themselves according to the models that I present, unlike many of the more numbers-driven studies about intermarriage, it does offer opportunities to delve into the cultural contradictions that are less evident in numbers-driven studies. This ethnography uses the compelling concerns of my informants as the starting point rather than beginning with a research question framed according to Jewish institutional policy questions or other external concerns. An ethnographer inevitably does privilege his or her own analytic concerns over those of the informants merely by authoring the descriptions of the informants' lives. But by starting from the informants' own experiences and self-understandings, I hope to balance more evenly the power dynamics between ethnographer and informant and to represent my informants with integrity, particularly since depictions of intermarried couples have often been objectifying. Starting from my informants' concerns pointed me right back to important sociological and anthropological questions about how we understand meaning and moral experience in modern society. The self-understandings, pressures, and conflicts that my informants experience resonate with important cultural themes, including secularization, identified by sociologists of American religion and historians and sociologists of American Judaism.

Analysis starting from ethnographic observation of the experiences of contemporary intermarried Jews, lived in both Jewish and American cultural contexts, is missing from the existing literature. Sociologist Sylvia Barack Fishman, in her well-received *Double or Nothing? Jewish Families and Mixed Marriage* (2004), uses qualitative methods to engage with intermarried couples, seeking to illuminate issues such as "the impact of mixed marriage on Jews and Judaism" (jacket copy). She voices concern that American openness to Jews might lead to the dissolution of a distinctive Jewish culture in the United States. Fishman and I share interest in some themes and specific organizations, and our informants' comments are strikingly similar. However, our questions, methods, and goals differ and yield divergent results. Fishman analyzes data from focus groups, interviews, and media studies in the context of literature on ethnicity and ethnic boundaries. I focus on a smaller sample of informants in order to identify dimensions of the experience of intermarriage that elude focus groups and questionnaires: What are the systems of meaning in which intermarried Jews live—not just Jewish ones but also American ones? How do those cultural patterns shape the specificity of individual experience as it unfolds amid the multiple discourses about intermarriage? How do those informants' self-understandings incorporate and pass beyond "meaning"? Fishman and I arrive at different conclusions about our informants, even though there is overlap in our informants' responses, because we start from different questions and employ different methodologies.

Another well-received book-length qualitative study of intermarriage, Keren McGinity's *Still Jewish: A History of Women and Intermarriage in America* (2009), begins with questions about meaning. McGinity examines the meanings that twentieth-century Jewish women attached to intermarriage and how their self-understandings as Jews changed over time in tandem with broader cultural and social changes in the United States. Data gathered through oral history and archival research support a more deeply contextualized reading of her subjects' intermarriages that draws upon the subjects' own lives as well as the social and cultural worlds that they inhabit. McGinity's findings call into question some longstanding conclusions about intermarriage, such as the claim that religious differences contribute to a greater likelihood of divorce (which I will discuss in chapter 1). Her study also exemplifies how research questions and methods directly shape a study's conclusions.

Ethnography extends our understanding of the contexts in which informants live by involving informants' social worlds more directly. While meaning frequently occupies qualitative social scientists' attention, meaning is not necessarily the principal feature of our lives. Social scientists attend to meaning because they are trained to use it as their primary interpretive frame (Seeman 2004). But as anthropologist Don Seeman argues, interpreting the meaning of our informants' lives is a way of imposing a coherence that does not necessarily reflect their experiences. "Meaning," anthropologist Arthur Kleinman (1997) writes, "is understood as a cognitive response to the challenge of coherence" and "places greater value on 'knowing the world' . . . than on inhabiting, acting in, or wrestling with the world" (320). In addition, researchers' focus on meaning tends to overemphasize the thoughts and feelings of the individual, regarded as the ultimate arbiter of meaning. I argue that while meaning is a significant part of my informants' experience of Jewishness, other elements of their lives that they are less readily able to articulate remain extremely important for them. Moral experience, for my informants, comprises the claims of family, culture, religion, and self.

A numbers-driven study of the Atlanta Jewish population in 2006, commissioned by the Atlanta Jewish Federation, helps to contextualize my informants' self-understandings. For example, of the Atlanta intermarried households with children, 39 percent are raising them as Jewish only, 15 percent as Jewish and "something else." These families' choices to raise children in Judaism seem striking because in Atlanta, with its relatively large population of evangelical Protestants and megachurches, raising children only in Christianity might be easier. However, according to many of my informants, living in the South raises their awareness of their Jewishness. One Jewish woman who had grown up in the South told me that, in high school, she regularly found notes from classmates in her locker informing her that she was bound for Hell because she was Jewish. A Christian woman married to a Jewish man, both of them from the Northeast, told me that they had made a point of joining a synagogue in Atlanta because of the pressure that their children's evangelical Christian friends put on them to attend their church. While they would not have felt such urgency about synagogue membership in the Northeast, she said, in Atlanta they felt that they needed to provide their children with their own religious community. Thus, when this 2006 study reports that substantial portions of the population that includes my informants agreed that it was "very important" to be Jewish (Ukeles Associates 2007), my informants' stories add depth and context, explaining why it might be so important to be Jewish.

No other book in this field has started from contemporary intermarried couples' perspectives and experiences rather than from policy questions reflecting Jewish organizations' priorities. This book is meant to provoke critical thinking for several audiences in different ways. First, it offers students and scholars of religion, Jewish studies, gender studies, and social science insight into how research questions and methods matter. The experience-near ethnographic frame that I apply shifts both the questions and the answers when compared with the quantitative and even other qualitative methods that have been applied to the topic of intermarriage. Simply choosing a different methodological and analytic starting point moves this book away from previous research on the topic of Jewish intermarriage. For example, my informants' experiences made clear that previous studies have underestimated the significance of the broader context of American religion. Previous research based on questions about the policy agendas of Jewish institutions instead has relied on sociological theories about ethnicity that have rendered a shallow picture of the experiences of intermarried couples. This ethnographic account offers insight into the processes of religious change and cultural assimilation in everyday life and the interaction of religious norms and personal choice in lived experience. By drawing our attention to important overlaps with American religion and other areas of study, the ethnography of Jews and Judaism opens up new questions in Jewish studies, complementing the more dominant approaches of historical and quantitative research. Contemporary Jews understand themselves and interact with their social, cultural, and moral lifeworlds in ways both continuous with and distinct from historical modes. Understanding contemporary Jews' sense of being in the world requires the depth of the ethnographic approach, even as survey research helps to situate ethnographic findings within the context of a larger population.

Second, this book is meant to speak directly to intermarried couples and their families. I hope that they will find in it a portrayal of their concerns and experiences that is accurate and dignified. Perhaps they will also gain insight into the ways in which discourses about intermarriage, laden with judgments about "good" and "bad" Jews, affect their choices and self-understandings in ways that they had not recognized. Experience-near ethnography necessarily involves portraying the experiences of my particular informants rather than making generalizations about all intermarried Jews. While no ethnography can hope to resonate with every reader in every way, I hope that readers will find my portrayals of my informants to be fair.

This book is also for those who are concerned about American Judaism and want it to enjoy a healthy and vibrant future—a desire that I share. I recognize that this book addresses a controversial topic and that some readers may be distressed at its deconstruction of categories and concepts upon which much of American Jewish life has been built. I hope that my study can contribute in a positive way to the policy debates that I describe. Intermarriage may be an important issue for the future of Judaism, but recycling inaccurate images of intermarried Jews and their families does not help to ensure that Judaism will have a future.

My central concern goes beyond particular policy debates, however. As I argue throughout the book, American Jews "think with" intermarriage. More is at stake in intermarriage discourse than is directly acknowledged: questions of the nature of Jewishness, the ties that bind Jews together in a free society, and the language that contemporary Jews may use to describe their commitments and experience need much more sustained and direct attention than they have received. These questions are more expansive than debate about intermarriage allows, and they affect a greater number of Jews than such debate lets on. The exploration of these questions does not necessarily have to lead to the kind of openness to intermarriage depicted in chapter 2's description of the Dovetail Institute for Interfaith Family Resources. But it does require that we move beyond debate that focuses simply on the boundary-crossing practices of intermarriage and address more directly a question that sociologist of American Judaism Marshall Sklare raised in 1964: "What do you stand for when you wish to remain separate?" (52). And we need to ask not only what we stand for, but who we are.

Ideas sometimes substitute for direct knowledge gained through experience (Lippmann [1922] 1997). At its best, social science can help us see this gap between the world of ideas and the world of lived experience and begin to make our understanding of society more realistic. The gap between intermarriage as it is portrayed in discourses and as it is lived by intermarried Jews has consequences for real people's lives. Intermarried Jews, the subject of intense scrutiny for decades, serve as symbols of American Jews' fears of assimilation even as real intermarried human beings live their lives, attempting to fit into a community that is ambivalent about them or walking away from it. Studying the gap between discourse and lived experience can help illuminate how and why such disjunctures happen—how they can be ways of working out widespread cultural anxieties through specific figures—and may be able to help us imagine our way out of such gaps too. As I will suggest in the afterword, one way forward may be to create opportunities for Jews from different backgrounds to develop personal relationships with one another. Not only might such personal contact help to moderate some of the vitriol in intermarriage discourse, but it might also begin to supply answers to the larger existential questions about the nature of Jews' ties to one another.

Talking like Americans, Talking like Jews

At a pub in Des Moines, I celebrated my birthday with two new Jewish friends, Heather and Kimberly. All three of our birthdays fell within the same week, and we seized this opportunity to let our husbands take care of our small children while we shared uninterrupted conversation for a couple of hours. The three of us attended the same synagogue that Abe did. Heather and Kimberly both have Jewish husbands. For a while, our talk focused on Judaism. Even though I was a graduate student in religion at the time, I had not initiated this line of conversation; it emerged spontaneously.

Heather said, "Judaism should be whatever I think is meaningful. To me. I decide what rituals I'm going to do, and I decide what they mean."

Kimberly agreed, giving an example. "In my household, we keep kosher—we only buy meat that was raised humanely, that had a happy life. It may not have the *hechsher* [certification of being kosher], but officially kosher meat may not be humanely raised anyway. This is about caring for animals, and there's definitely a basis in Judaism for keeping kosher this way." Still, she acknowledged that her view was unorthodox. "I tell people that we keep kosher, but if we were having the rabbi over to our house, I would explain to him what we mean by 'kosher' since it's probably not what he expects." Kimberly drew a straight line between her personal convictions and Jewish values about the treatment of animals. As Heather had explained, commitment to Jewish rituals mattered, but the terms of that commitment she and Kimberly managed on an individual basis.

The fact that we were talking about the meaning of Judaism over a weeknight birthday dinner at a pub marked this conversation as Jewish, not something that you'd expect to hear at just any dinner table in America. Nevertheless, I was struck by how deeply American it was as well. As Conservative Jews, we were in theory committed to Jewish law and normative interpretations of it. Redefining *kashrut*, or the laws concerning kosher food, and observing Jewish ritual according to personal preference rather than God's commandments would not be considered legitimate interpretations of Jewish law by many observant Jews. But in the context of American ways of talking about morality and religion, these interpretations made sense. Dominant American moral and religious discourses emphasize the autonomy of individuals, even as actual individuals find that such language encompasses only some of their experiences and that it fails to capture their deeply held commitments to interests greater than themselves. As my conversation with Heather and Kimberly shows, and as the work of Steven M. Cohen and Arnold M. Eisen (2000) also shows, American Jews who are firmly situated within normative Jewish communities and who see themselves as continuing normative Jewish practices use this individualistic language.

These individualistic strands of American culture conflict with vague, monolithic conceptions of Jewish tradition, community, continuity, and identity. Both academic and popular discourses about intermarriage use these terms as if they were universally understood. Even the meaning of intermarriage itself is muddy in these conversations. Sociologist Bruce Phillips, professor of Jewish Communal Service at Hebrew Union College–Jewish Institute of Religion in Los

Angeles, recognized that the word intermarriage means different things in different contexts. In 1997, he published a typology of intermarried couples to help achieve greater specificity in conversations about intermarriage: Judaic mixed marriages, dual religion, interfaithless, Christo-centric, Judaeo-Christian, and Christian. These categories he named to identify couples' religious practices and identities, with the understanding that there is a wide range of possibilities (Phillips 1997). His terminology does not often appear in popular discourses, even though policymakers and scholars may have it in mind when they discuss intermarriage among themselves.

This muddiness in terminology contributes to the longevity of the intermarriage-as-assimilation narrative. Scholarly findings about intermarriage have not been uniform by any means, but they have yielded a more complex picture than is reflected in local conversations among Jews, both intermarried and in-married, and in media discourses. Even as a great deal of energy and money is invested in encouraging intermarried couples to deepen their involvement with Jewish institutions, the cultural shorthand used in media discourses and many local conversations (such as the one I described with Abe, in which intermarriage means "assimilation") directly and powerfully undercuts the work of Jewish outreach. My informants recognize in this narrative a way of speaking about intermarriage that does not reflect their reality. Being part of a local Jewish community in which these discourses are present, even if not dominant, raises their awareness of being both insiders and outsiders simultaneously. Using this cultural shorthand undermines the goals of bringing more intermarried couples into Jewish institutions.

As Kimberly's and Heather's comments show, contemporary Jews disagree about the content of Jewish tradition. I discovered no consensus on precise definitions for any of these seemingly monolithic concepts of Jewish tradition, community, identity, or continuity among my informants; and the historical record further discounts the idea of a monolithic tradition, as Jews have debated these concepts for centuries. Even though these terms frequently appear in American Jewish media accounts as well as private conversations among Jews, investigating them reveals a lack of consensus about their meaning among contemporary American Jews.

Nonetheless, my intermarried informants often felt that Jewish tradition and Jewish community were concrete entities that had the power to sanction them as "good" or "bad" Jews, loyal or disloyal to Judaism, transmitters of Jewishness to the next generation or weak links in the chain. My informants often did not realize that these conceptions of Jewish tradition and Jewish community deny the conflict and variety in contemporary and historical Jewish experience and that discourses that invoke these terms rely on the terms' power to encourage conformity to the norms that they imply. My intermarried informants talked about Jewishness and moral commitment as endogamous Jews do, which is surprising because American Jewish discourses about intermarriage suggest exactly the opposite.

Dominant cultural narratives about intermarriage as assimilation deflect attention from the similarities between intermarried and endogamous Jews, and they do so for an important reason. The voluntaristic, pluralistic setting of the contemporary United States makes it difficult to reach consensus about the meaning and nature of Jewishness. Equating assimilation with intermarriage allows the illusion of consensus by denying the influence of voluntarism and pluralism over all American Jews, instead attributing individualism and assimilation primarily to intermarried couples. This narrative relieves endogamous Jews from anxiety about the meaning and nature of their own Jewishness. As often as this narrative is repeated in American Jewish media and local communities, it frequently meets resistance from Jews who argue that intermarriage does not necessarily signify assimilation. In this way, intermarriage discourse is a proxy for working out anxieties and meanings attached to assimilation and Jewishness for American Jews in general, without pressing them to claim those anxieties and meanings for themselves.

American Jews are not the only ones asking questions about the meaning and nature of moral experience and communal belonging. The sociology of religion asks exactly these questions about Americans in general, most thoroughly in Robert Bellah and his colleagues' *Habits of the Heart* (1985). The tensions of individualism and belonging with which my informants contend resonate with those experienced by white, middle-class, native-born Americans (Bellah et al. 1985; Madsen 2009) and "moderately affiliated" American Jews, whether or not they are intermarried (Cohen and Eisen 2000). That my informants' experiences are similar to those of other white, middle-class, native-born Americans generally and to those of endogamous American Jews specifically points to the significance of the contexts of American religion and American Judaism. Recent sociological literature on lived religion and secularization has continued to explore these tensions of autonomy and obligation. Historical processes of secularization in our increasingly complex society have led us to understand religion as a private, personal matter. This transformation in how we understand religious authority supports our American cultural emphasis on the language of individualism, even though this language is unable to capture our deeply felt attachments to community, family, and religion.

Sociologist Richard Madsen (2009) argues that, for middle-class, native-born, white Americans, religious individualism is the American religion, despite its shortcomings. From Orthodox Jews to evangelical Christians, Madsen finds common descriptions of individuals' religious participation as the consequence of their active, voluntary choice; their emotional experience of God;

and their journey toward forms of religious experience different—whether more restrictive or less so—from ones they already knew. This emphasis on personal feelings and choice echoes Protestant Christian understandings of religion as faith, which requires the believer to enter actively into relationship with God. By highlighting the subjectivity of each person as the salient element of his or her experience, the varied languages of American individualism reinforce a modern Protestant Christian emphasis on belief or faith above practice as the central element of religious experience.

For Jews, this idea of religion as faith is complicated by a sense that Jewishness is also kinship. My informants' comments suggest that they recognize that belief is often seen as the most important part of religion, but their own experience tells them that Judaism is not only that. Similarly, while the "moderately affiliated" American Jews in Cohen and Eisen's *The Jew Within: Self, Family, and Community in America* (2000) looked to the "sovereign self" as their religious authority, they also spoke of their sense of Jewishness as being innate, as did my informants. While American Jews experience their Jewishness in this multifaceted way, the language available to them to express their experiences is more limited: even though American culture emphasizes individualism as an ideology, intense social pressure to conform limits individual Americans' choices in practice, as Margaret Mead ([1942] 1975) points out in her anthropological study of American culture. Being American, then, means adopting individualism and the Protestant view of religion as the primary lens for understanding one's own experiences. The language of individualism has deeply penetrated American Jews' consciousness so that, at least for non-Orthodox Jews, it is inextricable from their conception of their own Jewishness.

I found further demonstrations of this tangle of conformity, choice, and community. Even though my purportedly individualistic intermarried informants resisted clerical and communal disapproval of their marital choices, they did not ignore it. Religious institutions and norms continued to be relevant to their lives. They argued with them and sought religious experiences and connections with religious communities. Just as the narrative of intermarriage as assimilation obscures the role of individualism in endogamous Jews' lives, it also obscures the role of Jewish norms in intermarried Jews' lives. Individualism was the idiom through which my informants related to religious norms. These intermarried couples maintained Jewish traditions, but they did so in their own ways and for their own reasons. They insisted that maintaining traditions was of great importance to them, even as they replaced their content with newer, American ideas.

I identified two perspectives with which intermarried couples engaged as they developed their self-understandings and practices: universalist individualism and ethnic familialism. Universalist individualism emphasizes the conscious choice of religious commitments, rooted in notions of fairness, the unity of humanity, and the autonomy of individuals. Ethnic familialism values these elements but organizes religious identity and practice around the unity of the family and visceral, emotional connections to religious traditions. It describes commitments based in an inchoate but deeply felt sense of "what you are," a responsibility to the Jewish people that could not be clearly articulated but is nevertheless compelling. My informants drew upon both of these models at different times and in different contexts, though most of them relied more heavily on one or the other. These categories, universalist individualism and ethnic familialism, are tools that allow us to explore the striking anxieties that many American Jews continue to feel about assimilating into American culture: at home in both American and Jewish cultures, Jews still often feel somehow apart from them. Intermarried Jewish-Christian couples and, to a lesser extent, rabbis and Jewish educators strive to understand Jewishness in a way that they perceive as authentic to both Jewish and American cultural values.

As my intermarried informants integrate Jewish religious practices and traditions with American individualism in their lives, discourse on intermarriage frequently seems oblivious to the realities of the lives of the people about whom they ostensibly debate. While most of my small, nonrandom sample of intermarried informants raise their children as Jews (something they see as demonstrating their commitment to continuing Jewishness), American Jewish leaders disagree about the status of these couples and their children in the community. Because the Reform, Conservative, and Orthodox movements of Judaism, to which many but not all American Jews belong, strongly disagree with each other over fundamental matters such as who is a Jew and the nature of Jewish legal authority, these movements are unable to agree with each other about the circumstances under which intermarried couples should be accepted in the Jewish community as a whole. This stalemate points out the futility of the monolithic terms *Jewish community* and *Jewish tradition* in these discourses. These movements do not fully agree on what Jewishness is, so they are also unable to agree on the significance of intermarriage for Jewishness.

Despite policymakers' discussions about the status of intermarried couples and their children, many of these couples are raising their children in Judaism with or without Jewish institutional approval. They sometimes do so not as members of Jewish congregations but with the help of organizations such as the Mothers Circle or Pathways, new groups that serve intermarried couples specifically without making demands on them about religious practice or loyalty. In choosing to have Jewish families, my intermarried informants go against the grain not only of the Jewish community's understanding of Jewishness but also of the practices of the majority of intermarried couples in America who do not raise their children as Jews. They carefully construct arguments about why they are doing religion in the ways that they are, whether as a two-religion household or as a family with one religious identity, even without all family members' belonging to the religious community. They raise their children in both religions or only Judaism because these choices seem to them to be the best way to handle conflicting commitments to themselves, their families, and their sense of where they fit into a history of people and religious traditions, demonstrating a complex interplay of individualism and conformity, self and belonging.

As my informants managed their choices and commitments, they felt that they had to answer to intermarriage discourses—to answer for being a "good Jew" or a "bad Jew." Many intermarried people I spoke to, as well as some rabbis who officiate at interfaith weddings, mentioned that they had heard comments that intermarriage "gives Hitler a posthumous victory." Aware of the portrayal of intermarrying Jews as disloyal, of intermariages as losses to the Jewish future compounding those of tragedies past, both the intermarried Jews and their non-Jewish spouses underscored how important it was to them to contribute to the next generation of Jews. They did not want to be seen as disloyal or to see themselves as disloyal. Simply continuing to be Jewish and to have Jewish children, regardless of their Jewish beliefs or practices, helped them to understand themselves as good Jews. Raising Jewish children was, for them, the clearest signal of their Jewish loyalty. Beyond that, the meanings of Jewishness were not fully clear.

The multiple overlapping communities to which my informants belong also struggle with the meanings of Jewishness. Their conflicting understandings of it are rooted in broad sociological and historical changes affecting Jews since the beginning of modernity and culminating in the conflict between individualism, often rendered as assimilation, and peoplehood. Jewish religious thinkers have given deep consideration to the role of the individual's relationship to God as well as to the Jewish people's relationship to God—for example, the "Lonely Man of Faith" described by Rabbi Joseph B. Soloveitchik (1965). But in discourses on intermarriage, these complex understandings of the relationships of people to God and to one another have been flattened into a debate about assimilated individual Jews and the Jewish community.

All these historical and social changes have given Jews a kind of existential whiplash. What does it mean to be born into a Jewish community when individuals can choose whether or not to identify as Jewish, an option that was not available to Jews some generations ago? How do Jews understand Jewishness if they do not feel that they are commanded by God to observe Jewish law? Under what circumstances might Jewish law or tradition override an individual Jew's own preference concerning where to live, whom to marry, or which school to attend? Jews who observe Jewish law may experience less inner conflict about these questions, but those who do not see Jewish law as binding do not have it so easy. By marrying non-Jews, intermarried Jews have made a choice that, in cultural shorthand, represents other choices as well. But as I learned over the course of my research, couples who intermarry are not necessarily making all the other choices implied by their intermarriage. Instead, intermarriage is just one of many choices made both in connection with and independently of other aspects of one's life.

Researching Selves

The constant awareness of the link between assimilation and intermarriage in Jewish discourses was a factor in my informants' responses to me as a researcher. Some expressed discomfort with what they perceived to be researchers' agendas and worried that Jewish organizations would use information that they provided to condemn intermarriage or intermarried couples. My own status as an intermarried convert to Judaism helped some of them to feel less threatened by my academic interest. While this book is not an autobiography, I would like to explain how certain aspects of my identity and experiences shaped my relationships with informants and how they, in turn, reshaped me.

When I began studying intermarriage, I was engaged to become intermarried. My informants were often pleased to know that I was like them and had had, or would have, similar experiences. At that time, I felt that my informants and I were really more different than alike, relying on my own unthinking assumption that other intermarried Jews were assimilated—not me. When I was twenty years old, I had converted to Judaism "for no reason," as a friend from my Atlanta synagogue put it—meaning that I had not converted for marriage. I was raised as a practicing Roman Catholic child of intermarried Roman Catholic and nonpracticing Lutheran parents, and I converted to Judaism in the Conservative movement. The conversion process began early in my time as an undergraduate at Brandeis University and ended in New York after about a year and a half. At least one of my informants had also converted to Judaism and later intermarried. Perhaps I wasn't as unique as I thought.

Still, my experience did not parallel the cultural clashes described in popular and widely read books on interfaith relationships (for instance, Paul Cowan and Rachel Cowan's *Mixed Blessings: Overcoming the Stumbling Blocks in an Interfaith Marriage* [1987]), nor did the religious misgivings and reversals some of my informants described seem to apply to my spouse and me. My nonreligious husband participated amiably in Shabbat (sabbath) dinners and Passover seders and tolerated keeping a kosher kitchen. We had agreed before we were married to raise our children in Judaism. In our household, Jewishness was primarily situated in religious practices. In contrast, some of my Jewish informants seemed more similar to what some of my friends at Brandeis had called "bagel Jews": for them, Jewishness was more often rooted in cultural and familial traditions than in religious ones. Questions about belonging to religious institutions and combining rituals from Judaism and Christianity in the home did pose significant challenges for these informants.

Eventually, I found that I did share some important experiences with my informants, such as an awkwardness in my relationship with Jewish institutions. As a Conservative Jew, I didn't know where my husband and I would be welcome once I decided to join a synagogue. When we did choose one, some members assumed that my husband was Jewish and that I was not, evidently because he has dark hair and I have reddish-blond hair. It was strange to feel others applying stereotypes about the physical appearances expected of Jews and non-Jews to us. The Christmas tree also became a source of ambivalence. We didn't have one until, just as my informants told me would happen, our son was born. Then my husband bought a small rosemary plant that Home Depot had pruned into a Christmas tree shape, potted, and wrapped in red shiny paper, and he hung a few small ornaments on it. In later years, we went to friends' or relatives' homes for what some of my informants called "Thanksgiving with a Christmas tree." Regardless of what we did each year, I had the deeply discomfiting, and paranoid, feeling that the entire Jewish world was watching and judging us. Many of the intermarried Jews I spoke with expressed similar feelings.

Being a woman with a non-Jewish background raising a Jewish child made it easy for me to take part in settings among similar women, such as the Mothers Circle, where I spent time among non-Jewish women married to Jewish men and actively engaged in religious activities. My informants and I also shared demographic elements, such as regional mobility and middle-class status. Like many of my informants, I was not deeply rooted in the place where I lived but had moved around, following occupational and educational opportunities. My family had ricocheted back and forth from the South to Alaska, a strange pair of cultural and climatic opposites, following the pattern of such mobility established by and among Americans for generations. Some of my informants, both Jews and non-Jews, had grown up among Jewish friends, family, and neighbors. I had known almost no Jews at all until starting college at Brandeis University, where some 60 percent of the student body was Jewish.

My connections to Jewishness sometimes came to feel more tenuous than those of my informants because I had only choice and practice, not the history of family and kinship that my informants could claim. This gave me greater freedom in that I had no Jewish family members to oppose my intermarriage but also the disturbing sense that being a "good Jew" was much more difficult because it depended on my creating ties to a deep historical tradition out of thin air. This combination of freedom, choice, tradition, and kinship featured prominently in the talk of the intermarried—and in-married—people I met and talked with.

These convergences of my informants' experiences with my own helped me to understand how deeply we were all affected by discourses about intermarriage, as well as powerful feelings and habits that we could not fully articulate and that we enacted in sometimes self-contradictory ways. For example, if the Jewish community does not fully and unquestioningly accept Jewishly identified children of intermarriage, what does it mean to create Jewish children whose Jewishness is contested? Why do intermarried Jews say they are responding to existential anxiety about the Jewish people's dying out by raising their children as Jews and doing it in ways that have not been traditionally acceptable to the Jewish community—with non-Jewish women, with little or no Jewish practice, and without regard for traditional definitions of Jewishness? When asked to articulate the meaning of these claims or their relationships to one another, my informants sometimes resorted to platitudes or silence. But in the context of their lived experience, and in conversation with one another, they talked about these conflicts using the languages of universalist individualism and ethnic familialism.

The categories of intermarried and endogamous prevent us from seeing the ways in which American Jews in both categories are fundamentally American. This book tells the stories of a small group of intermarried Jewish-Christian couples and connects them with those of in-married Jews as well as other Americans. While intermarried couples do contend with some issues that are less significant for in-married couples, their styles of moral reasoning have much in common. The debate about intermarriage, and the implicit debates within it about Jewishness and the responsibilities of Jews to one another, reveal a lack of appropriate categories in American culture to talk about Jewish peoplehood among Jews who are thoroughly American. For my informants, these discourses' portrayal of them denied the existence of these contradictions. The paradoxes of my informants' experiences of Jewishness, including their sense of obligation to other Jews and their insistence that only they could determine their own religious lives, are largely absent from these discourses on intermarriage. This book focuses on them, using ethnography to explore the paradoxes of Jewishness in contemporary America.

1

Defining Judaism
by Debating Intermarriage

The narratives about intermarriage in contemporary discourse echo those of the mid-twentieth century, despite significant changes in American Jews' lives since then. A narrative of intermarriage as assimilation was born from a convergence of sociological theory about assimilation, immigration, and ethnicity with Jewish historical and religious understandings of intermarriage. These threads reinforced one another in media produced by Jews for consumption by other Jews. Media, scientists, and Jewish religious experts contended and cooperated with one another to shape American Jews' understandings of themselves and each other through this narrative, creating a sense of a shared reality and communal boundaries. For American Jews, debate about intermarriage has functioned since the second half of the twentieth century as a proxy for a larger and more difficult discussion about the nature of Jewishness itself.

Policymakers, rabbis, and journalists have not only chronicled but also shaped American Jewish life through a lens of assimilation and decline. From 1950 to 2011, American Jewish print media depicted social scientists' and religious experts' attempts to understand and shape American Judaism. A search of the website of *The Jewish Daily Forward*, a New York–based publication that bills itself as "American Jewry's essential newspaper of record," showed that it published approximately four hundred pieces in 2009 and 2010 that mention intermarriage, including op-eds, opinion columns, editorials, letters to the editor, interviews, news reporting, and feature articles. Late twentieth- and early twenty-first-century news and magazine items tell stories of rabbis debating whether to perform interfaith weddings, local federations deciding how to allocate money for outreach, and sociologists attempting to quantify how many people were intermarrying and whether intermarried Jews were affiliating with the Jewish community. The Jewish Telegraphic Agency, which describes itself as "the definitive, trusted global source" for topics "of interest to the Jewish people," and local Jewish newspapers regularly cover intermarriage-related stories. Jewish popular and "self-help" literature offer suggestions for preventing intermarriage or making the best of it once it has occurred.[1] The perspectives of intermarried laypeople who affiliate with the Jewish community are represented to some extent in these discourses on websites such as Interfaithfamily .com, which describes itself as "the online resource for interfaith families exploring Jewish life and the grass-roots advocate for a welcoming Jewish community." Through these sources, as well as those in many other outlets, scholars, policymakers, rabbis, volunteer-organization leaders, laypeople, and journalists participate in a debate about assimilation already under way for two centuries. Even though the social circumstances of American Jews' lives in the 2000s are vastly different from those of previous centuries, the central issues with which Jews struggle remain consistent.

Since the 1960s, Jewish media coverage of events both directly and tangentially related to intermarriage has demonstrated the intermarriage-as-assimilation narrative. It has also steadily increased anxiety for many American Jews. Each time a new study on intermarriage is released or a celebrity with some connection to Judaism (such as Chelsea Clinton) grabs public attention, pundits raise questions about the place of intermarried Jews and their offspring within the Jewish people. In 2011, the attempted murder of Arizona congresswoman Gabrielle Giffords, a member of a Reform congregation and the daughter of a Jewish father and a Christian mother, provided a poignant opportunity to recirculate questions about the Jewishness of children of intermarriage. As her story unfolded, many Jews claimed Giffords as a "member of the tribe" despite the contested status of patrilineal descent, the inheritance of Jewishness from a Jewish father. (Jewish law holds that only a Jewish woman can transmit Jewishness to her children, and Conservative and Orthodox Jewish organizations do not recognize people as Jews by patrilineal descent.) The decision of Reconstructionist Jews in 1969 and of the Reform movement in 1983 to recognize the children of Jewish fathers as Jews embodied the disagreements of liberal and conservative Jews about the authority of tradition and the legitimacy of change, as I will detail later in this chapter. These disagreements are painful to many Jews: on the news website *The Huffington Post*, one Conservative rabbi expressed helplessness, as if it were beyond the power of Conservative Judaism to figure out how to include patrilineal Jews in Jewish communities in a satisfactory way (Miller 2011). Similarly, intermarried Jews' status within Jewish communities is also contested: intermarried Jews are often blamed for their disaffiliation, or lack of membership or participation in Jewish organizations. Though surveys do indeed show that intermarried couples are less likely to affiliate with Jewish institutions (Dashefsky, Sheskin, and Miller 2012), this discourse treats the unaffiliated and the intermarried as largely overlapping categories, even though plenty of Jews who are not inter-married likewise do not affiliate with Jewish institutions.

The anxiety about the ambiguities of assimilation has motivated some to apportion blame for intermarriage. In a 2009 piece in *The Forward* called "Time for Straight-Talk about Assimilation," Jack Wertheimer, a professor of American Jewish history at the Jewish Theological Seminary of the Conservative move-ment, draws on sociological studies of American Jewry and declining member-ship in and donations to "most established organizations" to argue that "vast populations of American Jews are steering clear of organized Jewish life" (Wert-heimer 2009). Affiliation with Jewish organizations, he implies, indicates an individual Jew's commitment to Judaism; failure to participate indicates assimi-lation. Wertheimer furthermore connects the unaffiliated to the intermarried and points out that most children of intermarried couples do not identify exclu-sively as Jews: "Few would dispute that the Jewish community has a far better chance of retaining the allegiance of individuals raised in homes in which both parents are Jewish than in those where one parent identifies with a different reli-gion." He leaves it up to the reader to make the connection between intermar-riage and the vast populations of American Jews who avoid Jewish institutions.

Shortly after the publication of "Time for Straight-Talk," Wertheimer debated Adam Bronfman, managing director of the Samuel Bronfman Foundation, in the pages of *The Forward* (Wertheimer and Bronfman 2009). The foundation's web-site proclaims that it "seeks to inspire a renaissance of Jewish life," emphasizing that "all Jews are a single family" and that "vibrant Jewish communities are open and inclusive." In "Straight-Talk about Assimilation: An Exchange," Bronfman counters Wertheimer by asserting that intermarriage does not necessarily imply assimilation. In the contemporary United States, he says, intermarriage is the result of taking full part in a multicultural society: "Jews do not marry non-Jews in an effort to assimilate. We do so, as I did, because we fall in love." Further, Bronfman says, intermarriage reflects an individual Jew's relationship to his or her Jewish background and to the wider American society in which he or she grew up, not assimilation in the sense of purposeful rejection of Judaism or the Jewish people. Resisting Wertheimer's association of the unaffiliated with assimilation, Bronfman argues that many "traditional Jewish institutions" offer no "relevant and compelling" answer to the question "Why should I be Jewish?" The Jews whom Wertheimer might regard as assimilated, Bronfman reminds us, come from diverse Jewish backgrounds and experiences. They did not grow up in "vibrant Jewish communities" nor in the kind of close-knit Jewish communi-ties that Wertheimer says strongly discourage intermarriage, so they never made a choice to leave Judaism. Bronfman suggests instead that social opportunities to meet and fall in love with a broad variety of people, some of whom are not

Jewish, and problems that turn people away from Jewish institutions together play important roles in the incidence of intermarriage. But none of these factors is equivalent to assimilation, and many other factors contribute, too.

Wertheimer replies that intermarriage and disaffiliation are the result of personal choices—individual Jews' prioritizing themselves above the Jewish people. "Jews of all ages are *choosing* to inter-date," responds Wertheimer. "They actively place themselves in situations where the likely outcomes will be intermarriage." Choosing to date a non-Jew has consequences, he writes: "I would not hesitate to advise that such a decision would vastly complicate" the Jewish life of any individual and his or her children. "I would further explain that Jews committed to a Jewish future have not abandoned the millennia-old continuity strategy of endogamy," he continues, pointing out that intermarriage is far less common among Jews who belong to communities with norms that oppose intermarriage—ones in which Jewish leaders "dare to speak of such choices as inimical to Jewish life." In contrast, Jews who actively choose intermarriage, he says, do so because they are influenced by social norms that emphasize "individual gratification" over "the ties binding people together." Hoping that Jews will completely immerse themselves in Jewish community and Jewish life, Wertheimer redefines the familiar American idiom of personal choice by saying that Jews can choose to resist assimilation: "As with all choices, that means embracing some things and forsaking others." In this view, because individuals' personal choices are the basis on which the fate of the entire Jewish community rests, communal or institutional needs should supplant what individuals might perceive as their own personal compelling interests. In intermarriage discourse, such communal and institutional constraints on personal choice are frequently advocated. Strikingly, God's commandments against intermarriage are rarely mentioned (as I will discuss later), even though covenant with God is traditionally the basis of Jews' obligations to one another.

The claim that individual Jews have a responsibility to make personal choices that align with the interests of Jewish institutions paradoxically follows a strong current in American moral reasoning. As sociologist Robert N. Bellah and his colleagues describe in their bestselling book *Habits of the Heart* (1985), middle-class Americans resist responsibilities and commitments that are not of their own choosing. Instead, they understand themselves to select commitments that give them satisfaction on a personal level and frame these commitments as independent and free choices, even when they have been shaped by history, memory, and community as well as structural factors beyond their consciousness. When Wertheimer asserts that Jews should choose to constrain their range of action, he expresses his argument for Jewish traditionalism in an American cultural idiom. But these two elements work against each other because American individualism emphasizes freedom and independence and Jewish traditionalism emphasizes unchosen obligation.

Even though Wertheimer emphasizes the role of individual choice, structural changes have strongly contributed to the conflicts evident in his exchange with Bronfman. Since the mid-twentieth century, Jews have experienced undeniable social and economic success in the United States; and they may now choose their professional, social, and academic endeavors without external limits. American Jews have also formed new self-conceptions due to the nation's changing patterns of marriage and of ethnic and religious diversity. While Jews may previously have seen themselves as a distinct ethnic group, other white Americans often viewed Jews' as well as their own ethnic difference as mainly symbolic, chosen rather than ascribed (Sarna 1994; see also Sollors 1987; Waters 1998). Additionally, American cultural and social-structural emphasis on democracy, pluralism, and choice (Hatch 1989) heavily influence American Jews' interpretations of Judaism (Cohen and Eisen 2000). Their lack of involvement in Jewish organizations and lack of religious observance does not diminish their sense that they are part of the Jewish people and share in its collective identity. They see themselves as free to choose whether to belong to Jewish institutions based on personal considerations such as their feelings about the rabbi, not because of a sense of obligation to the Jewish people. They report greater interest in home rituals, such as Shabbat (Jewish sabbath) dinner, than in synagogue worship that clergy or other leaders control (Cohen and Eisen 2000). But these preferences, framed as personal choices, are shaped by American cultural ideologies, not invented anew by each individual Jew. At the same time, these changing cultural attitudes and social opportunities have led to Jews' having different experiences and therefore different assumptions about what is reasonable and what matters. Rhetoric of individual responsibility denies such cultural and structural changes and attributes these changes' effects simply to personal choices.

The argument about individuals, peoplehood, and responsibility on display in the exchange between Bronfman and Wertheimer echoes a long history of similar arguments concerning intermarriage, assimilation, and the future of Judaism. Jewish media's representation of local, regional, and national Jewish institutions' concerns about the impact of intermarriage on Judaism's present and future has remained oddly static since at least the 1960s. Even though claims about the dangerously individualistic nature of intermarried Jews have been contested by people such as Bronfman, these claims continue to be repeated.

While pieces like the exchange explicitly link intermarried Jews' purportedly extreme individualism to their supposed assimilation, other pieces do so implicitly. For example, a 2010 article that appeared in *The Forward* titled "New Study Finds That It's Not a Lack of Welcome That's Keeping the Intermarrieds Away" immediately suggests a familiar narrative of intermarriage: it implies that "intermarrieds" fail to participate in Jewish institutions because of some fault within the intermarried people themselves. The article does not blame Jewish institutions, although accompanying comments from two representatives of Jewish outreach institutions protest that the intermarried people with whom they work frequently say that they have felt unwelcome in Jewish institutions. Its opening paragraph clearly conflates intermarriage and assimilation: "Since at least the 1990s, one of the chief concerns of the American Jewish community has been the problem of intermarriage. With the perception that an increasing number of American Jews are marrying outside the faith, the problem of how to stop the attrition has been a major preoccupation" (Beckerman 2010). The article's focus on intermarriage as assimilation is striking because its ostensible topic is a recently completed study for the Foundation for Jewish Camp that focuses on recruitment for midwestern Jewish camps. The author dismisses as "fairly obvious" the study's main finding that "those who were committed to raising their children as Jews—whether the couple was Jewish or interfaith—were more likely to send their children to a Jewish camp." Instead, he emphasizes its incidental finding that intermarried couples felt "welcome" in Jewish settings, in contrast to the contrary claim of Jewish outreach organizations. Perhaps this incidental finding seemed important, given that one of the study's authors was Steven M. Cohen (Cohen and Veinstein 2010), who is widely known for his sociological studies on American Jewry and particularly intermarriage. Focusing on differences between "purely Jewish and intermarried couples," *The Forward*'s reporter summarizes: "Cohen's conclusion was that most interfaith couples feel like they have an open invitation to be part of Jewish life. The real problem, he said, is that they feel like they don't know what to do with that invitation. 'It's not that they feel unwelcome, but that there is a competence barrier,' Cohen said. 'They feel that their kids will be expected to do things they don't know how to do, and they themselves don't want to be part of a community where they don't know the choreography'" (Beckerman 2010). Perhaps highlighting intermarriage rather than the study's "obvious" findings about likely campers appealed to the newspaper's readership because the topic was familiar and touched a raw nerve.

The article underscores its attention to intermarried couples' faults by including the opinion of another sociologist known for her work on intermarriage, Sylvia Barack Fishman, who "agrees with Cohen that the problem is not that synagogues are unwelcoming. 'Very, very few non-Jews who are married to Jews say they feel they were insulted or treated in a bad way,' Fishman said. She also added credence to the theory that competence was the bigger problem, saying that many of these non-Jews who didn't feel insulted also said they were turned off when they couldn't understand the Hebrew or strange songs being sung" (Beckerman 2010). Fishman depicts intermarried couples as ignorant of the "choreography" of Jewish life, but there is no suggestion that single Jews or endogamous couples might also lack such knowledge.

Regardless of who was or was not welcomed by whom, *The Forward*'s article taps into a cultural narrative about intermarriage that apportions blame for intermarriage and assimilation and that highlights Jewish institutions' lack of success in slowing down intermarriage rates. It retells this narrative in a cultural shorthand, expecting readers to fill in much of the story based on what they already know. Relying on some of the same shorthand, the Foundation for Jewish Camp study described in the article had taken up the question of welcoming and intermarriage in a narrower fashion, as part of a conversation among policymakers and scholarly policy advisers. Programming that brings intermarried couples into greater contact with Jewish institutions, Cohen told me in an email conversation, helps to create friendships, encourage interest in Jewish topics, and teach "the inner choreography of Jewish life." Its success is actually rooted not in its welcoming, he said, but in the way it helps intermarried couples' Jewish familiarity and social networks to germinate. As Cohen's explanation shows, his analysis of these social interactions is deeply intertwined with the goals of particular Jewish organizations. But *The Forward*'s coverage of his analysis sidesteps this context in favor of an implicit story about intermarried Jews.

Cultural shorthand depends on consumers and users who are familiar with a topic and can therefore fill in the rest of the story. The Jewish camp article built on three decades of Jewish public discourse that characterized intermarriage as a "crisis" (McGinity 2009, 190f). Though the article quotes representatives of two outreach organizations, it does not include the views of intermarried people. Instead, it uses intermarried Jews and their families in a symbolic way. Not all intermarried people lack the kind of Jewish social networks and familiarity that would allow them to feel comfortable within Jewish organizations. Jews who lack Jewish social networks and familiarity may be assimilated, but they are not necessarily intermarried. Yet in this discussion of social networks, the term *intermarried* does not simply mean "couples that include one Jewish spouse and one non-Jewish spouse." It means "couples who are assimilated"—that is, those who are disconnected from Jewish communities, organizations, and practices. In this cultural shorthand, not all assimilated Jews are intermarried, but all intermarried Jews are assimilated.

News articles that discuss incidental findings of Jewish policy studies are not really focused on the studies themselves. Rather, media coverage of such studies provides an opportunity to retell the narrative of intermarriage as assimilation. Media coverage of a 2005 study of intermarried families and their children in Boston (Gan, Jacobson, Preuss, and Shrage 2008) drew attention to what some saw as a surprisingly high rate of intermarried couples' raising their children exclusively in Judaism. This study was evidently of interest to readers of Greater New York's *The Jewish Week* (Saxe, Kadushin, and Phillips 2006), not because they were about to participate in Boston's Combined Jewish Philanthropies planning sessions but because the story contradicted the familiar expectation that intermarriage would lead to assimilation. While nearly 40 percent of Boston Jews were intermarrying, about 60 percent of these couples were raising their children as Jews. Even this "optimistic note," as the study's principal investigators called it, perpetuated the intermarriage-as-assimilation narrative.

Helplessness, disapproval, confusion, and self-contradiction abound in these examples from recent discourses about intermarriage. Such feelings remain fresh and raw among those who express them. Yet when viewed against the deeper history of discourses about intermarriage, these recent examples sound strangely familiar. It is curious that Jewish discourses still express the same feelings in largely the same ways, even though many other important aspects of Jewish life in America have changed (McGinity 2009, 203).

Converging Sociological, Historical, and Religious Narratives

Jews have been wrestling with the pressures of assimilation for centuries. Biblical and rabbinic texts depict concerns about maintaining the stability and integrity of the Jewish people (Cohen 1999), and Jews in the contemporary United States have continued to debate this topic, wrestling with the tensions among their group loyalties, identification, and obligations and their desire to enjoy the broad opportunities of an open society. During the second half of the twentieth century, American Jews worked out these tensions by discussing intermarriage. The themes of their discourse have remained remarkably consistent across the decades, revealing the resilience of anxieties and ambivalence about assimilation despite changes in the circumstances of Jews' shared and individual lives.

The pressures of assimilation in the United States have been different from those that Jews encountered before modernity. European Jews lived in bounded and semiautonomous communities until western European countries and the United States began granting them citizenship during the eighteenth and nineteenth centuries. After this process, known as Emancipation, had begun, questions arose about how Jews could maintain their distinctiveness within an open society that was culturally dominated by Christianity. Broad social changes such as a growing ideology of individual choice and autonomy affected Jews and Christians alike (Bellah [1970] 1991).

These changes gradually improved Jews' relationship with Christians and Christianity. In the distant past, Christian church rules forbade and punished intermarriage as severely as Jewish law did (Adelman 1991; Fishberg [1911] 2006; Maitland 1898), but modern Jews and Christians had more choices. Intermarriage rates depended heavily on local circumstances, and in many places were quite low (Barron 1946; Drachsler 1920; Fishberg [1911] 2006; Geffen 2009; Levenson 1989; Lowenstein 2005; Sowell 1981). Jewish leaders worried about the consequences of intermarriage and began to identify it with population loss: Jewish-Christian marriage was considered out-marriage because children from such marriages frequently were not raised as Jews (Hertz 1991; Kaplan 1991, 208; Rose 2001). The Christian identification of children of Jews was exactly what Jews considered assimilation—and what they feared most.

Decreasing social distance between Jews and non-Jews prompted Jews to wonder again what distinguished them from other Americans who also valued religious freedom, economic mobility, and educational achievement. Non-Jews' social acceptance of Jews increased, and antisemitism decreased. Particularly after World War II, Jews increasingly enjoyed opportunities to interact with each other and with non-Jews openly and comfortably (Berman 2009; Dollinger 2000; McGinity 2009; Moore 1981, 1994; Sarna 2004). For Orthodox Jews, there was a simple answer to the question of Jewish identity in a dominantly non-Jewish society: Jews were a people united by their mission to serve God through observance of God's commandments. But for more liberal Jews, as the external forces that had ensured Jews' separation from non-Jewish society all but evaporated, the inner commitments and interests that held them together grew more difficult to articulate. To what degree could Jews be part of the society around them while still remaining distinctive as Jews, both collectively and individually? To what degree did they even want to be part of societies that had visited persecution upon them for centuries (Baron 1957)? The Reform and Conservative movements, neo-Orthodoxy, and myriad others that came later each set forth its own vision of the relationship between Jews, individually and collectively, and the societies in which they lived (Dahlstrom 2006; Endelman 1990, 1997; Katz [1973] 1998; Levenson 1989; Scheindlin 1998).

Responding to the cues of the society around them, Jews described themselves in varying ways, referring to their race, religion, people, and ethnicity (Goldstein 2006). Yet none of these descriptors captured the full experience of Jewishness. So in the nineteenth and early twentieth centuries, American Jewish leaders drew on social science as a way to justify Jews' separateness and to resist assimilation (Berman 2009; Hart 2000). They appealed to then-prevailing theories about race and eugenics to argue that intermarriage was biologically and morally harmful to the Jewish people (Hart 2000). Between the first and second world wars, studies showed that "the more homogenous a couple, the more likely their marriage was to succeed and stand as a foundation for a stable society" (Berman 2010, 96). In this view, Jews' endogamy was their way of contributing to the strength of American society. As sociologists found a sharp rise in intermarriage rates beginning in the 1960s (McGinity 2009), a narrative of intermarriage as assimilation became engrained in the American Jewish public consciousness (Berman 2010, 102–103).

Sociological narratives about assimilation, such as Milton Gordon's *Assimilation in American Life: The Role of Race, Religion, and National Origins* (1964), provided a basis for predicting the decline of the Jewish population as it grew increasingly comfortable within American society (Phillips n.d.). Early twenty-first-century social scientists argued that Jews' group existence was threatened by declining antisemitism, non-Jews' increased social acceptance of Jews, and structural changes to modern societies that assume the individual to be the basic unit of society (Cohen and Eisen 2000; Fishman 2004). The social and cultural changes that Jews were experiencing also affected other Americans. American Jewish discourses, however, focused narrowly on attempting to predict the fate of the Jews.

Sociologists writing in the pages of the popular Jewish magazine *Commentary* used this narrative of assimilation and decline to explain the changes that American Judaism was undergoing. In the mid-1950s, Herbert Gans introduced the concept of "symbolic Judaism" to explain how Judaism would change in its American context. A cultural shift was happening, he argued. Second-generation Jews were torn between their parents' eastern European immigrant world and the American one into which they had been born. Their children, the third generation, were fully American. Subsequent generations would be further removed from the immigrant experience in which Jewishness enveloped one's life. American-born Jews of American parents would experience Jewishness as symbolic Judaism, a weak concoction of Jewish objects and rituals removed from their original context and used for emotional succor (Gans 1956a, 1956b). Gans (1979) later extended the concept of symbolic Judaism into symbolic ethnicity, applying the same principles to other immigrant ethnic groups in the United States. Sociologists studying American Jews interpreted symbolic ethnicity as a sign of decline and assimilation. Yet Gans's symbolic Judaism is not far from sociologist of religion Robert Bellah's ([1970] 1991) description of modern religion, in which individuals customize religious symbols to respond to their own needs and experiences. The same facts, viewed in Bellah's frame, might have yielded an understanding of Judaism as being in the process of transformation. Sociologist Calvin Goldscheider (2010) has argued for just such an understanding, pointing out that it makes sense for contemporary Jews to cohere in different ways than they did a hundred years ago because the circumstances of their lives have also changed.

Marshall Sklare, the founding father of American Jewish sociology, critiqued narrow Jewish communal approaches to assimilation and intermarriage and urged American Jews to recognize the breadth of the changes that they were experiencing. His sociological insights into American Jewish existence sometimes made other Jews uncomfortable. In a memoir, he recounted a Conservative rabbi's comment to him after the publication of his 1955 book *Conservative Judaism: An American Religious Movement*: "Young man, how dare you tell the truth about Conservative Judaism!" (Sarna 1993, 1). Sklare's articles in *Commentary* "helped to explain the American Jewish community to itself," wrote historian Jonathan Sarna (1993, 4).

In those articles Sklare pointed out that rabbis and social scientists in the 1960s had pathologized intermarrying Jews. For instance, psychology professor Louis Berman's *Jews and Intermarriage: A Study in Personality and Culture* (1968) emphasized what Berman understood to be pathologies associated with intermarriage, a view that undergirded his argument for endogamy. Similarly, Jewish community leaders depicted intermarrying Jews as status seeking, assimilating, and hostile toward their parents (Sklare 1964). By doing so, they placed blame for assimilation and intermarriage on only the individual Jews themselves, not on Jewish institutions or broader social change, just as Wertheimer did in his 2009 article in *The Forward*. Elements of such portrayals did reflect some intermarrying Jews' feelings. During the 1960s and 1970s, certain Jewish women chose intermarriage as a form of rebellion against their parents, part of a larger drive for self-determination and pursuit of personal meaning (McGinity 2009, 139). Some American Jews who grew up during this period explained that their intermarriages were part of their alienation and rebellion against their Jewish parents' "materialism" (Fishman 2004, 19–27).

Portraying intermarriage as the result of personal failures shifted responsibility for intermarriage onto individuals and away from the Jewish community but did not necessarily reflect reality, and Sklare (1964) predicted that an increase in intermarriage would force the Jewish community to deal with the question "What do you stand for when you wish to remain separate?" (52). This desire to remain separate depended upon ideas about categorical difference between Jews and non-Jews (Berman 2010), as I will discuss; but as intermarriage discourse unfolded over the second half of the twentieth century and into the twenty-first, it also drew a categorical distinction between endogamous and intermarried Jews. The latter distinction depended upon the conflation of intermarriage and assimilation and implied that endogamous Jews were exempt from the individualism of assimilated/intermarried Jews.

Sklare (1970) also critiqued what he called the "discord" approach to discouraging intermarriage, which he saw as another way of avoiding the question of what made Jews different from non-Jews. Rising divorce rates in the 1920s and 1930s had spurred scholars during the 1930s and 1940s to attempt to understand the factors most essential to happy marriage. They determined that "shared culture," interpreted to mean religion in particular, was fundamental (Berman 2009, 59–61). Jewish leaders seized on this finding in the 1950s and 1960s, contending that marriage was hard enough "without introducing yet another potential disharmony, such as a mate of a different faith." Thus, Jews should marry each other to eliminate a potential source of marital strife (Sklare 1970, 53). With the discord approach, Jews could argue for endogamy on a scientifically founded, pragmatic basis, one that avoided arguing from religious authority and that dodged charges of ethnocentrism.

The discord and divorce rates of intermarried couples continue to occupy the attention of social scientists and, since at least 1925, rabbis and the Jewish press (McGinity 2009, 42, 56, 114). Fishman (2004) highlights the "special tensions" that she argues her intermarried interviewees experienced, citing findings from the 2001 American Religious Identification Survey (ARIS) that "interfaith households are three times more likely to end in divorce as families in which both parents share the same faith" and 1990 National Jewish Population Survey results showing that "Jewish mixed-married households are twice as likely to end in divorce as Jewish inmarried households." Based on these survey data, she concludes that religious differences must "contribute to greater spousal tensions" (44–45). McGinity (2009), however, disputes these statistics and suggests that, rather than religion, her subjects' divorces resulted from economic or political differences, infidelity, or gender inequality (164–165, 274–275n48). McGinity's findings suggest that including a broader social context in interpreting statistics about divorce helps researchers to avoid mistaking correlation for causation.

The discord approach has persisted for nearly ninety years, even though it is ineffective at persuading Jews to avoid intermarriage. Sklare argued in 1970 that this approach failed to persuade Jews who observed happy intermarriages and unhappy in-marriages. Worse, as Sklare pointed out, the discord strategy failed to address the larger question of what constituted a particularly Jewish marriage other than its inclusion of two Jews. Because Jewish leaders had misunderstood why Jews intermarried, he argued, their strategies to combat intermarriage were ill-fated. Continuing attention to the discord approach suggests that its attraction is not in its effectiveness but in its reinforcement of the idea of categorical difference between Jews and non-Jews. By valorizing Jewish in-marriage, it suggests that Jews share a special way of being that makes marriage between them succeed and that makes marriage with non-Jews fail. It aligns well with the tribalism that Cohen and Eisen (2000) describe.

Broader analyses yielded greater understanding of how Jews were changing with American culture. Sklare (1964) highlighted a study by Rabbi Henry Cohen ([1962] 1974) at the University of Illinois, which showed that the value system of some Jews had turned from traditional Judaism to a more secular and universalistic "Academic Commitment," an individualistic "religion" of academic and professional values (50). Recognizing this shift in values would allow Jewish leaders to devise strategies that responded more directly to the facts on the ground. Sklare (1964) interpreted this cultural shift as assimilative, however, predicting that the children of such academic Jews would intermarry at a high rate even with two Jewish parents because they were raised without a committed, strong foundation in Judaism.

As Jewish leaders avoided grappling with the questions that Sklare raised, divisions arose between leaders and laypeople. Jewish parents worked to maintain good relationships with their intermarried children, while blaming intermarriage on bad religious schools, rabbis, or synagogues (Sklare 1970). In turn, Jewish leaders blamed Jewish parents, particularly mothers, for failing to produce the "properly" Jewish children that institutions and leaders deemed necessary for the perpetuation of the Jewish people (Berman 2010; McGinity 2009, 94). Mid-twentieth-century American Jewish institutions sought to control the formation of Jewish children to ensure that they would remain properly Jewish. Day schools, summer camps, youth groups, and university Jewish studies programs thus attracted new emphasis once the mid-1960s rise in intermarriage rates came to light. In 1999, Birthright Israel began sending young Jewish adults on trips to Israel in an effort to ensure their avoidance of intermarriage and assimilation. These efforts stemmed from Jewish leaders' sense that Jewish parents alone could not be entrusted with the important task of ensuring their children's continuing proper Jewishness (Berman 2010). More recently, Fishman (2004) found that the children of parents who insisted upon Jewish endogamy were more likely to marry Jews, while intermarriage was the more likely result for children of parents who did not attempt to intervene in their dating or marriage choices (34–38). In 2012, websites such as Preventintermarriage.com (Packouz 2008) and Interfaithfamily.com ("Tips for Talking to Your Children about Interdating" 2013) advised parents to warn their children of the difficulties that interdating and intermarriage would bring to their lives as Jews. These two websites come from very different institutional backgrounds: Preventintermarriage.com carries the Orthodox "inreach" group Aish HaTorah's logo, and Interfaithfamily.com is meant to be a resource for Jewishly identified intermarried couples. That they dispense similar advice points to how strong the parental role is thought to be and continues the earlier line of reasoning in which intermarriage is a measure of Jews' success or failure as parents.

Many Jewish parents, however, resisted leaders' insistence that they attempt to direct their children's marital choices. These parents' loyalty to the Jewish people did not outweigh their attachment to good relationships with their children, and even Jews who opposed intermarriage were unwilling to "face an estrangement between themselves and their children over intermarriage" (Sklare 1970, 52). And because the parents were not religiously observant themselves, Sklare wrote, such a demand would have made them feel uncomfortably ethnocentric and hypocritical. Parents' discomfort had to do with the contradiction of Jews' support for their own full integration into an open American society even as they sought to preserve their cultural separation from it (Dollinger 2000; McGinity 2009, 114). To the extent that parents of intermarrying Jewish women opposed intermarriage, McGinity (2009) found, their opposition was based on group loyalty rather than religious views (93). Sklare (1970) argued that the Jewish community avoided inquiring too deeply into the meanings of and reasons for intermarriage because doing so would make plain the contradictions of American Jewish life that were too uncomfortable to address openly. Adamant opposition to inter-marriage could render Jews vulnerable to charges of separatism, while too little opposition suggested a lack of interest in their own heritage.

Rather than face the ambivalence and anxiety that lay behind the question of what differentiated Jews from non-Jews, people began to develop strategies to integrate non-Jews into Jewish families. Some Jews in the 1970s planned inter-faith weddings and sought ritual legitimation through rabbinic officiation. Such gestures were symbolic, not meant to imply that the marrying couples intended to observe Jewish law, because the non-Jewish spouse would have converted to Judaism in that case. Yet rabbis did not generally regard rabbinic officiation at weddings between Jews and non-Jews as acceptable, and conversion for the sake of marriage was undesirable according to Jewish law. Moreover, requiring conversion could imply that Jews saw Judaism as superior to the non-Jewish spouse's religion, reinforce stereotypes of Jews as insular, and conflict with American values of egalitarianism and universalism (Sklare 1970, 57). Jews who sought rabbinic officiation could rely upon the 41 percent of Reform rabbis (in 1972) who were willing to officiate (McGinity 2009, 129) or, according to a New York Jewish newspaper, Jewish officiants who had no connections to synagogues or even rabbinical credentials. In 1973, the New York–based *Jewish Week* dra-matically alerted readers to the existence of "fraudulent rabbis" who offered to officiate at interfaith weddings despite their lack of official recognition as rab-bis. "These men are vultures who are exploiting for financial gains the tragedy of Jewish parents whose children are about to marry a non-Jew," cautioned Rab-binical Assembly executive vice president and Conservative rabbi Wolfe Kelman (Rosenblatt 1973). "Legitimate" rabbis and Jewish social workers warned the Jewish community away from them. These religious experts and Jewish families did not understand themselves to have the same interests.

Like Sklare and Gans, sociologist Charles Liebman also analyzed cultural change and the conflicting desires of American Jews. In *The Ambivalent Ameri-can Jew* (1973), he described the divided feelings of Jews who wished to be fully American and yet separate from America. He argued that their approach to Jew-ishness was untenable and that a survivalist frame was imperative for Judaism's continued existence. The feelings that he described were quite similar to those that Gans described among second-generation American Jews. But by the time Liebman's book was published, the third generation, by Gans's account, should have been comfortably practicing symbolic Judaism. The conflicted feelings that Gans had described in the mid-1950s and had theorized as an artifact of second-generation Jewish experience had remarkable resilience for later generations as well. It was not clear whether the predicted decline of Jewishness and increase in assimilation were occurring, but fear of them persisted.

Debating Intermarriage through Media Discourse

The intermarriage-as-assimilation narrative has anchored Jewish discourses for decades. Focusing on intermarriage in an instrumental and functional way rather than acknowledging the inherent contradictions in American Jews' experiences may have been an attempt to contain the religious and cultural dissonance among American Jews, but it was unsuccessful. Even the attempt to devise a coherent Jewish communal strategy against intermarriage would reveal deep disagreement, as the more recent inreach-outreach debate (which I will explain later in this chapter) shows. But as dissonance spilled out in that debate, many participants continued to assume a categorical difference between Jews and non-Jews and between endogamous and intermarried Jews that precluded full recognition of these contradictions that faced all American Jews.

Some Jewish religious experts in the 1970s continued to address intermarriage in instrumental and functional ways, ignoring the broader social context that had enabled intermarriage to increase. These religious experts hoped that individual Jews would choose to limit themselves in order to preserve the existing structure of Jewish institutions—the same argument that Wertheimer would offer in 2009. When synagogues, rabbinical associations, and secular Jewish organizations came together to sponsor the 1976 National Conference on Mixed Marriage in New Jersey, many of its speakers described intermarrying Jews in the same terms that Sklare had rejected earlier ("2-Day Conference to Explore Threat to Jewish Survival" 1976). For example, Conservative Rabbi Robert Gordis, professor of Bible and philosophies of religion at the Jewish Theological Seminary, portrayed intermarrying Jews as rebellious against parental authority and desperate for non-Jews' social acceptance. Increased Jewish education and home observances could help prevent intermarriage, he said, but conversion should also be emphasized since it would not be possible to entirely eliminate intermarriage (Gordis 1978, 127–132). Left out of his account was any mention of intermarrying Jews' subjective experiences, such as love for their non-Jewish spouses ("Intermarriage the Price of Open Society?" 1977).

Some Jewish leaders experimented with ways to adjust traditional institutions in order to mitigate the assimilative power of intermarriage. Beginning in

1975, Reform rabbi Roy Rosenberg, leader of the hundred-member Daat Elohim synagogue in Manhattan, accepted intermarried couples without requiring conversion of the non-Jewish spouse. In 1979, Rosenberg wrote in *Sh'ma* magazine that Daat Elohim "fill[ed] a perceived need in the lives of those whom it serve[d], in the process preserving and passing on the Jewish heritage in family lines where it would otherwise be lost" (Gallob 1979, 27). Rabbi Rosenberg focused on intermarried couples' interest in Judaism rather than their failure to meet the standards of Jewish law. Yehuda Rosenman, director of Jewish communal affairs for the American Jewish Committee, wrote that intermarrying Jews were not necessarily trying to cut themselves off from the Jewish community but saw their marriage choices as separate from religion. They wanted "acceptance and understanding from the Jewish community" (Lester 1978, 41). The *Omaha Jewish Press* ("Report Studies Intermarriage" 1979) reported that the American Jewish Committee's study "Intermarriage and the Jewish Future," released in January 1979, said that a "spiraling" intermarriage rate threatened the Jewish community (11). It recommended both conversion of non-Jewish spouses and the welcoming of non-Jews into the Jewish community regardless of conversion.

This approach was controversial even among those who valued pluralism within Judaism. In a letter to *Sh'ma*, Modern Orthodox rabbi Haskel Lookstein argued against giving "sanction to intermarriage not only by officiating at a wedding but by inviting the couple to participate fully in a Temple of Universal Judaism," adding that "it is not Judaism" (Gallob 1979, 27). Lookstein was known for his willingness to work with non-Orthodox Jews: he was later described as "one of the few Orthodox leaders to defy the growing resistance to pluralism" and said that he felt that Orthodox rabbis needed to "work out a solution to our problems" along with Reform leaders (Mark 2008). But Daat Elohim's openness to intermarriage went further than he was willing to go. Rosenberg responded that the model was realistic and that he expected Daat Elohim to join the Union of American Hebrew Congregations (UAHC) when its membership was large enough (Gallob 1979). Both rabbis felt the future and definition of Jewishness itself to be at stake in their responses to intermarriage.

In the United States and Israel, liberal and Orthodox Jews clashed over religious authority and legitimacy through their debates about intermarriage and patrilineal descent. At the 1980 annual meeting of the Orthodox Rabbinical Council of America (RCA), its president, Rabbi Sol Roth, argued that intermarried Jews and rabbis who officiate at intermarriages should be excluded from leadership positions in Jewish organizations. Roth also protested the Reform movement's consideration of a rule of patrilineal descent, which would count as Jewish any child who had one Jewish parent and who was raised as a Jew, rather than the traditional determination of Jewishness through the mother ("Reform Rabbis Unanimously Back Israel Assault on PLO in Lebanon: Defer Decision on

'Jewish Fatherhood'" 1982).[2] "This breach of Jewish law by Reform leaders would create a sect which would erroneously regard itself as Jewish but whose Jewish identity would not be acknowledged by the mainstream of the Jewish people," said Roth (3). Orthodox rabbis in Israel also resisted the idea of patrilineal descent, seeking to legally restrict those eligible for the Law of Return to those born to Jewish mothers or converted according to Jewish law. Because Israel's Law of Return offered automatic Israeli citizenship to any Jew, this restriction would disqualify Reform converts to Judaism for Israeli citizenship under that law, the argument being that Reform conversions did not adhere to Jewish law. Further, Conservative rabbis would have to adhere to standards for conversion set by Israeli Orthodox rabbis. Many Reform and Conservative rabbis understood this effort to be an attempt to discredit their legitimacy (Yaffe 1977), and they resisted it—so much so that the Conservative movement considered recognizing patrilineal descent in the mid-1970s specifically to help the children of intermarried Soviet Jewish men immigrating to Israel qualify for citizenship under the Law of Return. In 1976 Rabbi Solomon Goldfarb wrote in an article in *Conservative Judaism* that, in Israel, many such children were not counted as Jews. He asked, "Why, in the light of the liberation and relaxation of the prohibitions against intermarriage, do we still insist that only the child of a Jewish mother be considered a Jew?" (Yaffe 1977, 27). According to a news report, the Conservative Rabbinical Assembly's Committee on Jewish Law and Standards planned to consider the question of patrilineal descent, and its members were surprised that Goldfarb, who was reportedly resistant to change in ritual and practice, had proposed it. "These are new times in Jewish life and we are faced with new demands especially in matters concerning the Jewish family," Goldfarb wrote (ibid.). Conservative Jewish leaders' consideration of patrilineal descent suggests that the idea may have appealed more broadly than later portrayals would admit.

In 1983, the Reform movement formally recognized patrilineal descent. As Goldfarb, a Conservative rabbi, had done, the Reform movement characterized its decision as a response to what it saw as the needs of the time. It was a watershed in the debate on intermarriage. The Central Conference of American Rabbis (CCAR) argued that, in the past, rabbis had adopted changes that fit the needs of the time. Now they, too, felt compelled to bring Jewish practice into line with current values. As the first movement to ordain a woman rabbi (Wertheimer 1993, 105), the Reform movement was committed to equality between men and women. It recognized that the world now offered equality and freedom for Jews, social contact between Jews and non-Jews, changes in family structure and gender roles, and an increase in "mixed marriages" (Central Conference of American Rabbis 1983). Furthermore, because the matrilineal principle was rabbinic, not from the Torah, there was precedent for patrilineal descent in the Bible. And in the contemporary United States, children from intermarriages already existed. Thus, the CCAR felt "morally obliged to make provisions for the offsprings of such a union when either the father or mother seek to have their children recognized and educated as a Jew." Finally, by requiring "positive acts of identification," the decision went beyond the requirements of traditional Judaism so that even someone who was Jewish by matrilineal descent would have to demonstrate his or her Jewishness by, for example, celebrating a bar or bat mitzvah.

The patrilineal descent decision responds to a specific American, even Protestant, context. It acknowledges the centrality of choice, in addition to ascribed ties, melding sociological and religious reasoning in its redefinition of Jewishness. The CCAR made clear the importance of the American context in its explanation of how it understood Jewishness:

1. We do not view birth as a determining factor in the religious identification of children of a mixed marriage.
2. We distinguish between descent and identification.
3. The mobility of American Jews has diminished the influence of the extended family upon such a child. This means that a significant informal bond with Judaism which played a role in the past does not exist for our generation.
4. Education has always been a strong factor in Jewish identity. In the recent past we could assume a minimal Jewish education for most children. In our time almost half the American Jewish community remains unaffiliated, and their children receive no Jewish education.

For those reasons the Central Conference of American Rabbis . . . declares that the child of one Jewish parent is under the presumption of Jewish descent. This presumption of the Jewish status of the offspring of any mixed marriage is to be established through appropriate and timely public and formal acts of identification with the Jewish faith and people. The performance of these mitzvot serves to commit those who participate in them, both parents and child, to Jewish life. (Central Conference of American Rabbis 1983)

With this upheaval of the traditional Jewish definition, the Reform movement implicitly recognized that the United States had thrust upon Judaism a new definition of religion. Being Jewish by birth was no guarantee that anyone would choose Jewish beliefs or actions. By broadening the circumstances by which one could be considered Jewish by birth and including a requirement for Jewish actions as well, the CCAR had attempted to merge American and more traditional Jewish ideals as authentically as it could.

With this contested expansion of the boundaries of the Jewish family, the boundaries of the Jewish people grew unnervingly nebulous for Jewish leaders, although less so for laypeople. Before the introduction of patrilineal descent, the Jewish community generally had agreed on rabbinic law's definition of a Jew as one who is born to a Jewish mother or who has converted. Jews under this broadly accepted definition made up "the Jewish people." This construction is religious, ethnic, and familial all at once. In traditional terms, each Jewish family is meant to continue the Jewish people and its covenant with God (Lamm [1980] 1991), functioning as one of many interdependent links in a chain of Jewish families going far into the past and future. Debate about intermarriage grew increasingly tense as the furor over patrilineal descent made clear the depth of Jewish leaders' divisions. But while the Conservative movement chose not to follow the Reform movement's lead, a 1988 study found that non-Orthodox Jews largely accepted patrilineal descent, whether or not their leaders resisted it (Cohen 1988).

Unnerving religious disagreements shifted into debates about social scientific studies of American Jewry in the 1970s and later. Focusing on these studies rather than contentious religious issues gave the appearance that Jewish leaders were unified in their commitment to mitigating the effects of intermarriage—even if such unity was among only the leaders, while the followers married non-Jews more than ever. Social scientific studies of American Jewry typically obtain data when Jewish federations commission demographic studies in order to plan how to distribute their funds among the various social service programs that they operate. These studies collect information about Jews' affiliations with and activities in synagogues and other Jewish institutions, along with data about intermarriage rates, in order to understand the local Jewish community. These studies respond to the federations' perceived needs and usually avoid explicitly prescribing specific religious content in their policy recommendations. But the data that the studies collect about intermarriage regularly become part of the same debate about religious legitimacy that both preceded and followed the Reform movement's adoption of patrilineal descent.

The extent to which debates about such questions of religious legitimacy and authenticity are recast as scientific and policy discourse is remarkable. One might assume that opposition to intermarriage or devotion to community cohesion is deeply rooted in devotion to God and Torah. Oddly, neither God nor Torah is mentioned in most examples of intermarriage discourse discussed in this chapter. Of three essential facets of Judaism—God, Torah, and Israel—only Israel, in the sense of Jewish peoplehood, is explicitly featured in this heated controversy about what people owe to one another and to their ancestors and descendants. Instead, the conversation is framed in a utilitarian way, concerning the best method to ensure Jewish continuity but not necessarily any particular content. In this context, Jewish institutions simply seek to determine the most efficient way to reach the goal of ensuring the existence of enough Jews to support Jewish institutions in their existing forms. This utilitarian focus builds on a longstanding foundation: since the 1950s, rabbis have been using statistics rather than religious prescription to explain the need for endogamy. The proliferation of these numbers has had a strong impact on American Jews' consciousness of intermarriage and helped to construct intermarriage as a problem that could be solved (Berman 2009, 44–45, 69n202). Mid-twentieth-century and later Jewish leaders determined that producing such Jews through institutional programs based on social-scientific data was preferable to the unpredictable results of individual parents' efforts (Berman 2010). Some social scientists used surveys for activist purposes as well: in a 1977 article called "The American Jewish Population Erosion," Harvard demographer Elihu Bergman predicted that by 2076 there could be only 10,420 American Jews left. Even though Bergman later admitted that his methodology was flawed and his conclusions were exaggerated, he had achieved what he said was his goal of getting American Jews' attention (Kaplan 2009, 167).

Soundly constructed or not, demographic studies' data about intermarriage have been controversial because people have interpreted them according to their existing beliefs about intermarriage and assimilation. Jewish social surveys in the 1970s documented that intermarriage was increasing and that it had begun to occur equally among Jewish men and women. A debate over the surveys' statistical data and their meaning emerged. The surveys came to be implicitly regarded as holding symbolic power to see into the Jewish future, carrying the authority of science. Indeed, news reports about the surveys emphasized their scientific authority: "While the survey itself was carried out several years ago, the computerized analysis was completed only recently at Bar-Ilan University in Israel by Prof. Bernard Lazerwitz, a research expert who used the university's giant IBM computer to reach his conclusions" ("Losses from Intermarriage Replaced, Analyst Reports" 1977, 6). Several major surveys of the American Jewish population supplied statistical data for discussions of intermarriage from the 1970s onward. These included the National Jewish Population Study (NJPS), carried out in 1971, 1990, and 2000–2001; the American Jewish Identity Survey of 2001; and the American Jewish Committee's Survey of American Jewish Opinion, carried out annually from 2000 to 2006. The earliest of these studies was widely publicized in the mid- to late 1970s.

When the 1971 NJPS results finally became widely available in 1977, the Jewish media reported that, contrary to popular wisdom, intermarriage was actually less of a problem than had been believed. The researchers had concluded that the low Jewish birthrate was more to blame than intermarriage was for population shrinkage. The majority of intermarried Jews' children, said Fred Massarik, NJPS's scientific director, were raised as Jews ("Intermarriage Not the Major Threat, Jerusalem Dialogue Scholar Asserts" 1978). The 1971 study reported that 9.2 percent of American Jews were then intermarried; and of those who had married between 1966 and 1972, 31.7 percent intermarried. But the study defined intermarriage as "a marriage in which one or the other partner was identified with a non-Jewish religious-cultural viewpoint *at the time that he/she met his/her future spouse*," so that only born Jews marrying born Jews counted as endogamy. Thus, while it was troubling to most that nearly a third of new marriages were intermarriages, that figure could be assumed to include some conversions to Judaism, and even some of the nonconversionary couples were still affiliating with the Jewish community (Council of Jewish Federations and Welfare Funds 1973).

Those who were already convinced that intermarriage was a threat continued to regard it as such, assailing the construction of the NJPS study that downplayed the threat of intermarriage. In a 1979 issue of *Commentary*, David Singer, who was then associate editor of the *American Jewish Year Book*, argued that Massarik's interpretation of the statistics reflected an impossibly rosy view of intermarriage that would only "buoy the accommodationist spirit." This approach would obscure the fact that intermarriage was, in Singer's words, "a threat both to Jewish group survival . . . and to the continuity of generations within the family and the ability of family members to identify with one another." Singer (1979) argued that, rather than "attitudes—how many non-Jewish spouses identify as Jews; how many intermarried couples plan to give their children a Jewish education," the surveys should have measured "behavior" (52). He was arguing for a more traditional definition of Jewishness in which behavior means "observance of Jewish law and custom," and his claim might even have excluded people who would be considered Jewish according to Jewish law. The construction of the survey itself was a site of conflict about the definition of Jewishness.

It made sense that the NJPS had focused on attitudes, given modern American conceptions of religion as focused on faith and belief rather than actions. Sociologists later found that across religious groups religious identification in the United States essentially is based on attitudes more than behaviors. For example, many more Americans say they go to church than actually do so (Hadaway, Marler, and Chaves 1993, 1998). As members of American society, American Jews who follow this pattern of religious membership might see nothing unusual about it nor any reason why their religious membership should be considered illegitimate. In addition, measures of behavior reveal that exogamous and endogamous Jews are not completely distinct in their religious observances (McGinity 2009, 127). Singer's argument demonstrated that two different definitions of religion were already operating in American Judaism: a traditional Jewish one favoring behavior, identification across generations, and group survival; and an American one, rooted in personal attitudes, that was shaping many Jews' practices and beliefs.

However, social scientists and media commentators generally did not view intermarriage as part of the same set of social changes that had affected all American families or even as merely one of many threats to Judaism. This stance contrasted with that of the popular Jewish press, which in the 1970s covered the threat of intermarriage alongside the dangers of the oppression of Jews in the Soviet Union, the state of Israel's constant threat from its neighbors, the Zero Population Growth movement, women's expanding public and workplace roles, and the concomitant shrinking average family size. American Jews worked together on behalf of Jews imperiled in other parts of the world, but on personal matters such as childbearing and family structure, they were more divided. Milton Himmelfarb, a senior staff member at the American Jewish Committee and a contributing editor at *Commentary*, blamed Jewish women for the declining Jewish population, saying that their use of contraception was the problem. In the early 1970s, the Jewish Population Regeneration Union urged Jews to have larger families to counteract the effect of the Zero Population Growth movement, which urged people to consider the environmental impact of their family size (Staub 2002, 261–262). Demonstrating the longevity of these concerns, the Conservative movement made a similar plea in 2006, enjoining families to have a "mitzvah child" (one more child than they had originally planned) to help offset the continuing slowdown of the Jewish population (Moline 2006).

Women's increased workforce participation, delayed marriage, and the lower birth rate affected American society at large as well as Jews.[3] Writers for the new Jewish feminist magazine *Lilith* noted that the Jewish "population panic" coincided with women's increased career aspirations and the need to change contemporary Jewish family structures (Frank 1978, 12). Jewish men had enjoyed increasing autonomy as they became middle-class Americans, but Jewish women were relative newcomers to it, along with other contemporaries of the second-wave feminist movement. Feminist writers argued that Jewish men displaced their ambivalence about assimilation and Judaism onto Jewish women. The opposition of the non-Jewish woman, the *shiksa*, to the Jewish woman, cast as the "JAP" or "Jewish American Princess," demonstrated their worries "about becoming American men," anthropologist of American Judaism Riv-Ellen Prell (2003) argues. The ambivalent Jewish man could choose a feminizing Jewish woman, who would threaten him with her demands to make the "right" choices, such as a Jewish marriage partner and to have Jewish children. Or he could choose a nonthreatening shiksa who would demand nothing but who "[would make] it impossible to continue Jewish life" because she did not contribute to the continuity of Jewish tradition through the family. The genesis of such stereotypes coincided with the 1960s increase in intermarriage (Sarna 1994, 55–58), showing that traditional notions of the Jewish family were being questioned for many reasons, not only because of intermarriage.

Scholars have continued to examine the role of gender stereotypes in inter-marriage. Fishman (2004) argues that Jews absorb negative stereotypes about Jewish men and women and choose to intermarry because of them. McGinity (2009), in contrast, argues that "actual negative experiences" with Jewish men in her Jewish women interviewees' lives were more likely than stereotypes to have contributed to their intermarriages (165). Such gender analysis never-theless leaves intact the terms of the debate about "defects in the contracting parties" who may be influenced by stereotypes. The stereotypes mark Jews as different, but the question underlying intermarriage debates is whether and how Jews as a group are different from the rest of American society.

As women sought to expand their roles in public life, Americans more gen-erally focused on their personal fulfillment. This 1960s and 1970s individualism saw intermarriage as a matter of individual happiness rather than group loyalty (McGinity 2009, 113–114). At the 1976 National Conference on Mixed Marriage, rabbis and sociologists tried to integrate their awareness of this cultural shift into their understandings of American Judaism. Rabbi Arthur Hertzberg (1978), a historian and past president of the American Jewish Congress, explained that American Jews regarded marriage and intermarriage, like religion, as a pri-vate decision and not a "total break with the Jewish community" (11). At the same conference, Brooklyn College sociologist Mervin Verbit (1978) argued that this private Judaism was "the real threat" to the Jewish community because it changed the definition of Jewishness. He asserted that the "Jewishness of the Jewish community is not merely a characteristic of the individuals who make it up" but that it is "a characteristic of the community itself" across the world, through history, and as defined by Judaism as a religion (97). Verbit felt that contemporary Jews' lackadaisical attitude toward intermarriage would gradually change the nature of Jewishness itself by positioning individualism, instead of Jewish peoplehood, as a first principle. While he recognized that individualism grew out of sociological processes of secularization, he felt that the Jewish com-munity had to resist it because "an individualistic definition of Jewishness is too internally contradictory" (100–101). For the good of both the Jewish people and Jewish individuals, Verbit urged emphasizing Jewish unity over and against the individualism of the broader culture. Thus, he suggested, while individual Jews might have unique subjectivities, they ought to restrain them. This tension between individualism and group loyalty was already present in American cul-ture long before the 1970s and continues today, as I will discuss in later chapters.

Instead of understanding the changes to Jewish expression as having emerged from these social transformations, Jack Wertheimer (1994) identified intermarriage as a kind of "deviant" family structure (30). In a *Commentary* arti-cle entitled "Family Values & the Jews," he lambasted what he saw as the Jewish community's failure to resist and remedy individual Jews' failure to get and stay married, bear multiple children, ensure that the children stayed Jewish, and remain geographically close to family. He included intermarriage as one among many sociological facts that he understood to be the result of Jews' personal and communal failures. Sociologists Michael J. Rosenfeld and Byung-Soo Kim (2005) point out that young adults who move away from their communities of origin are likely to have greater independence from their families and are therefore more likely to have an interracial marriage or same-sex union. Wertheimer implicitly saw such independence as a threat to what he understood to be "Jewish family values."

These contested ways of talking about intermarriage continued into the 1990s and 2000s with the same emotional intensity and scientific scrutiny. Some people read the continuing rise in intermarriage rates as a clear sign that the scales had been tipped in favor of assimilation. The 1990 NJPS reported that 52 percent of born Jews who married between 1985 and 1991 had married non-Jews who did not convert to Judaism (Kosmin et al. 1991, 13), although there was debate about whether this figure was accurate. Nonetheless, the percentage was repeated over and over, taking on a life of its own as a symbol of assimilation and communal threat. In response, meetings of Jewish elites, comparable to the 1976 National Conference on Mixed Marriage, continued into the 1990s (McGinity 2009, 175–176). The statistics attained intense symbolic power in these discourses; in a powerful and concrete way, they confirmed people's fears about the Jewish future.

Recognizing the power that the numbers had gained, some scholars attempted to debunk the statistics. Egon Mayer (1994), a sociologist who studied intermarriage and directed the Jewish Outreach Institute, described a 1984 study that had been used erroneously to support claims that intermarried Jews would not have Jewish grandchildren, a fate widely seen as the sign of imminent communal demise. The study's sample comprised thirteen intermarried people in Philadelphia whose parents had also been intermarried and whose children were not of "the Jewish religion." People who had intermarried parents but who were married to Jews and/or raising their children as Jews were excluded from this sample. "So at least some of their parents (who had intermarried) had Jewish grandchildren," Mayer concluded. The sample's boundaries were not the only problem: the phrasing of the question was also faulty. The study did not ask if their children were *Jews*, which Mayer thought would have elicited a positive response. Citing other surveys' findings that many Jews tend to answer that they are Jewish but that their religion is "none," he highlighted the fact that secular ethnics made up a large portion of Jews in the United States, intermarried or not, and that people with two unquestionably Jewish parents who are secular ethnics are still Jews by any commonly accepted definition of Judaism. Finally, even within this sample of thirteen people who said they were not of the Jewish religion, some fasted on Yom Kippur and maintained mostly Jewish social circles. Again, the concomitant operation of different definitions of religion and Jewishness rendered the picture of intermarriage murky.

Mayer implied that studies of intermarriage continued to function as a sort of Rorschach test or ideological mirror, reflecting whatever viewers wanted to see about the state of American Judaism. He suggested that Zionist anti-Diaspora ideology motivated the researchers behind this "lachrymose" interpretation of intermarriage: "Why the eagerness to write off possibly hundreds of thousands of people who may well think of themselves as Jewish or have the potential to do so? And why is this being done by the very people who claim to be so concerned about the quantity as well as the quality of the Jewish future?" Echoing Sklare's words from thirty years earlier, Mayer said, "Writing these people off often masks the as yet insufficiently explored issue of disaffection among the descendants of the in-married. Not only do the grandchildren of the intermarried opt out of Jewish identification, so do Jews marrying other Jews, in proportions that have yet to be measured" (50).

Mayer's suggestion that statistics on intermarriage served as a Rorschach test dovetails with David Schneider's ([1968] 1980) concept of folk science. Americans' theory of kinship, Schneider argues, in part depends on a folk scientific notion of genetics. Presented with contradictory information reflecting actual scientific knowledge of genetics, Americans nevertheless cling to their original, inaccurate folk theory. Mayer's argument about the uses of statistics on intermarriage makes a somewhat similar point: because statistics have the authority and legitimacy of science and confirm a preexisting fear of cultural extinction, they are difficult to refute and so continue to be used.

In addition to the statistics' scientific authority, their repeated use by Jewish media helps to cement their importance in media consumers' minds. The familiar narrative of intermarriage as assimilation anchors the reporting on these statistics so that media consumers grasp these facts within the context of their relevance to Jewish continuity rather than in the context of the studies in which the statistics were generated. Sociologist William Gamson (1999) argues that elite media organizations serve as gatekeepers for facts, so that the facts that they choose to convey to the public become the only facts to which the public has access. The idea that media repetition of certain facts constructs the reality that media consumers know, in combination with folk science, helps explain why the narrative of intermarriage as assimilation has such staying power.

Alternate Narratives

The narrative of intermarriage as assimilation has persisted in Jewish public discourse despite the development of competing sociological theories. Sociologists of religion have devised a wide variety of interpretations and predictions about religion in the modern world, and for each one that suggests that religion is in some kind of decline, another suggests that religion is as strong as ever but in different ways (Berger 1998; Casanova 1994). So, for example, sociologists have applied to Judaism ideas about the transformation of religious authority, the privatization of religion, and a resurgence of public religion (Davidman 1991; Goldscheider and Zuckerman 1986; Kaufman 1991; McGinity 2009). Religious decline, too, may be seen in the 2008 American Religious Identification Survey's finding that a growing number—15 percent—of Americans claim no religion at all, even if they do possess religious beliefs (Kosmin et al. 2009). The same study found that the number of people claiming Judaism as a religion has declined, although many still continue to claim Jewishness as ethnicity ("Catholics on the Move" 2009). By 2028, religious "nones" could represent 25 percent of the American population, if current trends continue (Kosmin et al. 2009). If American Jews are leaving Jewish religious institutions behind and assimilating, they are doing so in the company of many other likeminded Americans.

Alternative understandings of intermarriage as part of a transformation of Judaism (Goldscheider and Zuckerman 1986; McGinity 2009) and of religion more generally have failed to supplant the intermarriage-as-assimilation narrative in Jewish public discourse. Instead, that narrative depends on understanding Jewishness as ethnicity, not religion. So while we read some particular aspects of American Judaism as we do a Rorschach image, as a personal response, intermarriage has come to function as a definitive litmus test for Jewish commitment, although one more commonly thinks of religious commitment than of ethnic commitment. But ethnicity has been a more convenient way to mark Jewish distinctiveness because it does not depend on anyone's having particular religious beliefs. While intermarriage is religiously forbidden, avoidance of it can mark socioreligious boundaries without reference to religious content. Responses to intermarriage in Jewish public discourse therefore both reflect and avoid acknowledging the religious split that has already taken place.

Sociological theory underpinning the inreach-outreach debate (Kaplan 2009, 171; McGinity 2009, 203–209) exemplifies this emphasis on ethnicity over religion. Categories of "central" and "peripheral" are key parts of the debate, and they reflect sociological theories about ethnic groups (Fishman 2004, 145–146). Jewish policymakers consider whether Jewish continuity would be better served by performing outreach (persuading Jews they often designate as "peripheral" to join Jewish institutions) or inreach (concentrating financial resources on the "central" Jews who already participate actively in Jewish institutions). Given findings from Jewish community demographic studies that link endogamy with greater participation in an array of Jewish activities and institutions, the intermarriage-as-assimilation narrative understands unaffiliated, peripheral Jews as intermarried and central Jews who already participate in Jewish institutional life as in-married (Dashefsky, Sheskin, and Miller 2012). An application of this theory can be found in Wertheimer and colleagues' creation of the categories of "core" and "lowest common denominator" (the periphery) with which to categorize the American Jewish populace (McGinity 2009, 210).

Discourse about intermarriage displaces questions about what holds Jews together and how they might talk about it onto intermarried Jews, often holding endogamous Jews exempt from them, as if the changes of modernity affect only those Jews who choose to be affected by those changes. In Jewish public discourse, intermarried Jews symbolize for American Jews as a group their ambivalence about their success in the United States and the contradictions that it brings. The very commitments that led to Jews' success in this country—for example, their investment in building a politically liberal society that would accommodate religious freedoms and equal opportunity—undercut their certainty about the basis of their group loyalties and boundaries (Berman 2009; Dollinger 2000; Goldstein 2006; McGinity 2009; Staub 2002). Attributing assimilative desires and habits to intermarried couples, rather than recognizing the ways in which all Jews are affected by questions about assimilation and the meaning of Jewishness, renders unnerving questions about the future of Jewish existence in the United States less threatening. It also perpetuates a sense that monolithic constructions of Jewish community, Jewish continuity, the Jewish people, and Jewish tradition reflect shared meanings among most or all Jews.

Intermarriage represents issues that are fundamental to the structure of Jewish peoplehood. Anxiety and anger about intermarriage are linked to anxiety about Jewish survival amid changes thrust upon Jews by modernity. Regardless of what statistics about intermarriage say, they continually evoke this anxiety. Jews in earlier times and other places also have worried about the survival of their people, and historically American Jews have consistently rallied to the cause of imperiled Jews in other countries. As Simon Rawidowicz (1986) wrote, Jews throughout history have feared that their own generation was the last and that when they died, so would Jewish tradition and values. Nevertheless, generations of Jews continued to study, extend, and in their turn fear for Jewish tradition. Rawidowicz thought of this as a double process of ever-dying and everliving: as much as Israel was the "ever-dying people," its dread of death ensured its vitality. These inseparable and self-renewing processes are also visible in the contemporary United States as the United Jewish Communities responds to the "crisis" in Jewish affiliation rates with efforts to create a Jewish "renaissance" through promotion of Jewish education and identification (Wiener 2001).

The American context projects that dread of dying into a new arena: instead of physical survival, continuing peoplehood is at stake. In other times and places, Jews have lived in relatively self-contained communities within relatively hostile host societies. While antisemitic sentiment still exists in the United States, it does not have widespread popular support, nor is it engrained in public institutions. Instead, contemporary American Jews now enjoy abundant acceptance and goodwill from American society to the extent that many non-Jews want to marry them. Some Jews experience this situation as a threat to Jewish survival: if non-Jews marry into the Jewish people, they disrupt the traditional stream of Jewish kinship. Some Jews hope for the possibility that these spouses will become new Jews. Some Jews simply see an opportunity to marry whomever they love, without restriction or proselytizing. If intermarriage is indeed a threat to Jewish survival, it is a new kind of threat that has nothing to do with Jews' physical safety. Other situations that have captured American Jews' attention and energy, such as the rescue of Ethiopian Jews, have involved donating money, volunteering, and lobbying congressional representatives. Activism about intermarriage mainly takes place through the persuasive and analytical voices that participate in the multiple discourses on the subject.

The American Jewish media's discussion of intermarriage from the 1960s to the present has aimed to persuade readers that the Jewish community is under siege from within. The parties involved in these discourses have been gripped by the reality of trying to reconcile two cultural worlds, American and Jewish, which hold equal part in their lives but use different languages, symbols, and reference points. Each cultural world has demanded allegiance and exacted consequences for failing to meet its demands. What is at stake is at once personal, familial, and cultural. At the personal level, nostalgic and identity elements connect Jews to their Jewish background within a familial and cultural context that is intrinsically both Jewish and American. Neither of these cultural elements can be separated from American Jews' self-concept. The fact of intermarriage has forced Jews to ask what Judaism is in this American context. But attempts to define Judaism in the United States have led to only diffuse answers and partial agreements.

In contrast to these discourses that reveal ideological statements and representations about intermarriage, the ethnographic approach that I pursue in the remainder of this book allows us to ask how traditional ideas about Judaism, Jewish community, Jewishness, and different understandings of fairness and individualism factor into the religious lives and choices of intermarried people. By balancing American, Christian, and Jewish cultural and religious thought and practices, my intermarried informants understand their families' religious lives, broadly speaking, in two ways, which I call universalist individualism and ethnic familialism. While my informants' experiences do not neatly fit into only one or the other of these models, the categories reveal elements of their lives left out by discourses about intermarriage and help illuminate the irreducible category of Jewishness in America.

2

American Contradictions

Conversations about Self and Community

As my intermarried informants developed their self-understandings and practices, they took into account a wide range of factors: intermarriage discourse; their own feelings and experiences; and American cultural ideas about religion, community, the self, and gender. Couples and individuals combined these factors in ways that were sometimes contradictory but responded to their needs and experiences as they understood them. These couples' conversations and experiences showed that the meanings of marriage between Jews and Christians were not as easily or clearly defined as American Jewish discourses about intermarriage have suggested. My informants both resisted and accommodated such discourses as they sought to reconcile the contradictions of American Judaism, community, and individuality.

Spending time among intermarried couples in a variety of settings allowed me to observe a wide spectrum of self-understandings and practices, bounded on either side by models of religious experience and self-understanding that I call *universalist individualism* and *ethnic familialism*. This chapter and the next examine the logic and emotion behind these models. The couples drew from each model, to varying degrees, as they connected to religious communities and preserved what they understood as their personal integrity and authenticity. The models help us understand how different emphases on particular cultural themes result in different practices and choices within a family; they are not meant to capture the essence of any family's being. Most people draw from both categories and do not fall strictly into one or the other. However, by using these categories to understand their lives, we gain insight into how discourses affect people's self-understandings and practices and how people manage all of these factors when some of them contradict one another. The voices of intermarried individuals and couples presented in chapters 2 and 3 bring these contradictions to life in a way that many of us can relate to.

I present first the universalist individualist perspective and then the ethnic familialist perspective. The universalist individualist perspective draws upon themes in American culture that emphasize the unity of religious teachings, resistance to authority, and Protestant Christian ideas about the individual's right to interpret religious teachings. This perspective stresses egalitarian gender roles and a carefully rational, choice-focused approach to religious beliefs and practices. At the same time, universalist individualists see what they call "heritage" as playing an important role in their religious lives. They explain that respect for "both sides" of each individual's heritage is a kind of fairness.

Ethnic familialism also honors heritage and fairness but understands the relationship between these concepts differently. People taking this perspective were more likely to look at fairness in terms of the group, not the individual. Because Jews are more anxious about their demographic prospects than Christians are, many who took this perspective explained that it was fairest for them to identify with the Jewish part of their children's heritage, not the Christian side. Those who followed this perspective tended to adopt more traditional gender roles and experiential rather than choice-centered religious practices. Both perspectives clearly responded to American Jewish intermarriage discourses.

Both perspectives also demonstrated the importance of women in determining a family's religious choices—particularly the family's Jewishness. As Orthodox Rabbi Z (discussed in chapter 5) put it, "My guess is that if women are the Jewish partner, they're more actively Jewish; if the women are the non-Jewish partner and the husband is Jewish, the women are more actively Jewish [even though the women themselves are not Jewish]. . . . In most cases, the woman is leading the man." Chapters 2 and 3 will explain how and why.

Prophetic Outcasts

On a Friday night in January 2006, a group of self-described "interfaith" couples and Jewish and Christian clergy gathered for a communal Shabbat dinner at a building shared by a church and a synagogue in Bethesda, Maryland. This group of approximately one hundred Jewish-Christian couples, mostly white and middle class, had come together from all over the United States for the weekend. Their aim was to discuss ways to make dual-religion families work. All were participants in a weekend conference entitled "How Interfaith Families Can Thrive and Contribute in a Polarized World," held by the Dovetail Institute for Interfaith Family Resources. The interfaith families gathered here inoculated one another against the claims of normative religious discourses that expressed disapproval of their choices, instead insisting that they possessed a more enlightened viewpoint.

In supporting one another and framing their experiences in a way that reflected positively on their choices, these couples demonstrated their awareness of discourses about intermarriage and Jewishness. Some couples responded to such discourses by asserting their integrity as individuals, the truth of universalism, and a vision of community based on these principles, all of which they felt were essential to any conception of religion. They suspected religious norms and institutions of conspiring to rob them of their autonomy. Others acknowledged individualist and universalist values but also felt a responsibility to demonstrate that they were "good Jews," not assimilated individualists. Yet their commitment to Jewishness was often hard for them to articulate or explain, in sharp contrast to the carefully delineated, if sometimes unconventional, religious ideas that some other intermarried couples espoused. Commitments to individualism and Jewish norms were hard to reconcile, but most of my informants felt that they had to do so somehow. American and Jewish cultural discourses about family, individuality, and religion created difficult contradictions for them.

While not all of my informants belonged to, or even knew of, the Dovetail Institute, many agreed with its distinctly American approach to religion and family. The organization's journal, *Dovetail: A Journal by and for Jewish/Christian Families*, explains in its mission statement that "Jewish and Christian perspectives can dovetail." The journal advocates the sharing of "ideas, experiences, resources, and support" to enhance "communication for interfaith couples, their parents, and their children." It recognizes that intermarried spouses bring differing, potentially conflicting, perspectives to a marriage, as the discord approach that Marshall Sklare described also recognized. Instead of discouraging intermarriage, however, Dovetail seeks to help intermarried couples "make peace in their homes and communities." The journal was founded in 1992 by Joan Hawxhurst (1998), a Protestant married to a Jewish man (1).

In supporting Jewish-Christian families, the Dovetail organization emphasizes that such families can be configured in many ways, arguing that the best arrangement for any given family is whatever that family feels is best. What is distinctively American about this approach is the organization's claim that there are no definitive answers and that communication is key. While Americans are often unable or unwilling to explain their moral commitments in substantive terms, saying that their convictions are personal and private, they are convinced of the value of communication. Agreement on religious matters may not be necessary or even possible in this view, but the common good is served simply by acknowledging and understanding others' points of view (Bellah et al. 1985).

For the conference participants, the meaning of interfaith was as flexible as Dovetail's mission statement intended it to be. The term *interfaith* also appeared to be somewhat exclusive of strictly normative religious observances, as I learned at the communal Shabbat dinner. When I chose kosher food from the kosher and nonkosher buffet options, my Jewish and Christian dinner companions, whom I had never met before, expressed surprise. This choice seemed to mark me as especially religious and in their eyes might have been incongruous with my being intermarried. Because we had all attended this conference to learn about ways to make interfaith religious lives work, I wondered what the term *interfaith* meant to my companions, given that they seemed startled at my observance of religious norms. The term's meaning grew even more nebulous as I overheard a couple discuss their son's impending wedding. A woman asked about the engaged couple, "Is that a diversity situation?" *Diversity* appeared to be a synonym or euphemism for intermarriage. I surmised from these conversations that *interfaith* was akin to *multicultural*, a value with which my informants seemed to identify, but that it was not normatively religious.

The next morning, I learned more about the relationship of the term to normative Judaism and Christianity. I attended a discussion group of about two dozen people, middle-aged and younger, about ways to avoid "confusion" and the responsibility to "model" interfaith life for others. We gathered in a circle of folding chairs in the function hall of the combined church-synagogue and introduced ourselves. Two couples in the group were not yet married. Many of the participants were raising their children in both spouses' religions. These couples hoped to inspire each other and themselves to view intermarriage as a positive force and a special privilege over and against normative religious rhetoric critical of intermarriage.

After the group members introduced themselves, the session's moderator, Nancy, noted that their comments demonstrated "practical, political, and prophetic aspects of interfaith."[1] The discussion to follow would not merely highlight pragmatic ways in which intermarried couples could resolve disagreements over conflicting religious celebrations; it would valorize "interfaith"— multireligious—families as epitomizing and surpassing the religious insights of the normative traditions from which they came. Participants in this discussion clearly were contesting some religious leaders' and institutions' arguments against intermarriage.

"Interfaith families are outcasts, like the prophets were, and like the prophets, interfaith families are contributing to *tikkun olam* [repairing the world]," said Nancy, referring to a Jewish mystical concept that has been extended by some contemporary Jewish and Christian groups to mean "social justice" generally. Her comparison of the intermarried discussion participants to biblical prophets suggests not just that the intermarried couples had special religious understanding but that they possessed special access to God. They felt that their moral outlook was holy—not only as legitimate as normative religious traditions but surpassing those traditions in the sense that this outlook recognized both individual persons and the unity of humanity as ultimate values. Another woman added that even her rabbi had acknowledged the prophetic nature of interfaith relationships, although he still advised couples to raise their children in only one religion. She remarked that refusing to choose one religion over another was a form of "idealism," a way of focusing on the religions' teachings without being encumbered by their rules. With this comment, she suggested that "teachings," or religious beliefs, outweighed "rules," or religious behavioral norms, practices, and institutions. Similarly, a number of my informants characterized normative Judaism as overly focused on rules without attention to their "meaning."

Next, two invited panelists told their story to the group: Jude, who was Jewish, and his wife, Tabitha, who was Catholic. Long married, Jude and Tabitha were raising their children in both Judaism and Catholicism. Jude described to the group his nine-year-old daughter's reflection on being part of an interfaith family, clearly delighted at her insight. "Our daughter said, 'If I'm Jewish and Catholic, and I marry someone who's Buddhist and Muslim, our children would have four religions!' I thought this was so profound. It showed that, contrary to what people say, being raised in both religions is *not* confusing. My daughter can identify with more than one religion without being confused. She gets that it's the individual and humanity that matter, not the religion." Here Jude commented that normative religious institutions and their representatives, such as priests, rabbis, and their professional associations, who forbade intermarriage ignored the importance of both individual persons and the world beyond the religions' own membership. Instead, he suggested, these figures were more concerned with preserving their own power over their members and false divisions between their members and non-members. One of the ways in which they did this was to claim that children raised in multiple religious traditions would be confused. Sociologist Sylvia Barack Fishman (2004) observed a similar push back against warnings of children's confusion at a Dovetail conference held in Chicago in 2002 (94). Repeating his daughter's comments was Jude's way of reassuring the assembled interfaith couples that the "scare tactics" of opponents of intermarriage were disingenuous and did not reflect the truth of intermarried families' experiences.

Tabitha added that religions teach the same ultimate truth, as Jude believed their daughter's comment to have shown. She explained, "The religions aren't incompatible or contradictory. Catholicism came out of Judaism. The ethics and morals are very similar. That's why we marry each other! For Jude and me, even ethnically we're more alike than different. Both of us are from working-class immigrant families where our grandparents didn't speak English, so we relate to each other's backgrounds." Like Jude, Tabitha argued that religious institutions and norms created false divisions between members of different religions by focusing on what makes them unique. Fishman (2004) noted a similar argument made at the 2002 Dovetail conference by a fourteen-year-old child of intermarried parents, who said, "Judaism and Christianity are really almost identical: they're only separated by about three laws—and one God!" (140). Jude and Tabitha emphasized their similar backgrounds and outlook on life throughout the discussion, saying that because of their similarities as individuals and their recognition of their religions' shared teachings, their multireligious household ran smoothly. Yet the descriptions they offered of their religious backgrounds did not sound terribly similar at other points in the discussion: Tabitha spoke with warmth of the liberal, activist Catholic community she was raised in, and Jude recalled his Orthodox upbringing in a Jewish neighborhood. But here they emphasized the aspects of their backgrounds that were shared or similar.

Jude and Tabitha's argument that parents could teach children to understand their identities as inherently multiple conflicted with the advice of many religious leaders, but it resonated in other contexts, from multicultural education to raising multiracial children to contemporary American political ethics. Activists committed to their multiracial identity lobbied the U.S. government to permit them to claim more than one racial category on census forms, arguing that a single category alone did not represent their experiences or self-understanding (DaCosta 2007). Just as multiracial children were often pressured to choose one identity lest they have one assigned to them by society (American Academy of Child and Adolescent Psychiatry 2011), multireligious children felt pressure to choose one religious identity. But children should resist such pressure, Jude suggested, for their own good. He believed that, from an early age, children could see that religious values such as tolerance and acceptance reach beyond any one religion, suggesting that these values are natural and obvious to anyone. One teenager explained at the 2002 Dovetail conference that she felt "lucky" to have more than one religion as a resource in her life: "we know that if one 'truth' turns out not to feel like the truth to us, there are other versions of the truth we can think about and maybe believe in" (Fishman 2004, 94–95). In this view, the contention that religious identity should be single is faulty because it ignores every religion's own universalist teachings.

According to this outlook, because norms found in more than one religion were identified with ultimate truth, intermarried couples had special access to such truth because they approached it from more than one standpoint. The inference was that the imaginary person in Jude's daughter's comment who had four religious backgrounds would not only clearly see the similarities in those religions' teachings but also have deeper religious understanding than someone with only one or two religious backgrounds might have.

Despite its arithmetical simplicity, Jude and Tabitha's interpretation of the basic oneness of religious truth is at odds with some major teachings of classical Judaism and Christianity. Christianity has had a complex history of contradictory stances toward other religions. Its relationship to Judaism has been particularly fraught because of the concept of supersession (the claim that Christianity is the New Israel and thus replaces Judaism) and because of Christians' historical denigration of Jews for what they considered Jews' refusal to recognize Jesus as the messiah. After the Holocaust, a serious effort arose to stop anti-Judaism, as seen in publications by the World Council of Churches in 1948 and Vatican II in 1965 (Cross and Livingstone 2005a). But some Christians have continued to try to convert Jews and other non-Christians, which leaders of these groups strongly oppose (Niebuhr 1999). This troubled history may help to explain why most Jews see belief in the divinity of Jesus as a boundary that they will not cross (Edelstein 1994). Some Jews have not even recognized Christianity as a monotheistic religion because of its trinitarian God. Even so, Judaism avoids restricting salvation to Jews only. For example, observance of the Noachide Laws, a set of universal moral laws in Jewish tradition that prohibit offenses such as idolatry, blasphemy, bloodshed, and theft, is understood to constitute moral conduct for non-Jews (Schwarzschild, Berman, and Elon 2007).

Christianity and Judaism each bear complex, multifaceted, and at times contradictory relationships to one another and to other religions. These relationships have developed and changed over many generations and in many different contexts. Nevertheless, many couples at the Dovetail conference overlooked their religions' centuries-held historical, structural, and theological differences in favor of what they saw as more fundamental similarities. Instead of the broader sweep of "universal truth" that they claimed, Dovetail conference participants' views reflect a narrower swath of religious teaching: the Protestant conception of a universal priesthood of all believers and a particularly American Protestant emphasis on individuals' moral and psychological improvement; religious tolerance; and individuals' right to interpret religious teachings for themselves, with or without the approval of religious institutions (Cross and Livingstone 2005b). Jude and Tabitha were unafraid to challenge arguments against intermarriage with which they assumed their audience was familiar. They felt free to substitute their own judgments where normative religious views contradicted their experiences.

This reductionist move toward universalism facilitated a corresponding move toward individualism. Its logic worked as follows: if all religions promulgated the same ethical teachings, then there could be no significant distinctions between religions. Exclusive religious practices, such as communion rituals in which only church members could participate, were based on the failure to look past false distinctions and recognize universal ethics. All that legitimately could be left, in this reckoning, were the universal ideas and the individuals who lived them out. Thus, individual persons were more important than religious rituals or norms.

Tabitha felt a responsibility to teach others her understanding of universal religious truth through modeling because in her view some people were blinded by religious norms to the special insights that intermarriage offered. "We're always modeling openness to religious ideas for our extended family. And we're modeling how to accept people the way they are, by not asking them to become another religion," she said. By modeling acceptance and openness, Nancy added, Jude and Tabitha were also modeling respect for humanity and individualism. Tabitha, Jude, and Nancy not only resisted arguments against intermarriage; they countered with their own vision of its meanings and possibilities.

According to Nancy, modeling these insights from the experience of intermarriage would benefit not only religious leaders, who might awaken to unrealized religious truths, but also American popular culture, which was plagued by shallowness. Interfaith life centered on living out these deep values, she continued. American culture more broadly seemed to equate interfaith with the view that "everyone should get along," which she saw as not a religious view but a cultural one. Nancy pointed out an instance of this view on the television show *The OC*, which aired from 2003 to 2006. This prime-time drama, centered on a group of California teenagers, had made pop culture waves when it introduced "Chrismukkah," an irreverent blend of Christian and Jewish holiday symbols (discussed in Kaplan 2009, 161–166). In one Chrismukkah scene, a teenage boy places candy canes and menorahs side by side on a mantel, delighted that he and his family can have both. In another scene, a teenage girl presents her Chrismukkah invention: the "yarmuclaus," a velvety red, yarmulke-shaped Santa hat with white faux fur around the edge and a white faux fur ball on top. As of early 2008, the yarmuclaus could still be purchased on the WB television network's online shop, even though *The OC* was no longer in production, demonstrating that it had endured as a humorous way of promoting tolerance—even syncretism. Nancy, however, disliked this portrayal of an interfaith holiday celebration because it ignored the "serious" religious basis of such celebrations in favor of a "shallow cultural" understanding. When celebrated together, she said, these holidays ought to teach peace, universal respect, and the unity of humankind.

Nancy's description of these holidays stood in ironic contrast to a more traditional understanding of their meanings. While Hanukkah is a minor religious holiday for Jews, it commemorates the conclusion of a Jewish civil war fought over the issue of assimilation. Christmas is far more important in the Christian religious calendar, with its celebration of the birth of Jesus, the son of God—the very subject of Christian proselytizing efforts. Nancy's understanding of these holidays differed substantially from how more traditional Jews or Christians might describe them.

Nancy went on to discuss what she saw as a failure to recognize these holidays' real teachings. A priest-rabbi team calling itself "the God Squad," she explained, had recently appeared on the television program *Good Morning America* to argue that only members of their respective religions should observe Christmas and Hanukkah. The intermarried couples at Dovetail felt that the God Squad's rejection of holiday blending constituted a breach of religious authenticity: how could these clergy call themselves people of God while rejecting and excluding people who wanted to celebrate their religious holidays together? The God Squad represented an "uneducated" viewpoint, said Nancy, "stuck in the old defensive ethnic" model.

While the God Squad probably would describe its view differently, Nancy's characterization depicted the extent of what she saw as misunderstandings of interfaith life. Rather than fairly representing Hollywood or the God Squad, her comparison was meant to build solidarity among the people present. They felt misunderstood and shortchanged, whether religious authorities rejected intermarriage or secular American culture celebrated it, because they did not see their self-understanding reflected in either depiction. Because the simplistic Hollywood approach and the ethnic approach that "forces people to stay in old irrelevant boxes" were all that most people knew of interfaith marriage, "we have to grapple with that when we model," Nancy said.

In Nancy's understanding, Dovetail participants' complex blending of religions to arrive at open, tolerant unity had been endorsed by God: "At different times, people have needed God's word in different ways. So there have been different covenants and different interpretations." She explained that the reason for the existence of multiple religions was that God spoke to people in the ways that they would be able to understand, which varied across time, but that God and God's messages remain unchanged. Interfaith families were modeling these different renditions of God's word in a "prophetic" way. Even though clergy and religious institutions often saw the couples as wrong-headed and dangerous to their communities' cohesion, they themselves felt that they demonstrated the true core of these religions' teachings.

Indeed, one woman present, Laura, believed that the Virgin Mary had directly given her divine approval to transcend religious exclusivity because love for and between individual persons was a higher value. Laura was a devout Catholic and was troubled by her sense that Catholicism was exclusivist, especially since she had married a non-Catholic. She went to see a visionary in Yugoslavia (as it was then called) "who was seeing the Blessed Mother appear" and asked the visionary what Mary had to say about Laura's marrying a non-Catholic. According to the visionary, Laura recounted, "Mary said it would be very hard, but that [Laura's husband] did not have to convert." She also talked to her priest during one Christmas season, early in her marriage, and he said that her husband did not have to become a Catholic: the important thing was that she loved him.

"Yes!" Tabitha agreed. "The most important thing is that you love each other and not your religion." The claims of religious norms had to be subordinated to love between individuals.

This aspect of the participants' conversation highlights the deeply individualistic and universalistic strains in American culture, which I will discuss in more depth later. These values are so strong that, to the participants, it seemed natural to consider them at least as important and valid as their religious traditions' norms, and they offered a powerful response to religious claims with which the interfaith couples disagreed. But they nevertheless sought connection with their religious communities and employed strategies for doing so.

Redrawing Boundaries

Prioritizing universalism over the specifics of any particular religion helped couples to resist disapproving comments about their intermarriage. Resistance was not their only strategy; they also reframed key religious concepts in order to construe religious boundaries as more open than others might understand them to be. Even some clergy who were intermarried understood love between individuals to be more important than religious traditions were. Michael, a Presbyterian minister, was married to a Jewish woman, Deborah. Although they were raising their children as Jews exclusively, he remained committed to Christianity for himself and led an evangelical congregation. "Christianity is individual," he said. "It doesn't have to cover the whole family."

His congregants wondered how a Christian minister could head a Jewish family that did not share his beliefs or practices, but Michael and Deborah did not see their religious differences as a problem. Their children were being raised in only one religion, so the parents felt that the children would clearly understand their own religious identities. The interfaith component of the family was in Michael and Deborah's spousal relationship, where they could discuss faith and negotiate as needed. "I model for my evangelical Christian congregants that you can be strongly Christian without the whole family being Christian, and we can be strongly in Judaism too," Michael said.

For Michael, *modeling* meant teaching ways of being Christian or Jewish that would seem unfamiliar to many normative Christians and Jews. "My congregants are old progressives and young Koreans who are very conservative. I manage the conservatives' objections to interfaith marriage by teaching scriptures that undercut Christian certainty about being the only way to salvation. Christian certainty is part of mainstream Christian culture, but it isn't necessary to interpretation of the Bible or Christianity." He interpreted Christianity as being tolerant of non-Christians rather than viewing them as condemned to Hell for being unsaved.

Despite Michael's modeling and teaching, his congregants did not let go of their Christian certainty so easily. Often they would assume that Deborah was a messianic Jew and that the children would become Christian eventually. "My evangelical congregants see our raising children as Jews as an opportunity for the children to accept Jesus when they're thirteen or fourteen," Michael said. "I say no. This is identity formation. The goal is for the children to be and stay Jewish, not for them to choose as young adults." Even though he was a Presbyterian minister, to him and his family there was nothing wrong with his being the only Christian in his nuclear family.

Joint participation in both Jewish and Christian rituals helped many of the couples in this discussion to model respect for each other's religions as well as to enhance their family's experience of them. Directly countering the claim that religious boundaries had to be maintained for the integrity of the religious community, participants in this discussion argued that they better understood and appreciated their religions when they crossed or erased such boundaries. "Our children are exposed to Christian rituals and church. They respect it and know the common ground between Christianity and Judaism," said Deborah. Michael credited himself with "energizing" Deborah's parents' practice of Judaism. He advocated for a sabbath observance, so the whole family took up the practice of having Shabbat dinner and lighting Shabbat candles at Deborah's parents' house. Even though he was not Jewish, Michael could urge his in-laws and his Jewish immediate family to have Shabbat dinner together every week because he found the rituals meaningful for them as a family. The fact that he was a devoted Christian had no bearing on his practice of Shabbat or the meaning he found in it because its meaning could be universally understood.

While they crossed boundaries, participants also redefined key religious terms so that their boundary blurring was a fulfillment rather than a transgression of religious norms. Decoupling religious beliefs and rituals was an important part of this move. Michael admitted that the divinity of Jesus remained an irreconcilable point of disagreement between Jews and Christians, but by separating ritual performance from belief, his family could move comfortably between Christian and Jewish contexts. One discussion participant distinguished between religion and tradition: "Tradition is more like ethnicity or culture, so theology shouldn't get in the way" of participating in other religions' rituals. Another participant clarified, "You can practice together without having to believe the same. Shabbat is a *practice*." These remarks suggest that religious ritual should be open to anyone who finds it meaningful—in other words, that it should be both individual and universal.

Similarly, Jude said that his own Jewish practice was energized by the inter-faith context of his family. "If I'd married a Jew, I wouldn't be as religious. I would have been lazy about it. Being married to a Catholic, I'm responsible for the Jewishness in the family, so I have to know the religion and do it and keep learning." McGinity (2009) found similar sentiments about "increased devout-ness" among both Catholics and Jews (180–181). Jude's interest in continuing Jewish practices in his family was rooted in the universalism that he discerned in Judaism, a perspective that became important to him in the context of his interfaith marriage. His upbringing in Orthodox Judaism, with Yiddish-speaking grandparents and a fully Jewish neighborhood, had done less to secure his Jew-ish practice than his having a Catholic wife. Their individual interests, fam-ily relationships, and universalistic interests shaped their religious practices more than the religions' norms did. Their experiences taught them that tradi-tions, practices, and ethnicities that seemed specific and exclusive to just one religion—for example, Shabbat or Christmas—were just the container, not the contents. Rather, the contents of any religious practice were universal respect for others and the unity of humanity. The "container" of religious ritual, prop-erly understood, should be open to anyone who finds it meaningful.

Some people in the circle commented that even the divinity of Jesus did not have to be a stumbling block for interfaith families. Why not, they asked, just bracket the issues of salvation or Jesus' divinity and agree that each fam-ily member can have his or her own equally valid view? This claim emphasized the location of religious belief and practice within the individual, not the fam-ily or community. It resisted the claim that a religiously divided family would be confusing or otherwise undesirable and rewrote family unity as a matter of collective interest in religion more generally rather than membership in one religion. One woman suggested that as long as members of an interfaith family were religious in some way, they were united more than they were divided: "The problem isn't the two religions; it's religion versus the secularism of American culture." This claim echoed a concern among Catholic leaders in the 1980s that individuals within a family should have "faith," whatever faith that might be, in opposition to secularism (McGinity 2009, 172). By focusing on their spiri-tual lives, even though they did not share one religion, families could avoid the commercialism and consumerism that many people here saw as characterizing secular American culture and constituting the opposite of spirituality. Their spiritual lives would follow the Protestant model of personal discernment and judgment, allowing each family member to use his or her conscience as the arbiter of religious truth. With this redefinition of family unity, the discussion participants resisted messages conveyed about the confusion of children with multiple religious attachments while continuing to view unity as important in their own way.

"My interfaith parents chose Judaism for me," said Sharon. "I choose both religions for my kids. Kids will choose for themselves what they want at some point anyway. Having a choice made for you gives clarity and puts off ambiguity and struggle until later in life. If kids are brought up in both, they have to figure it out at a young age." In this view, personal preference, which could be discerned through struggle, mattered more than religious norms in a person's religious decision making. Nancy summed up: "So parents should figure out how they want to go, and the kids will adapt." In other words, whether parents chose to raise their children in one, two, or no religions, the children would eventually make their own choices anyway.

Most of the couples taking part in this discussion and others over the weekend said that they had been aware of a lack of acceptance of interfaith relationships from early in their relationships. At least two interfaith couples who were dating and contemplating marriage attended this discussion session in order to learn what issues they might face and how other couples were handling them. These couples worried about how their families might react to the idea of having more than one religious tradition in the family and how they would negotiate religious life-cycle ceremonies. Wedding arrangements, as informants outside the context of this conference said, were just the beginning of the negotiations. The couples would have to negotiate their own potentially conflicting wishes about being married in a church by a minister or under a *huppah* (Jewish wedding canopy) by a rabbi, or both, along with their parents' and grandparents' wishes or demands. Conflicts over these options were often smoothed over by choosing a secular location and officiant—for example, they might have a judge perform the wedding in a park.

The birth of children, many informants said, awakened latent wishes for baptisms or *brit milah* (circumcision) that had seemed alien before but became impossible to ignore. Because they could not please all of their parents and grandparents without doing things that were wrong for themselves, contradictory, or impermissible for the clergy involved, they knew that some combination of these people would have to be disappointed or kept in the dark. Family unity was thus redefined in terms of not just the number of religions a family might have but also the generations to which unity pertained. Anthropologist Bradd Shore (2005) argues that the formation of a new family entails the "challenge of creating a new miniature society with a distinctive set of traditions and coordinating practices" (185). For these couples, unity with one's spouse took precedence over unity with one's parents.

Most participants in this discussion said that they had talked early on in their relationships about how they would raise their children because they were aware of conflicting desires and expectations—their own, as well as those of their families, clergy, and religious institutions. Jude and Tabitha said that they had discussed how to raise their potential children even before their first date. After these early discussions about childrearing, the couples repeatedly turned outward for help with and validation of their choices. Their worries combined with fears that their future children would be confused by having parents of different religious backgrounds and that the children would opt for no religion at all rather than either or both of the ones in which they were raised. But Dovetail conference presenters emphasized that this fear of confusion was unfounded: their children were not confused by their families' religious arrangements, whether they were raised in multiple religions or only one.

Enlightened Children

One panel demonstrated that while universalism and individualism had clearly been conveyed to the children of the Dovetail conference participants, these values were not the only ones by which the participants organized their religious lives. "Heritage," as the panel participants put it, mattered deeply as well. This panel was composed of the teenage children themselves. Responding to questions about their interfaith upbringing, they described a Sunday school program designed especially to convey the kind of open exploration of religious ideas that the adults had described in the earlier session. The interfaith couples' resistance to religious boundaries had clearly influenced the children's views. But the couples' resistance was tempered by their recapitulation of traditional religious institutions such as Sunday school. For the children, the tension between these two impulses was often resolved through tolerance.

Most of the teenagers' families were affiliated with the Interfaith Families Project (IFFP), a local organization for families who were raising their children in Judaism and Christianity. This organization ran a Sunday school "to teach, not preach," the "religious and cultural heritages" of Judaism and Christianity. The school strove to "expose children to the moral values, traditions, history, and wonder of Jewish and Christian religious life," using an "objective" viewpoint. By *objective*, IFFP seems to mean that the organization has no preference for any particular religious outcome: a child's choice of Christianity, Judaism, both, or neither would all be equally acceptable. The group's version of objectivity seems to be informed by the concept of fairness as it operates in American news media. An element of American egalitarian and individualistic ideology, this perspective assumes that there are two sides to every story and that the only way to be fair to both sides is to give each one equal time to make its case. The listener then discerns his or her opinion because there is no clear truth other than whatever persuades the listener. For IFFP, the purpose of religious education was not to bring up young Jews or Christians but to help interfaith children "feel comfortable" with the two religions and their "dual faith identities"

(Interfaith Families Project of the Greater Washington, D.C. Area 1996b). This model did not seem to promote the importance of struggle, which Sharon had mentioned as part of determining one's religious preferences. Instead, it placed a high value on communication, as did the adult participants in the earlier discussion group.

The construction of religious identity as both heritage and choice dovetails with the middle-class white American notions of kinship that anthropologist David Schneider ([1968] 1980) identified. This kinship system centers on the symbols of "blood" (ties created by the circumstances of birth) and "love" (ties created by choice). In Schneider's view, blood kinship derives from a biogenetic link in which children receive 50 percent of their genes from each parent and are thus related to them "by birth" (23ff). Many of my informants extended this understanding of their genetic heritage to religious heritage as well. Just as an American couple might say that their children are half Irish, half German, many of my intermarried informants say that their children are half Jewish, half Christian, as if religion is passed on genetically and is "what you are" in a literal, physical sense.

The blood theory of kinship aligns with modern Jews' racial self-understandings. At different times in American history, Jews have described themselves as a nation, as a religion, and as a race. Racial language was in use by the 1870s and persists even today (Goldstein 2006, 17; Hart 2000). From the late nineteenth century until the end of World War II, both Jews and non-Jews used racial language to describe Jewishness, though Jews did not easily fit into the black-white dichotomy in American understandings of race. This racial language helped Jews to explain their distinctiveness as a group as they attempted to fit into American society while also remaining separate, in part because of endogamy and residential patterns, and in part because of their nebulous sense of difference (Goldstein 2006, 1–7). But Jews have also used the language of religion to explain their connection to each other. Some early twentieth-century Yiddish-speaking Jews perceived a deep divide between those who identified themselves as "religious" and those who identified themselves as "secular" (Polland 2007). Even as these groups rejected each other's ideologies, they continued to use a common religious language to describe and analyze their lives and communities (Polland 2007). By the early twentieth century, racial language seemed to threaten Jews' status as white; and the languages of ethnicity, tribalism, and even genetic studies came to fill in for race (Goldstein 2006, 165–166, 223ff; Kahn 2010; Tenenbaum and Davidman 2007). Jews have continued to struggle to find the right term to describe themselves to one another and to non-Jews. Jewishness is religious, familial, ethnic, and national all at once, so Jews' experiences of it encompass more than any one of these categories (Goldstein 2006). But in order to represent themselves in a way that non-Jewish

Americans could comprehend (Berman 2009), Jews have also described Jewishness using narrower sociological categories—for example, Jewishness as only ethnicity or as only religion. The evolution of such language demonstrates that none of the modern categories that describe group bonds manages on its own to encompass Jews' experiences of Jewishness.

Schneider's blood and love model of kinship also appears to inform universalist individualists' idea that fairness requires that children should be taught each religious heritage equally. The idea of "fairness to both parents," of which the IFFP approach to religious education is an example, follows this genetic model by requiring the family to celebrate an equal number of holidays from each religious tradition. Under this model, interfaith couples' children are said to "inherit" traditions from both sides, so to observe only one parent's tradition would show a lack of respect to the parent whose traditions were not passed on. Fishman (2004) describes "the intermingling of Jewish and Christian holidays" as an example of what her "mixed-married" interviewees considered fair (61).

An African-American youth leader who said that he had converted to Judaism moderated the children's panel. With *tzitzit* (fringes worn by observant Jewish men) showing at his waist, he outwardly displayed his religious convictions more than the white teenagers on the panel did, and perhaps he had had more experience with the struggle model of religious commitment. An animated speaker, he appeared to be deeply engaged in thinking about religious education. He mentioned research about adolescents' new interest in connecting to God through religious traditions and praised the "maturity" in the young panelists' thoughts about God.

Personal religious struggle or connection to God was not a central theme of the panelists' comments, however. Most viewed themselves as primarily secular, unlike the adults in earlier panel discussions. For example, Jon considered himself "independent"—neither Jewish nor Christian. He saw his religious education's primary value in its contribution to tolerance and having an "open mind": "I believe in the values that God represents, but not God as a being. The values of God are about helping people."

Leah, another panelist, jokingly described herself as a "Cashew," for "Catholic-Jew," a term she said came from a *Saturday Night Live* TV sketch.[2] A student of IFFP since childhood, she was now in college. Reflecting on her experiences, she echoed the universalist sentiments that the earlier discussion group's participants had raised.

> God is connection between people, and the main tenets of religions are all about how to treat other people. War results from not recognizing that.

> I would not want to raise children in a strong one-faith household because I don't feel it myself. I'd rather have religious education for educational and tolerance purposes, to have my children be open-minded.

People should do Bible study because it's part of our culture, so if you know the Bible, you'll understand more. I experienced no pressure from IFFP to believe or practice anything.

From the claim that religions share the same essential teachings came views about the purpose of religious education. Religious education's value, in this universalist view, was in explaining the roots of cultural beliefs and practices and in encouraging tolerance for people of other religions, who were assumed to share the same values under the guise of their particular religions.

Adam, also a college student, had attended IFFP until age thirteen and had a Coming of Age ceremony as part of his religious education. His religious self-description, he said, was "bothie"—that is to say, both Jewish and Christian. Once he had described himself as "interfaith," but he later decided that this term was no longer satisfactory because he really was only Jewish and Christian, not a member of all faiths. Although his father is Jewish and Adam attended High Holiday services, Adam did not count himself in a *minyan* (the quorum of ten Jews required for certain prayers) because the community in which he participated did not consider him Jewish. As a self-described "bothie," he believed he could "find God" in experiences of ritual that he might choose to attend, such as a gospel church. Nonetheless, he did not feel devotion to any faith. On that subject, Adam sounded ambivalent: he admired people who had strong, devout faith, and he felt sad not to have it too. But IFFP had taught tolerance, openness, and respect for other people's faiths, with no pressure to believe or practice anything, and he was glad to have had that broad education. His religious identity was rooted in heritage, not beliefs, so it made sense to him that he was "both" instead of "neither."

These young adults spoke of their religions as being innate and passed down to them from their parents. They learned about and participated in Judaism and Christianity because these religions were their heritage. While personal choice was of great importance to them, they did not choose from any and all religions; they focused on the ones to which their families belonged. The adults who took part in the earlier discussion group had shared negotiations about respecting their children's religious birthrights, even when their children were expected to choose their own religious identities. They held up both heritage and choice as equally important.

Jake and Amy, two siblings on the panel, were raised in Judaism, their mother's religion. Their Italian Catholic father was supportive and wanted the children to learn "both sides," so they studied Hebrew in religious school and Italian in public school. They also celebrated Italian Catholic culture through Christian holidays. The siblings shared the view that "being knowledgeable about both religions is good," as Amy said, a value that extended to religions and celebrations beyond those connected to their family.

"I'd like to learn about Kwanzaa because it's a different holiday, so it has a different meaning. I'd like to learn what that's like and how it feels," said Jake.

"Broad exposure to different things is good. Having choice makes religion more meaningful," said Amy. They agreed that the Washington, D.C., area was a hospitable place in which to live as a multifaith family because it was accepting of people's being "so many things at once." This comment echoes Jude's appreciation for his daughter's view of her identity as inherently multiple and resists the view that Judaism and Christianity must be kept separate. It also suggests an appreciation shared among many of the conference participants for both a cosmopolitan outlook and a "cafeteria-style" religious identity.

What the panelists viewed as tolerance some others view as syncretism. In her analysis of the 2002 Dovetail conference, Fishman (2004) characterizes the combination of Jewish and Christian observances in the same household as syncretism—the piecing together of "new notions of ethnoreligious identity" from existing traditions—even though the Dovetail conference participants themselves insisted "over and over" that syncretism was neither their intention nor their practice (95, 140). I see a great deal of commonality between the comments of Fishman's informants and mine, but I think that her diagnosis of syncretism came too quickly. Even if we ultimately disagree with our informants' interpretations of their actions, we owe it to them to understand their lifeworlds in their terms. If multireligious families understand themselves as not syncretic, why is their self-understanding automatically wrong and the researcher's interpretation automatically right? Fishman argues that "the majority of mixed-married Jewish families" fail to adhere to the "lowest common denominator of Jewish identity," which she views as being the rejection of Christianity (138–139). While there is certainly room for more than one interpretation of the situation, this assessment reflects the inreach stance within the inreach-outreach debate (see chapter 1). "The suggestion that to be Jewish one had to remain distinct from all others denied the possibility that someone could intermarry and remain Jewish," McGinity (2009) observes about the inreach stance (212). Adopting such a stance prevents us from learning about the ways in which Jews experience their Jewishness outside of the pronouncements that institutions and religious experts make about which kinds of Jewishness "count" (Kaufman 2005).

My informants, like McGinity's interviewees, continued to view themselves and their families as Jewish, whether by choice or heritage, even when Christian practices were also part of their lives. Family attachments were at least as important a part of their religious lives as tolerance and understanding of others were. The panelists maintained that religion's primary attraction for them was the opportunity to gather with family members for holiday celebrations. Jon said that he enjoyed the religious holidays that brought his family members together. Family was also central to Jake and Amy's religious experiences. While their Italian Catholic father's family had not been happy about his marriage to a Conservative Jewish woman, both sides of the extended family traveled across the country to gather for religious holidays. Leah also reported that her extended family joined together for religious holidays. In this respect, the panelists' association of religion with family agrees with Cohen and Eisen's (2000) observation that the context of the family is absolutely central to contemporary Jewish expression (46).

The religious self-understandings that the panelists formed, and that IFFP encouraged them to form, comprised universalist, individualist, and essentially ethnic elements that revolve around the student's religious heritage. For example, Leah described her Coming of Age ceremony in the IFFP Sunday school, which took place when she was thirteen years old. To prepare for the ceremony, she researched and then presented reports about the lives and ideas of one Jewish woman and one Christian woman. Leah's IFFP ceremony was intended to both incorporate and replace bat mitzvah and confirmation. The organization's website describes the Coming of Age Program as an embrace of young adulthood and adolescence. Unlike the analogous Jewish and Christian life cycle rituals, the program does not involve a formal acceptance as an adult of either Judaism or Christianity. Rather, it emphasizes the uniqueness of the individual and the personal meanings that he or she has found. The goal of the program is to

- Discover and honor the unique spirit and qualities of each participant.
- Help each participant find ways to create a rewarding and meaningful life for both herself and her community.
- Honor the richness of each family's heritage and dual faith background and explore the meaning this holds for each participant.
- Examine what the Jewish and Christian scriptures and traditions mean to each participant intellectually, spiritually, morally and ethically. (Interfaith Families Project of the Greater Washington, D.C. Area 1996a)

The Coming of Age Program's description emphasizes self-discovery and personal meaning, an approach to religious engagement that is also common in mainstream religion as well. For example, Jewish adult education programs frequently feature programs entitled "Jewish Journeys." But in these cases, such an approach functions as a way into an existing normative tradition, not as something that is supposedly being invented.

The specific goals of the Coming of Age Program reflect what religious educators in some Jewish or Christian congregations might seek for their students—for example, working together for the greater good, making thoughtful and caring choices, introspection. But in this case, they are not situated as a response to God's command or call. Coming of Age Program students "explore belief in God (as one 'defines' God)," leaving the nature of God up to the individual (Interfaith Families Project of the Greater Washington, D.C. Area 1996a). The program encourages students to become introspective and socially aware adults, but it does not encourage them to become specifically religious adults (cf. Fishman 2004, 95, 140). The definition of religion is itself in question in the program's structure and philosophy because all judgments about meaning and spirituality are left up to the individual student. The only assumed element is heritage, which comes from a student's parents and is an accident of birth whose subsequent significance is up to the student.

Ironically, the adolescent children's presentations at the Dovetail conference innocently displayed both their parents' universalism and the kind of religious opting out that their parents and communities feared. Only one of the six teenagers identified with either Judaism or Christianity as her own chosen religion; one of the other five considered herself "half and half," and the rest were not religious. The value of religious education, they all agreed, was that it taught tolerance and open-mindedness. They felt that it was important to know about Christian and Jewish religious beliefs and history because they were the premise of so much of western culture. Either religion was fine, as far as these children were concerned, but choosing neither religion was fine too. Adam even seemed to feel sorry for people who were worried about intermarriage's effect on children's religious identity. At a Hillel discussion at his college, he said, "People said they couldn't imagine marrying someone who wasn't culturally Jewish. People are scared that their children won't come out right. But really it will be okay."

Some of the differences between the parents' and children's concerns about religion can be attributed to life-course differences. As people raise children, they tend to use organized religion as a support to a much greater extent than they did when they were single or childless. Teenagers like these Dovetail-affiliated ones may well experience religion as more central to their lives as they age. Some Conservative Jews in Minnesota whom Riv-Ellen Prell interviewed reported that they planned to involve themselves in synagogue life once they had children but reported that, without children, activities such as lighting Shabbat candles felt almost "silly" (Prell 2000, 48). McGinity (2009) notes that her intermarried Jewish women interviewees became more religious over time, aligning with a similar national trend, and that they became especially interested in Jewish activities that they could share with their children (178–179). But even if the perspective of the Dovetail teenagers changes over time, the intellectual, choice-focused approach to religion with which parents have raised them does appear to have made its mark on their thinking about religion.

While many of the people in the audience who asked questions and offered comments were still developing their thoughts about intermarriage, the speakers at the Dovetail conference exemplified the universalist individualist approach, aligned with a popular American understanding of religion. The majority of the universalist individualists raised their children in both religions or advocated doing so. Their model emphasizes that multireligious families are unified by their rational approach to religion. They expect family members to make their own informed decisions about their religious beliefs and practices while demonstrating respect for all religious beliefs. They believe that all religions essentially express the same sentiments or ideas and that people can and should participate in religious practices that are not their own to the extent that they choose to do so.

Mary Heléne Rosenbaum and Stanley Ned Rosenbaum's book *Celebrating Our Differences: Living Two Faiths in One Marriage* ([1994] 1999) provides a detailed model of universalist individualism in practice. They see religious identity as entirely individual and do not seek a unifying religious identity for the family. Instead, their family's identity is interfaith. As a couple, they share the aspects of each other's religious observances that do not contradict their own, demonstrating solidarity without sharing religious experience, and they foreground the sense that their family is composed of separate individuals with personal identities. Their model of intermarried family life is more highly developed and deeply intellectual than that of many of my informants, emphasizing thought and deemphasizing normative ritual practice.

As the book explains, in their life as an interfaith couple they follow two separate but parallel religious tracks: Ned is Jewish and Mary Heléne is a practicing Catholic. Their children are educated in both religions and encouraged to choose. The Rosenbaums describe the approach as "*both* parents [raising] all children in *both* faiths," arguing that this way the children "begin to think about making a serious religious commitment" as adolescents so that their "religious identity . . . is likely to be more mature and thought-through than one that's merely the continuation of a set of habits inculcated in childhood" (112–113). They express appreciation for ritual but see it as something they can bend to the needs of the family rather than something that proceeds according to its own history and logic. For example, the Rosenbaums describe their family's own rituals of reading aloud together on Friday nights, an activity that is based on traditional religious rituals but is not a full enactment of them. Their adaptation of religious traditions is meant to include all family members while not pushing practices or theology on those who differ.

The Rosenbaums see the commitment to a religious community as one made by individuals rather than the entire family. Ned and Mary Heléne may attend religious services together at a synagogue or church but never in a way that includes both as full participants. Their attendance is as individuals who choose to belong to the religious community, with each spouse as a supporter but not a member. In this way, they foreground the sense that their family is made up of separate individuals with their own freely chosen identities. Individuals exercise their consciences in deciding which aspects of their own religions they agree with or believe in, and parents require children to explore thoroughly before making a religious commitment.

Before that commitment, the child has no particular religious identity. Mary Heléne recalls a moment when her daughter asked about her religious identity. The mother responded, "'Your father is a Jew, your mother is Catholic; you are a little girl.' . . . We were saying, in effect, that choosing a religion is something you ought to be grown up for" (113). Like the IFFP Coming of Age Program, Mary Heléne Rosenbaum emphasizes the "choice" aspect of religious identity and downplays the role of heritage.

The Rosenbaums' book is written to exemplify how interfaith marriage can be done but also gently warns those considering intermarriage. Mary Heléne writes that initially she felt that intermarriage was a bad idea, but she changed her mind as she and her husband led parallel religious lives. Ned writes that he experienced the opposite. After becoming more observant of Jewish law, he began to feel that intermarriage was more challenging than he thought it would be when he was first married and nonobservant. He came to feel that Jewish observance ideally would involve the whole family and optimally would not be an individual experience. Still, his change of heart remained individually centered, not based on the needs of the Jewish community.

American Contradictions

Universalist individualism reflects themes of individualism and autonomy that have been present in American culture for generations. America's history as a settler society encouraged a cultural orientation toward the autonomy of the individual. It also engendered an American character that rejects the authority of traditions handed down from earlier generations in order to enable children to surpass their parents' status, as anthropologist Margaret Mead ([1942] 1975) explains in her study of American national character. This cultural "orientation toward a different future" includes a belief that when a child becomes an adult, he or she will "pass beyond" his or her parents and "leave their standards behind" (41). Dovetail conference participants implicitly relied on such American cultural assumptions in their sense that their universalist and individualist understandings of religious teachings were correct, despite resistance from normative religious communities and leaders, because they could see themselves as "passing beyond" these normative standards toward a "different future." Nancy's description of normative religious boundaries as "old, irrelevant boxes" and ethnic defensiveness suggests her sense that she and other intermarried couples had moved beyond these categories. Universalist individualists incorporate into their strategies for religious education this expectation that their children will choose differently from their parents.

But at the same time, Mead argues, an opposing emphasis pulls Americans toward conformity and away from innovation. "Educators exclaim patiently over the paradox that Americans believe in change, believe in progress, and yet do their best, or so it seems, to retard their children, to bind them to parental ways, to inoculate them against the new ways to which they give lip service" (41). According to Mead, American culture includes a tension between expecting children to reject traditions in favor of finding their own way and encouraging children not to venture far from their parents' traditions. Universalist individualists' use of the familiar model of the Sunday school to teach their children about religion, despite their own discomfort with religious norms, reflects this tension, as do the conversations at the Dovetail conference. For example, the intermarried adults worried that their children might reject religion entirely, but they nonetheless enrolled their children in a Sunday school program in which they learned that the value of religion lies primarily in its cultural relevance. Mead's observations about American culture highlight my informants' conflicting desires to resist religious norms and maintain connection to religious traditions, albeit ones that are reinterpreted to mean something different from what they might mean to others.

This tension also highlights the extent to which individualism, understood in different ways depending on the context, is an ideology in American culture. Universalist individualist discourses explicitly call attention to individual autonomy even as the people who engage in them recapitulate the forms of the very institutions they disavow, such as Sunday schools. In asserting the right of every individual to discern universal religious truths for him- or herself, universalist individualist discourses suggest that all people are equal in their ability to do so while also implying that the results of such introspection and spiritual seeking will ultimately be the same for everyone. Individualism as an ideology works in this fashion across many spheres of society, not just that of religion, according to sociologist John Meyer (1987). While many of us understand our lives to be organized mainly according to the choices that we make as individuals, in the typical life course most Americans pursue the same activities at the same points in their lives: for example, they attend age-graded schools and observe standardized retirement ages (Meyer 1987; Meyer, Boli, and Thomas 1987). But cultural ideologies of individualism highlight aspects of our lives over which we do have control and ignore or explain away institutional structures and patterns in which we participate without explicitly or consciously having chosen to do so.

Universalist individualist discourses interpret personal experiences as the result of pure choice and resistance to externally imposed norms. Yet institutional structures and patterns continue to influence them, not only in the form of Sunday schools but also in people's engagement with religion itself. Most Americans share a belief in God, whether or not they participate in or are accepted by normative religious communities. According to both the U.S. Religious Landscape Survey of the Pew Forum on Religion and Public Life (2009b) and WIN–Gallup International's (2012) "Global Index of Religiosity and Atheism," only 5 percent of Americans said that they did not believe in God or a universal spirit at all. Interestingly, many of those who said that they did not believe in God still identified with religious traditions, including Judaism and Christianity (Pew Forum on Religion and Public Life 2009a). Consider Adam, the young man who called himself a "bothie" even though he did not claim an abiding faith in either Judaism or Christianity. He could have described himself as belonging to neither religion but instead he understood himself to belong to both. Heritage is interpreted as religious because American culture valorizes religious affiliation. While many of my informants who are affiliated with Dovetail and IFFP feel that they are creating new, personalized ways of engaging with their religious traditions, in fact they do so with the same institutional structures and patterns that they criticize.

As much as they struggled with religious traditions' place in their individual and family lives, the Dovetail conference participants rarely spoke about the importance of membership in a local religious community, even though many of them did belong to churches and synagogues and a church and synagogue that shared a building hosted their conference. Their membership in these communities appeared to be peripheral to their personal religious experiences. This focus on the self, too, has roots in American culture. As Mead ([1942] 1975) explains, whether the American self rejects the past or clings to it, it ignores the context in which that self arose. Similarly, universalist individualist discourses emphasize the particular religious experiences of intermarried couples but tend to ignore the familial and social context in which their personal religious experiences are formed.

This emphasis on the individual without acknowledgment of the context in which he or she lives and is formed has inspired concern about the vitality of American communities. In his observations of America around 1830, Alexis de Tocqueville wrote, "Individualism is a calm and considered feeling which disposes each citizen to isolate himself from the mass of his fellows and withdraw into the circle of family and friends; with this little society formed to his taste, he gladly leaves the greater society to look after itself" (qtd. in Bellah et al. 1985, 37). Tocqueville saw this self-isolation as problematic for American community, and more recent scholarly commentators on American society have continued to worry about this aspect of American culture. Sociologists, philosophers, and political scientists have repeatedly described and analyzed the negative effects of individualistic ideology on the health of American community (Bellah et al. 1991, 1985; Putnam 2000; Walzer 1994; Wuthnow 1998). Universalist individualism emphasizes these currents in American culture that undermine the cohesion of religious communities. As the Rosenbaums ([1994] 1999) said, individuals join communities by choice, not as part of a family or by default. And among the IFFP teenagers, the religious choice can sometimes be "none."

Because this move toward individual religious autonomy gives subjective experience equal if not more significance than it does communal experience of religion, religious and communal norms shrink in importance if the individual does not find them personally fulfilling. Sociologist Robert Bellah ([1970] 1991) observes that even "for many churchgoers the obligation of doctrinal orthodoxy sits lightly indeed, and the idea that all creedal statements must receive a personal reinterpretation is widely accepted" (41). This emphasis on personal fulfillment continues earlier versions of American expressive and utilitarian individualism (Bellah et al. 1985). In this newer form of American individualism, the individual can manage and manipulate his or her private life to achieve greater fulfillment, freely choosing or rejecting commitments, including marriage, work, and religious membership, solely on the basis of "life-effectiveness." But, Bellah and colleagues point out, "What has dropped out are the old normative expectations of what makes life worth living" (44–48). In other words, the context in which self-fulfillment takes on meaning beyond the individual, whether in terms of history, theology, ethnicity, or something else, is missing. Some of the participants in American Jewish discourses about intermarriage denounced exactly this perceived lack of normative commitments among intermarried Jews.

The American cultural context clearly informs the ways in which universalist individualists frame their religious commitments as personal choices emphasizing self-fulfillment and commitment to the good of humanity. Scholar of American religion Wade Clark Roof (1993) describes baby boomers' emphasis on self-fulfillment and personal judgment. Their generation began to reach adulthood at the same time that American Jewish discourses on intermarriage expressed growing anxiety about individualism among Jews and its role in growing rates of intermarriage. It appears that, at least among Dovetail conference participants, these individualistic themes have made their way into the consciousness of younger generations as well.

As Bellah and colleagues (1985) worry that the growing importance of individualism in Americans' lives eats away at the fabric of American community, Cohen and Eisen (2000) likewise worry that it severely undermines American Jewish community. They feel that the "sovereign self" is likely to "contribute to the dissolution of communal institutions and intergenerational commitment" (12). Like many of my informants, theirs, who are "moderately affiliated" Jews

and are predominantly endogamous, also conceptualize religion as a customiz-
able and private realm of their lives, seeing themselves and not clergy or community as the final arbiter of their religious practices and identification. Cohen
and Eisen argue that American Jews today, unlike in the past, primarily experience Judaism in the "private sphere," with friends and family and within the
self. They make their decisions about Judaism based on the sovereign self on
an ongoing basis, rejecting the public sphere and institutional life as important
expressions of themselves as Jews. For them, Jewish practices and beliefs are
adopted to the extent that they are personally meaningful (Cohen and Eisen
2000). Even as individual Jews seek meaning in Judaism, they remain ambivalent about it.

Universalist individualism helps many of my informants explain their religious experiences and describe their religious decision making as legitimate.
Though religious traditions and communities supply the symbols and practices
from which they choose, my informants do not see these traditions and communities as having inherent authority. Nor do they view religious communal
norms and clergy as having power over their families' religious decisions, even
though they often want clergy and houses of worship to be available for their
life-cycle ceremonies. Bellah ([1970] 1991) observed a similar perspective among
Protestants in their "increasing acceptance of the notion that each individual
must work out his own ultimate solutions and that the most the church can do
is provide him a favorable environment for doing so" (43). Many of the rabbis
among my informants had difficulty with this view because they saw themselves
as upholding religious traditions and communities that had value beyond particular individuals' estimation of it. Yet this individualism is not the entire story
of American religion. Even those for whom the individual was the primary unit
of morality felt a desire for community and a sense of being part of the Jewish
people.

Re-creating Community

Many of my intermarried informants struggled to reconcile their commitment
to individual integrity with their desire to be connected to religious traditions
or communities. This tension was reflected in my observations at a synagogue
in Atlanta that I will call Shir Hadash (the pseudonym translates as "New Song"),
which put universalist individualist values into practice within an institutional
setting that spoke to people as individuals as well as a community. This Reconstructionist synagogue, founded by and for lesbian, gay, bisexual, and transgender (LGBT) people, viewed itself as unique because it welcomed people regardless
of who they were or the religious choices they made. Heterosexual intermarried
Jews, among others, also valued this environment, and over time heterosexual

members grew to compose the congregation's majority. This community privileged the individual, honored his or her feelings of religious authenticity as the primary source of religious legitimacy, and rejected the authority of traditional religious norms, as many of the participants in the Dovetail conference had done. In contrast to the attitudes expressed by many of the participants at Dovetail, however, the individualism of this community seemed to be rooted in feelings of exclusion from and oppression by normative Jewish communities rather than an intellectualized concern for individual rights. Sociologist Randal Schnoor (2006) and anthropologist Moshe Shokeid (2002) discuss the difficulties that gay, lesbian, bisexual, and transgender Jews face in reconciling their identities as "a minority within a minority," as one of Schnoor's informants put it (2006, 53). LGBT Jewish organizations made it possible for such people to experience a wholeness of identity in ways that had not been possible in organizations that were only Jewish or only gay, giving Schnoor's respondents what they described as "comfort and a sense of belonging" (52). The members of Shir Hadash, motivated by similar desires, re-created the familiar institution of a synagogue but shifted its self-understanding so that it met this particular community's needs. This community sought to maintain a shared self-definition, including a sense of Jewishness that both permitted intermarriage and included non-Jews as full members of the community who had a different relationship to the Torah than Jews had. By rethinking religious boundaries, this community attempted to balance the needs of the individual with the integrity of the group.

In a dining hall at the church in which Shir Hadash met, several dozen people gathered to sit in two concentric circles of white plastic chairs. A well-known Reform rabbi, whom I will call Rabbi Green, had come to speak to the congregation about her views on spirituality, authenticity, and interfaith issues. Recognizing the prevalence of Jewish continuity discourse in American Jewish life, she told the group, "I'm not interested in boundaries; I'm interested in spirit." Like the Dovetail conference participants, Rabbi Green resisted the emphasis on boundaries between Jews and non-Jews and between intermarried and endogamous Jews that so frequently occupied intermarriage discourse. Some boundaries within Jewish communities had begun to fade away already, she noted, saying that the atmosphere surrounding intermarriage had changed to allow people to feel "authentic in who they are." She challenged her audience: "*The* spiritual question is when God says to Adam, 'Where are you?' It's not that God didn't know, in a geographical sense, but [the question highlights] the sense of relationship or spiritual journey. Where was God? Or my deepest self?" She invited the audience members to consider their relationship to God or to their deepest selves, if they chose to understand God in that way: "When did I hear that question 'where are you?' or feel drawn somehow? Where is my life? Is it what I want to be living now?" She offered handouts featuring passages from Genesis and from the writings of Rabbi Adin Steinsaltz, a scholar who is well known for a book that explains Jewish mystical concepts to a lay audience. Rabbi Green asked participants to discuss the following question in small groups: "Where have been the *ayecha* [where are you?] moments in your life?"

Participants earnestly shared their individual introspective processes with one another. Some minutes later, as they came together again into one large group, they mused about authenticity and community membership. Many commented that they felt relieved to belong to a congregation that consciously made itself a home for LGBT members. One way in which the congregation enacted its commitment to these members was by reciting a prayer at the end of services that acknowledged and honored their struggles, especially the difficulty of hiding their deepest identities. This prayer was meaningful not just to members who felt excluded from or oppressed by religious communities because of their sexual identity; it had been the catalyst for several heterosexual members to join Shir Hadash as well. For participants in this discussion, the prayer marked Shir Hadash as being profoundly different from other synagogues because it recognized that religious norms such as the prohibition of homosexuality, when enforced without respect for individuals, had harmful, oppressive effects. Such norms, they felt, pressured them to pretend to conform, which made them feel both disingenuous and deficient. In contrast, Shir Hadash accepted them as they were, which made them feel at home.

According to the discussion participants, Shir Hadash was completely different from other Jewish communities they had known. Echoing Adam Bronfman's comments in *The Forward* about Jews' reasons for avoiding Jewish institutions, one man, Alex, said, "This synagogue is the only one that I've attended that doesn't make my skin crawl."

Rebecca, who described herself as "a Teflon Jew," said that she grew up participating in Jewish activities but "none of it would stick." She commented that this community's Jewish practices felt genuine. "I don't feel like rolling my eyes at everything we do."

Abby, who said that she had grown up "Conservadox," meaning on the border of Conservative and Orthodox, told the group that she had found this community when she was struggling with coming out as a lesbian. The experience of being in a synagogue where she did not feel that she had to hide was so intense that she avoided the community for some time. Eventually, however, she felt ready to embrace it. "Growing up, I knew a lot about Judaism intellectually but never felt it." This community was the first place where she experienced Judaism spiritually and emotionally.

Gabe said that participating as a heterosexual in the congregation's reading of the prayer honoring LGBT members' struggles was helping him to learn about what it meant to be part of a community. Because the prayer is written in the first-person point of view, Gabe initially felt awkward saying, "I, as a gay/lesbian Jew." But he came to see that this prayer helped him to step outside his own ego to become part of the greater community.

Rabbi Green responded that the community allowed people to feel safe asking questions about authenticity—"being who you are deep down." Similarly, the important questions for interfaith relationships were "What's the authenticity? Who am I authentically?" Rabbi Green said, "Community can make it safe to ask those questions of yourself." Being an individual who made choices about religion could lead to terrifying isolation, she suggested, but those same choices made in the context of a supportive community could enable members to know themselves and God more deeply.

The topic of intermarriage arose, prompting Gina, a woman who was not Jewish but was married to a Jewish man and raising Jewish children, to venture that this discussion had just made her realize that, if she had lived in Europe during World War II, the Nazis would have come after her children. She thought that she might have denied that they were Jewish to try to save them. Gina said that she "often perform[ed] intellectual exercises" in which she considered "hypothetical scenarios" such as whether she would have been "courageous enough to join the civil rights movement." Beginning to cry, she said that her realization about the Nazis was emotional and not just intellectual. Her comment suggested that she had come to realize that being part of a religious community involved more than just her own choices. It also meant sharing its history and its suffering as well as its joys. Others began to cry along with her.

Gina's husband, who was sitting next to her, displayed no outward reaction to her intense emotional experience. Perhaps her realization was something he had already known because of his upbringing as a Jew or perhaps he was unwilling to experience or express feelings like hers in this setting. Speaking about their family's religious life, he said, "She's making it very easy—for me, anyway." He later commented, "Judaism is hard, and there are a lot of religions that aim at the same thing that are easier."

Across the circle, another man responded, "Wrestling with God is the whole attraction of Judaism," a sentiment with which many of the Dovetail group would have agreed and expanded to all religions.

Echoing the Dovetail conference participants' universalistic language, David said that the great thing about being in an interfaith marriage was that it connected him with another religion. He loved knowing that other religions taught the same values as Judaism. Religion and nature, he said, both provided him with a sense of connection, relief from loneliness, and freedom from the fear of death. The universalism expressed here was not just intellectual but existential and relational as well.

Rob, who was sitting next to David, worried about ultimate meaning in the face of death. He was "haunted" by the "ayecha question," he said, "because it's always comparative of where your life is now to where you might want it to be, measured on a timeline, because life is finite. If it weren't, then the question wouldn't matter."

This introspective discussion differed from the discussion sessions at the Dovetail conference. This group shared the Dovetail participants' emphasis on rational tolerance and respect for all people as well as their disdain for boundaries, which were usually seen as set by other people and an illegitimate exercise of authority over individuals. But members of this congregation expressed much more worry and doubt than were voiced at Dovetail. Shir Hadash carefully constructed itself as a safe space for people who perceived themselves to be unwelcome in other religious contexts because of their sexuality or other concerns. This religious safe space seemed to fill a need for community amid feelings of struggle and otherness that were not voiced so clearly among the Dovetail participants. Disavowing normative boundaries that community members perceived to be externally and illegitimately imposed, Shir Hadash created boundaries with which its members felt comfortable. The synagogue found its niche in welcoming people who felt alienated from most religious congregations, drawing on a language of individualism to create a community of like-minded people. Committed to both individualism and universalism, the community used Judaism as a common set of symbols and rituals, though not all members identified personally with that heritage.

The members of this congregation and the participants in the Dovetail conference correctly noted that intermarriage discourse does not necessarily reflect the lives of the people who are ostensibly its topic. The informants whom I describe in this chapter responded to this discourse by redefining religious belonging and community. While some might argue that these ways of framing religious experience can undermine the vitality of religious communities, the case of Shir Hadash suggests that universalist individualist discourses can support ties to religious communities for people whose lives deviate in some way from these communities' norms.

3

"What You Are"
and "What's in Your Heart"

While both the universalist individualist and ethnic familialist perspectives draw from Jewish and American cultural and religious orientations, they weave together the various strands in different ways. Families who adopted an ethnic familialist perspective generally were more closely connected to Judaism than to Christianity and often followed patterns that more closely resembled those of endogamous Jewish families. Their approach to their families' religious lives was comparatively less intellectualized and systematic than the universalist individualist one, emphasizing family and feelings more than rationality and self. While the two approaches differ in style, they share many key concerns: the appropriateness of religious mixing, fairness, the relative significance of heritage and choice, and the interplay of gender and family roles.

Ethnic familialism reflects an attempt to avoid or mitigate feelings of loss and disloyalty, concerns that not appear prominently in universalist individualism. The term itself emphasizes the importance of family and the sense of an ethnic relationship with the Jewish people in couples' decisions about religion in their lives. I use *ethnic* here in the sense of a conception of mythical shared ancestors (Porton 1994) because the mythic sense seemed to be most important to my informants. The notion has more to do with their emotional understanding of their roots than their contemporary group interests, which might be the foremost concern for some sociologists studying ethnicity. Ethnic familialists' conception of Jewishness intertwines race, mythic shared ancestry, and shared religious and cultural practices and beliefs.

Like universalist individualism, ethnic familialism often includes the belief that religions express generally the same values and that choice plays a part in religious belief and practice. But whereas universalist individualists redefined Jewish and Christian history and theology in order to align them with

American cultural and personal values, ethnic familialists set aside contradictions between the religions. They chose Judaism for their children, drawing
mental boundaries around their own use of Christian symbols and practices.
Often, in response to questions about which Jewish values they wanted to pass
on to their children, my Jewish male informants listed tenets such as the Ten
Commandments, "do unto others," and "be a good person," all of which Judaism
shares with Christianity as well as a diffuse American civil religion. Rarely did
they place these items in a specifically Jewish or even religious context.

Ethnic familialism entangles American and Jewish cultural values. Although
it starts with values particular to Judaism, it enacts them in a way particular to
the American setting. Yet this setting itself is the source of much ambivalence.
The freedom of religion that has enabled Jews to integrate into American society
has also offered them the opportunity to choose religious indifference. Before
the 1940s, Jewishness could be a state of being for Jews who lived in close-knit
Jewish neighborhoods of major cities, surrounded by Jewish friends and family
members (Moore 1981, 19–58). But with American Jews' movement to the suburbs, Jewishness became located in synagogues and Jewish community centers.
In the suburbs, Jews actively had to put themselves into the context of Jewish
referents. The experiential ethnic familialist model is a self-conscious effort to
create the sensory and spiritual experiences that in earlier generations might
have happened as a matter of course. Intermarried ethnic familialist Jews rely
on nostalgia as their guide for what they try to create, using memories of their
own Jewish childhoods or, lacking those, an imagined version of their parents'
or grandparents' Jewish childhoods. They also receive professional guidance on
these questions from religious experts like Mothers Circle leaders. Like universalist individualists, ethnic familialists hold a conception of Jewishness within
their families that strongly features American and Protestant Christian values
of fairness, individualism, and universalism. But it also includes a commitment
to Jewish peoplehood and religious continuity, bonds that operate outside the
language or practice of individualism.

Jewishness as "What You Are"

How is heritage understood and put into practice in family and community relationships and in child rearing? A free-form discussion group at the Dovetail conference, in which spouses described their religious upbringing to one another,
illuminated this question. Only two couples and I were present at this session.
Participants shared with one another their understandings of what it meant to
be in a religious community and part of a religious tradition. Their understandings were quite different from the universalist individualist perspective: belief
was far less central, and individual and communal experiences were far more so.

Alisa, who said that she came from a "nonpracticing Conservative" Jewish family, and Mitch, who was raised "mostly Reform," met for the first time at this session. They found that they had had very similar experiences. Both said that Judaism had seemed "contentless" to them as they grew up. Their families celebrated the High Holidays, Hanukkah, and Passover, and they ate Jewish foods, but neither sensed that there was any particular meaning to these activities. "You do the traditions because that's what you are," Alisa said, "not because of what you believe."

This conception of Judaism was incomprehensible to Mitch's Presbyterian wife, Diane. To her, religion meant practices that expressed deeply held personal beliefs, which members of a religious community articulated and shared. But she recognized that the Jewish community with which her family was affiliated seemed to assume that Jewishness was "what you are" rather than "what you believe." The community seemed to have expectations about behavior and belonging but not about religious beliefs.

Diane described her struggle to arrange their daughter's upcoming bat mitzvah within a Jewish community that felt strange to her. She worried that she would violate unspoken and unwritten communal norms of which she was unaware. No one had explained what beliefs were expressed in the practices of the bat mitzvah ceremony. Perhaps beliefs were not the focus; but if becoming bat mitzvah was so important, she wondered, why couldn't anyone explain it? The family's local Jewish community seemed to be full of assumptions about not only ritual protocol but also emotional connections and orientations that involved how Jews knew and felt that they were Jewish. Because she did not share these assumptions, Diane felt that she was always marked as an outsider.

We discussed fellowship, a term familiar to Diane from her Presbyterian background. Faith connoted belief and emotion mixed together. It could be articulated and explained, and in her experience people within the same community could come to a rough agreement on what it was and what it meant. Fellowship comprised the relationships within a community that came out of a shared faith. What Diane sensed in the synagogue was different: the Jewish version of faith was not often discussed as it was in the Presbyterian church, and the Jewish version of fellowship felt more like kinship ties than a community based on shared beliefs. (See Troeltsch [(1931) 1992] for a discussion of different ways in which Christians have understood fellowship.)

This sense of kinship (discussed in chapter 2) anchors the ethnic familialist perspective. This perspective admits belief and ritual performance but does not require them. As a newcomer, Diane focused on questions about the beliefs behind the community's practices and assumptions, even if her husband hadn't given them a second thought. But these were just the kind of questions that Sklare (1964) must have had in mind when he had asked, "What do you stand for when you wish to remain separate?" (52). When cultural contradictions become impossible to ignore, the traditions and assumptions upon which communal practices depend are called into question. Some might find such questions disturbing, but others find new ways to address them.

Learning to Be a Jewish Family

In creating an experiential mode of Jewishness, families drew on the expertise of Jewish educators and rabbis. I observed the interactions of non-Jewish women with such educators at the Mothers Circle as well as in other settings. The Mothers Circle gave non-Jewish women married to Jewish men support and knowledge to encourage them to choose Judaism for their families on the theory that women are most often the religious decision makers in families. Such institutional support helped participants situate their families as Jewish-only rather than mixed or assimilative, echoing mid-twentieth-century Jewish leaders' call for Jewish institutions to replace parents' judgment in the shaping of their children's Jewishness (Berman 2010). Otherwise, as the Dovetail conference had shown, intermarried couples who designed their own religious experience might mix Christianity and Judaism.

A project of the Jewish Outreach Institute, the Mothers Circle began as a pilot program in Atlanta and quickly spread to more than two dozen other cities. At its meetings, the group's facilitator followed a standard curriculum designed to identify and explain some of the assumptions that Jewish communities rely upon. She also invited the women to air their own concerns. They frequently discussed the assumptions about their families' religious lives that they detected in their interactions with their Jewish husbands and in-laws. These women's experiences and perspectives revealed how the "contentless" Jewishness that Alisa described appeared to non-Jews who lived within it.

At the Mothers Circle in Atlanta, some women discussed with one another what Jewishness was, just as Diane had done at the Dovetail conference. They sought to understand how husbands saw Jewishness. Some Christian women, seeing their husbands' lack of Jewish education, felt that it was up to them to learn and teach what some of them called the "strong traditions" of Judaism to their children and husbands so that their family's Jewishness would have integrity. (See also Fishman [2004, 50] and McGinity [2009, 184–185].) In contrast, the Christian women whom I categorize as universalist individualist refused to "give up" their own religious traditions, forcing their Jewish husbands to provide Jewish education and leadership within the families. Within many of these families, Jewish men explored ways to teach their children about Judaism, recognizing that their wives intended to transmit their own Christian religious traditions to their children.

The Mothers Circle women tolerated and worked around sometimes exasperating contradictions in their husbands' understandings of Jewishness. To the women, their husbands' and in-laws' reactions to Christian symbols and celebrations revealed inexplicable but apparently important assumptions about what it meant to them to be Jewish, which Fishman (2004, 64–68) and McGinity (2009, 191) also found. The women frequently wondered how their husbands could be ambivalent and apparently indifferent toward Jewish practices and beliefs while vehemently protesting any Christian symbols or practices in their homes. Over the course of the year, they came to understand, gradually and tentatively, that for their husbands Jewishness meant "what you are" rather than "what you believe." The Mothers Circle addressed this contradiction repeatedly, especially around the season of Christmas and Hanukkah, as I will discuss later in this chapter.

At one Mothers Circle meeting just before Passover in the spring of 2007, the women discussed their Jewish husbands' ambivalence toward Judaism. Six women had gathered at the home of the Mothers Circle facilitator, Denise. They sat in a half-circle on two deep sofas, chatting over coffee. In this session, the women were to acquaint themselves with Hebrew names and Jewish terminology related to conversion and baby-welcoming ceremonies, which most of their children had undergone. Denise coached the women as they took turns inserting their own distinctively non-Hebrew names into the Jewish pattern:

"Melanie *bat* John *v'*Ann. [Melanie, daughter of John and Ann.]"

"Cherise bat Michael v'Sharon."

"Alicia bat Steven v'Donna."

"Do you see how that works?" Denise asked encouragingly. The women shrugged awkwardly. Some of them seemed unsure that they believed the pattern was that simple.

"We don't know if my son already has a Hebrew name," Cherise said. "How do we find out? Is it written down somewhere? Did they give it to him at the *bris* [circumcision]?" Though all of the women present had experienced some kind of Jewish ceremony to welcome their children, many felt unsure about what had actually taken place. They felt unable to ask their husbands because the men also had only a vague idea and felt uncomfortable about the topic of Jewish ritual. That discomfort created challenges in raising Jewish children: their husbands insisted on Jewish households but resisted participating wholeheartedly in them. Their ambivalence reflected contradictions in American Jewishness and assimilation as well as a gendered division of labor, which I will discuss later.

"I don't know what my husband's Hebrew name is either," commented Alicia, a woman in her early thirties with a two-year-old son, Evan.

"Why don't you ask him?" asked Denise.

"Yeah, that would go over like a lead balloon," Alicia replied with a weary laugh. She did not elaborate, but the tone that she and the other women used to talk about this issue implied that their husbands were sensitive about such questions. Perhaps they experienced their wives' questions, to which they did not know the answers, as judgmental.

Alicia changed the subject. "Evan came home from the JCC [Jewish community center] preschool talking about the Easter bunny. He found out about the Easter bunny there, and now he expects it to come to our house. I don't know why they were talking about that at a Jewish school, or why I was able to buy two books about it there. But now my husband is afraid Evan will be confused." Her husband, she said, worried that Evan would not understand the difference between Judaism and Christianity or know that he was Jewish and not Christian. Worse, she implied, perhaps their son would feel deprived of fun Christian traditions such as the Easter bunny and Santa, especially if he was excited about them and then his parents told him he could not participate.

"My husband is like that too," said Cherise. "He's afraid of confusing our son who is only six months old! So he doesn't want us to have the Easter bunny. But I do! What's the harm in it? It's just a fun thing to do; it's not *religious*. So what are you all going to do for Easter?"

Most of the women responded that the Easter bunny would indeed visit, and they would dye eggs with their children. They saw it as fun for themselves and their children, and certainly not a way of sneaking Christianity into their households since they could imagine no religious message connected with the Easter bunny. And yet their husbands' apparently nonsensical objections nagged at them. How could a visit from the Easter bunny persuade their children of the divinity of Jesus? Their husbands claimed that the boundary they wanted to preserve was theological, but it seemed as if the real issue was something else.

Like the Easter bunny, the Christmas tree was also a source of marital conflict. It, too, could have been read as a secular symbol, part of an American cultural celebration that lights up an otherwise dreary winter. Rarely did any of my Jewish informants say that it symbolized the divinity of Jesus for them, though they often pointed to its "original" meaning as a Christian symbol. But the link between the Christmas tree's current usage and its theological origins did not seem to explain the marital acrimony that it inspired among many of them. Several Jewish husbands whom I interviewed expressed bitterness about having to "give in" to their wives' desire to put up a Christmas tree, saying that they did not want one but that it was so important to their wives that refusal would have caused too much tension.

To the Jewish husbands, the Christmas tree was a powerful symbol not of Jesus' birth, but of what the men themselves were *not*. Many feared that the tree's presence in their home would alienate their children from their Jewish heritage, and would mark them as being "non-Jewish" regardless of their Jewish practice; for, as Alisa and Michael said, Jewishness is "what you are." It was not the tree's "original" religious meaning that troubled these men. Rather, the tree symbolized a powerful assimilative majority culture, or even "two thousand years of persecution and . . . fears of annihilation" (McGinity 2009, 191).

For Jews, emphatically rejecting the Christmas tree has become a way to dramatize their subjective sense of difference and demonstrate unity with other Jews who also resist assimilation. But this move is largely subjective. Jewish distinctiveness is not necessarily found outwardly, although a folk theory of Jewish physiognomy persists (Glenn 2010). More often, it is internal, whether it is presumed to be carried in genes or blood (Kahn 2010; Tenenbaum and Davidman 2007) or simply in the mind in the form of "Jewish identity." The latter, a frequently used but imprecisely defined term, seems to rest on a nebulous but deeply felt sense of categorical difference from non-Jews. The "tribalism" or "historical familism" that Steven M. Cohen and Arnold M. Eisen (2000) discuss in *The Jew Within* suggests this categorical difference, "the sense that Jews differ from others, that they understand one another better, and that they can and should rely on one another in times of need" (187–188). Fishman (2004) reports that her interviewees felt that "being Jewish makes you different" and that intermarriage raised their consciousness of how far apart they and their spouses were (49, 53–54). American Jewish leaders in the mid-twentieth century were intensely interested in convincing their followers that such a categorical difference existed in order to discourage intermarriage (Berman 2010, 100). Many contemporary Jews have adopted this rhetoric even though they are uncomfortable naming specific ways in which Jews are different.

Intermarried Jews adopting the ethnic familialist perspective described feeling compelled to raise their children as Jews because they feared that otherwise their children would be different from them, unrecognizable, strange. I have already mentioned the Jewish father who said, "I felt like I would be forever alienated from my kid if he was in the Savior mode and I wasn't." He and his wife, a practicing Catholic, agreed that they would raise their child as a Jew, but his wife said, "I made the decision lightly and spent the next seven years struggling with it." She wanted to share her own religious faith and traditions with her spouse and children, but she and her husband also wanted to demonstrate their respect for Judaism by avoiding the mixing of Judaism and Christianity. In order to observe the boundaries set by intermarriage discourse while also honoring her own heritage, she devised a compromise: "My son has my spirituality under the guise of Jewish religion." Even though Catholic spirituality underlies their son's Jewishness, his avowed Jewishness enables his father to feel more deeply connected to him.

Intermarriage discourse invokes categorical difference most obviously in the discord approach discussed in chapter 1, which posits that Jews' and non-Jews' backgrounds differ so strongly from one another that their relationships will inevitably be strained. Even sociological studies that intend to be fair or sympathetic to intermarried couples often focus on the tensions that they experience and their relational problem-solving methods. For example, in "Intermarriage and Jewish Journeys in the United States," a policy study for which I served as an interviewer, subjects were asked about problems that they experienced and how they solved them (Dashefsky with Heller 2008). Fishman (2004) uses words such as *battle, skirmish, struggle,* and *complicated* and phrases such as "the great divide" and "through the looking glass" to describe her interviewees' relationships (59–60, 78, 96–97). Sociologist Bruce Phillips's (n.d.) analysis of the journal *Dovetail* finds that these foci also arise from the couples themselves as they describe their conflicts over holidays and life-cycle events and how they resolved them. But even though intermarried couples raise these topics on their own, they may not regard them as the central and most important feature of their relationships.

Such categories and assumptions affect both the conclusions that scholars reach and the lives of their subjects. As I showed in chapter 2, scholarly analysis filters into intermarriage discourse and affects the lives of real people who hear and respond to it—sometimes internalizing it, sometimes resisting it. Scholars do the same. I have described ways in which scholars have adopted the idea of categorical difference and the marital discord that results from it in their studies of intermarriage. Yet McGinity (2009) has shown that religious differences were minor if not irrelevant factors in the divorces of the intermarried Jewish women she studied. Additionally, we lose sight of other possible analytic frames when we focus on categorical difference. What might ground conceptions of Jewishness and connections between Jews if not the idea that Jews are inherently different from non-Jews? What might we find if we focus on the elements that bind intermarried spouses together in strong and loving marriages rather than fixate on what drives such spouses apart? For example, McGinity points out that her informants had become Americanized, not assimilated (105). To what degree does Americanness constitute categorical sameness for intermarried couples or for subsets of American Jews more broadly? Many American Jews are deeply formed by American cultural ideas about personhood and religion: 66 percent of those surveyed for *The Jew Within* agreed or strongly agreed that "My being Jewish doesn't make me any different from other Americans," and 77 percent disagreed or strongly disagreed with the statement "As a Jew, I feel like somewhat of an outsider in American society" (Cohen and Eisen 2000, 195ff, 216). Without placing these ideas about difference and sameness into the context of lived experience, we know little about what they mean to American Jews or intermarried couples. Ethnography can help us understand when and why sameness and difference matter and how our informants may hold these opposites in self-contradictory tension, perhaps to be resolved someday, perhaps not.

Nevertheless, a commitment to categorical difference, even when it was unclear what that difference actually was, lay behind the boundaries that my informants attempted to establish within their homes, families, and minds. As their concerns about their children's confusion made clear, the Jewish men were aware of the emphasis on strict separation between Judaism and Christianity in intermarriage discourse. Since they were unable to completely remove Christian practices or symbols from their homes—and because they in fact loved Christian members of their families—they tried to establish mental boundaries that delineated an awareness of themselves as Jews. Avoiding religious mixing was the way they chose to demonstrate that they were good-enough Jews, in contrast to the universalist individualists, who did not believe that distinguishing carefully between religions was important.

Intermarried couples who framed their participation in Easter activities as mere secular fun implicitly asserted that their own beliefs determined the activities' nature and significance. In other words, they thought they could render their participation "not Christian" simply by declaring it to be so. Fishman (2004) argues that this is essentially an exercise in self-delusion. In her view, when intermarried couples allow their children to participate in Christian activities such as Easter-egg hunts, the children become unable to recognize the categorical difference between Judaism and Christianity, even if the couple insists otherwise: "As their children grow up experiencing these activities in their own homes, they take psychological ownership of a Christian religious tradition" (68). Behavior, in Fishman's view, shapes belief. Her view corresponds to a traditional Jewish understanding in which observance of Jewish law may precede comprehension of the reasons for the law and indeed must take place regardless of whether such comprehension ever comes. These different understandings of religious activity raise the same disagreement I described in chapter 1 when I discussed concerns about whether the NJPS survey should have asked questions about behaviors or beliefs when determining whether respondents were Jewish.

This disagreement reflects a difference between a traditional Jewish understanding of religious activity and one that is not just American but fully modern. Processes of secularization and modernization that took place over the course of the seventeenth through nineteenth centuries joined with Protestant Christian ideas emphasizing individual autonomy, belief, and emotion to shape modern ideas about religion, persons, and the nature of society (Asad 1993; Casanova 1994, 21–22; Chaves 1994; Cross and Livingstone 2005b; Dumont 1982, 20; Yamane 1997). Protestant ideas about what mattered most in religious experience—the doctrine of justification by faith, universal priesthood of all believers, and the principle of private judgment—came to inform the modern western definition of religion itself as well as its idea of the individual (Bellah [1970] 1991, 36–45; Cross and Livingstone 2005b). It has been challenging for

Jews to translate Jewish life into a modern society based on these ideas (Batnitzky 2011). The idea that religious experience and authority are essentially subjective seemed to be part of my informants' sense that a mental boundary could be an effective way of maintaining their sense of themselves as Jews. In other words, the mental boundary was not simply a way for intermarried Jews to justify behaviors that a normative religious community condemned; it had deep roots in one of the cultures to which American Jews belong.

Ironically, even the assertion of categorical difference between Jews and non-Jews may be a performance of Americanness. Resistance to an assimilative majority culture, whether through beliefs, behavior, or heritage, constituted a measure of personal integrity for many of my Jewish informants. As they resisted participating in Christmas rituals because they felt that doing so would signal their disloyalty to Judaism, they performed an American script of moral self-assertion. In other words, their rejection of assimilation took place in an entirely assimilated way. American individualist ideologies celebrate "authenticity" and "standing up for one's beliefs" as opposed to conforming to the beliefs of a group. The American cultural "connection of moral courage and lonely individualism" is represented by heroic figures such as the cowboy and the "hard-boiled detective," who embody special virtue and serve their communities even as they remain isolated from them. In contrast, society is identified with corruption (Bellah et al. 1985, 145–146). When Jewish men resisted the Christmas tree and the Easter bunny, which their wives saw as harmless and essentially secular, they assumed an American moral stance of self-isolation that opposes dominant values and practices in American society.

Besides the theological argument against the presence of the Christmas tree that some Jewish men invoked, the specter of Jewish demographic catastrophe through assimilation and conversion to Christianity was also summoned. At one late November 2007 meeting of the Mothers Circle, another group of women met with group leader Denise and her husband Joe to learn about Hanukkah. They were perplexed by their husbands' objections to participating in Christmas activities with their families. Denise and Joe, both Jews, explained that sensitivity to Christian proselytizing boosted Jews' anxiety about Jewish-Christian boundaries. "Today I thought we could talk about the December dilemma," Denise said as the women sank into the soft couches. "Are there any questions you have about Hanukkah, any problems you and your husband are having figuring out how to make it all work? What do you do in your house in December?"

Since the term *December dilemma* was first coined in 1987, it has been widely discussed (McGinity 2009, 191–192) and has been the topic of outreach programs (Fishman 2004, 149). In Jewish educational circles, the term is a way of describing intermarried Jews' concerns about how to show respect and love for the Christian side of their family while maintaining integrity as Jews. In universalist individualist discourses, there is no dilemma because participation in another religion's rituals without believing in them is taken for granted. Many of my ethnic familialist Jewish informants, however, avoided Christian practices as a way of drawing a boundary around Jewishness without having to articulate its content. The dilemma arose in the conflict between their nebulous sense of Jewishness and their spouses' wish to maintain the Christian holiday practices of their childhoods.

The women looked around at one another to gauge who wanted to speak first. Then Michelle said in a strong voice, "I am a Christian, and we have a Christmas tree. That's just the way it is and how it's gonna be. My husband participates in Christmas—I always say it's like he converts two days a year, once for Christmas Eve and once for Christmas Day, and then he converts back to Judaism for the rest of the year."

This language of temporary conversion did not emerge at the Dovetail conference because the participants assumed that no conversion was needed to participate in the rituals of another religion. But because the Mothers Circle women were by definition raising their children as Jews, they and their husbands were concerned about identifying and maintaining boundaries around Jewishness. Yet without realizing it, Michelle had chosen words that struck at the heart of the American Jewish community's fear of assimilation, a worry that Jews might simply vanish into Christianity because they had failed to guard against it. The idea of converting two days a year implied that Jews could be religious chameleons at their convenience rather than being committed to a long shared history and interdependence with fellow Jews.

I wondered if Michelle's husband might strenuously object to this characterization of his participation in Christmas festivities. Jewish outreach professionals, who encourage Jews from "outside" normative Judaism to affiliate with Jewish institutions, often suggest that intermarried Jews raising their children as Jews can celebrate Christmas with their Christian family members and preserve the proper boundary if they simply hold their participation at arm's length. Jewish educators often encourage intermarried parents to tell their children that they are "helping Grandma and Grandpa celebrate their holiday," just as they help their friends celebrate their birthdays without mistaking them for their own. Exactly this language is advised by commentators for the Union for Reform Judaism (Appell, Chernow, Fink, and Farhi 2013), and Fishman (2004) also heard it frequently in her interviews with "mixed-married" couples (66). The distinction might well be lost on the Christian grandparents, but it was an important mental boundary for the intermarried Jew, another way of demonstrating subjective resistance to assimilation.

The other Mothers Circle members expressed their confusion about Jewish family members' objections to celebrating Christmas. Sheryl said in a perplexed tone, "My in-laws get really upset about our having Christmas at our house. It's weird. They see me doing all this Jewish stuff with the kids, but then just doing one thing that's Christian makes my in-laws start questioning my commitment to raising the kids Jewish."

Sandy agreed. "It's crazy that for this one day of the year, it's such a big deal that the kids go to their Christian grandparents' house and open presents, even though for the other 364 days of the year they're completely Jewish. I don't get it."

Joe offered an insider's perspective on the discussion: "I grew up in a town that was very multicultural, so even as a Jew—and I had no question that I was a Jew—I still participated in Christmas stuff with my friends growing up. I went to Christmas Mass with my friends. It was impossible to insulate yourself from other cultures there; you were in contact with them all the time. My parents did Santa in our house, and we were Jewish."

Denise echoed this universalistic view. "I sang Christmas carols in school," she said. "It wasn't considered a big deal then. That's just the way it was. Of course, now everyone freaks out about it." Denise and Joe tried to soften the appearance of Jewish opposition to Christmas by offering a universalistic view like that of the Dovetail conference participants: religious rituals and celebrations could be shared by people who did not share beliefs. After all, surely celebrating Christmas could not make one a bad Jew if even observant Jewish educators could participate in Christmas. Living in a multicultural and cosmopolitan environment, to this couple, meant actively participating in a diverse community and its religious rituals without necessarily believing in them.

"So that's what I don't get," Sheryl responded. "When both parents are Jewish, they can let their kids do Christian things, and they are comfortable with it and don't worry that it makes them any less Jewish because they're just participating in someone else's holiday. But if *I* do something Christian with my kids, suddenly it's like I'm trying to make them Christian, even though I've made it clear that they are Jewish."

The Mothers Circle women and their husbands had agreed that their children's religious lives would be strictly Jewish and would not be subject to the children's preferences, but the husbands and their Jewish family members appeared to be unsure that they could trust this agreement. Fishman (2004) describes the similar feelings of a Jewish woman who feared that her non-Jewish husband would "renege on their agreement" to have a Jewish home once they had children. In at least one case among Fishman's informants, a Christian spouse did come to realize that she wanted her children to have a Christian upbringing after previously having believed it to be unimportant; and in another, a Christian spouse developed an interest in Judaism (90–92). Christian in-laws also sometimes acted independently of an intermarried couple's expressed wishes to avoid Christian activities and symbols by bringing Christmas- or Easter-themed gifts to the Jewish-identified family's home (66–67). It is unclear to what extent my informants were aware that such cases existed, or whether they had imagined these possibilities.

Sheryl's comment rang true for the other women, who nodded in recognition. "Right!" Sandy said. "Like, we only do Christmas at my parents' house; there is no question of having a Christmas tree in our house. My husband said, 'Absolutely not.' So we don't have one. But I still don't see what the big deal is." She shrugged, resigned.

Joe explained, "The reason it's such a big deal is that, for so long, Jews have felt that Christians have been trying to make everyone Christian. Just last month Ann Coulter, this big Republican, was on TV saying she thought everyone in America should be Christian. And they asked her what about Jews, and she said they should become 'perfected Jews.' And Jews all over America were thinking, 'See, here we go again.' So it feels, like with the Christmas tree, it's one step towards them getting us to become Christian. Like, if they can get a Christmas tree in the house, then what could the next step be?"

The incident to which Joe referred had made headlines in the Jewish and secular media. Coulter, a right-wing conservative media personality already famous for making extreme comments about liberals, had said on a cable news television show that Jews should be "perfected," that Christians already were "perfected," and that the United States should be entirely Christian (Holden 2007). Many felt that she could not be taken seriously since she espoused views so extreme that few people would openly agree with them: for example, she also criticized the widows of men who had died in the September 11, 2001, terrorist attacks (Rutten 2007). Some in the Jewish press nevertheless felt that her comments reflected a latent antisemitism rampant in the United States or at least brought to the surface the truth about Christian beliefs about Jews. Others commented that her remarks showed that interfaith dialogue could never successfully overcome the problem of religious beliefs that fundamentally conflicted and wondered whether there was any point in interreligious conversation when there was disagreement on such basic matters as the divinity of Jesus ("Perfecting U.S. Jews" 2007; Wiener 2007).

Joe was not trying to suggest to the Mothers Circle women that their husbands felt that they were secretly antisemitic, but he hoped to explain the context of Jews' feelings about Christmas. It was not clear whether the women fully understood Joe's explanation since they did not share the feeling of being threatened that he described. Bracketing that difficult and confusing issue rather than attempting to resolve it, the conversation turned instead to a practical discussion of how to celebrate Hanukkah.

For the Mothers Circle women, creating a Jewish home required understanding not just Jewish traditions but also their husbands' unspoken assumptions and ambivalence about Jewishness. Whereas the men tended to depend on their innate Jewishness for their sense of identity, their wives felt that the choice to claim that Jewishness as the family's identity demanded serious effort. Even so, some of my Christian women informants felt that in making this choice, they disrespected their own heritage. They might have felt otherwise had their husbands been able to explain what Judaism meant to them, so that the reasons for giving up Christianity would be clear. But these men were often unable to articulate in depth their reasons for wanting Jewish children. Instead, they described the fun they had had in Jewish settings as children, and they implied that they feared disapproval from other Jews who might regard them as disloyal. Some ethnic familialist men seemed to want Judaism for their children because they wanted to relive their own childhoods or simply so that their children's experiences would seem familiar to them rather than an amalgam that included strange elements from Christianity. They felt that their own religious loyalties and identities had been shaped more by the accretion of their experiences in the context of their families, across their lifetimes, than by instruction in religious school or formal religious rituals. This experiential creation of Jewishness seems to align with the traditional Jewish focus on behavior over belief, even though my informants' Jewish experience did not necessarily center on observance of Jewish law.

Some of the women felt uncomfortable undertaking religious practices absent the accompanying beliefs. Linda, a Catholic mother of two middle school–aged children, said, "I wanted a huge Christmas tree, and we do have one. The kids enjoy decorating it and having it. But my husband is uncomfortable with it because he didn't grow up with it. And then we have to question our core beliefs at that point. Easter, too—we have Easter baskets, but I'm not sure if I should also insist on going to Easter services." By *core beliefs*, Linda seemed to mean something like "what we are," as Alisa and Michael had said, rather than theology. Her family's religious observances were not decided on the basis of how each member of the family felt about the divinity of Jesus and whether he was really resurrected on Easter Sunday. Rather, they were decided according to what made the family feel most unified and mutually supportive. Holiday religious observances were "usually my issue," Linda said. "I'm forced to think about it—like, if I ask for days off for the High Holidays. I'm not used to it. Sometimes I don't take the whole day off, and then it's awkward when the rest of the family is at services without me. If everyone were the same religion, it would be more automatic." Her core beliefs, as interpreted through these comments, seemed to relate to her desire to feel connected to her family more than her wish to attend worship services out of her own religious belief or duty to God.

Belief, practice, and belonging had a complicated relationship in the lives of my informants. Some of the Mothers Circle women and other non-Jews married to Jews were delighted to adopt Judaism's "strong traditions," as some of them put it, without committing themselves to belief in its tenets. This was one of the ways in which religion as "what you are" could be manifest in lived experience. Others were dismayed by their Jewish spouses' lack of "spiritual" involvement in their religion. Either way, the women moved past their confusion about their husbands' contradictory stances toward Jewishness by assuming leadership roles within their families.

Creating Experiential Jewishness

Despite their own complex feelings about Judaism, many non-Jewish women informants assumed Jewish leadership roles within their families, out of pragmatism as well as commitment to their families' choices. At another Mothers Circle meeting, I joined Denise, her mother, and Sandy to bake *hamantaschen*, cookies for the Purim holiday. Now halfway through the year-long Mothers Circle course, Sandy had been introduced to Jewish traditions associated with naming, life-cycle ceremonies, holidays, and the stories of Hanukkah and Purim. Despite feeling like a newcomer to Judaism, she said that her mother-in-law Ellen was already urging her to lead the family's Jewish celebrations. "Every time I learn how to do a new Jewish thing, she tells me that now I get to take over it for the family," Sandy commented as she rolled out the cookie dough.

"Why doesn't she say that to your husband instead?" I asked, cutting out circles of dough with the rim of a drinking glass. "He's the one who grew up with Judaism."

"He wouldn't know," Denise said.

Sandy agreed. "He doesn't know anything. He probably won't know what these hamantaschen are when I bring them home."

Joe, Denise's husband, was standing by the oven waiting for his poppyseed hamantaschen to come out of the oven. Poppyseed is a traditional hamantaschen filling, but no one else in the room, Jewish or not, liked it. "He'll know what hamantaschen are," Joe said. "That's one of the things you remember from being a Jewish kid. He'll know."

Joe's comment reflected exactly the kind of sensory childhood memory that mid-twentieth-century Jewish homemaking manuals had urged Jewish women to create (as I will discuss later in this chapter). More than any articulated intellectual or ethical commitment, these sensory experiences were to create children's ongoing allegiance to and love for Judaism. In essence, they would instill in the children an instinctive sense of "what they are" as Jews. To that end, the Mothers Circle included instruction in the preparation of holiday foods and activities, emphasizing ways to make them fun for children as well as their parents.

As we concluded our baking, Denise explained to Sandy and me that our next session would cover preparations for Passover: how to clean, cook, kasher (make kosher), buy kosher-for-Passover products, and discard or put away non-Passover foods. "My mother-in-law wants me to host all our family seders from now on," Sandy remarked. Denise nodded encouragingly.

"That's going to be a lot of work!" I said. "Is your husband going to help you with it?"

"No, he wouldn't be able to help with that," Sandy said.

Denise agreed, telling me, "He wouldn't know." She turned to Sandy. "But your mother-in-law can tell you what to do and what family traditions you can incorporate! You should ask her."

Non-Jewish women's leadership of Jewish practices in their homes is supported by gendered patterns of household and emotional labor. Routine domestic labor in American households is carried out by women, argues sociologist Arlie Russell Hochschild ([1989] 2003), in contrast to men's intermittently performed chores such as yard work or home repairs. Further, women typically provide men with more "behind-the-scenes" support than they receive, an imbalanced arrangement which men often claim that women choose (8–10, 210–11, 265f, 272). Sociologists continue to find that women perform more domestic labor than men do and that such labor is largely invisible to men. Such gendered patterns of household labor are clearly reflected in non-Jewish women's cleaning and cooking to create the home-centered Jewish rituals that take place as part of a routine, such as the weekly and yearly cycle of sabbaths and holidays. But because it is religious labor, the women claim it as their own and allow the men to avoid participating or contributing. When Denise and Sandy claimed that the men "wouldn't know anything about it," they replicated American gendered patterns of household labor as well as longstanding associations of women with religion (discussed later in this chapter).

Family Ritual and Meaning

Janice and Marie had been in the Jewish homemaker role longer than Sandy had and were happily taking on leadership roles in their families' religious lives. One summer day in 2007, in a bright, modern, suburban Atlanta home, I sat at the kitchen table with these two women, both of whom had converted to Judaism in the Reform movement and were married to men who were born Jewish. They had become friends through the Mothers Circle. Both were in their thirties, came from Catholic and Protestant backgrounds, and were raising their young children as Jews. Attractive, intelligent, and educated, they were like many of the Mothers Circle women who had left careers to become stay-at-home mothers. Janice and Marie enjoyed doing traditional home-making activities and crafts together and had even started a group to play mah-jongg, a Chinese game that became popular with American Jewish women in the 1920s, with some other local women (Olsen n.d.). Their Mothers Circle leader often laughed admiringly about their mah-jongg group.

Janice had spent the morning teaching Marie and me how to bake challah, the traditional Shabbat bread. We had already mixed and kneaded the dough. As we waited for it to rise, the conversation turned to the subject of celebrating Shabbat. "Have you done Shabbat lately?" Janice asked Marie.

"Did you see the screensaver on the laptop?" Marie laughed. "Did you see 'NO ENTERTAINING FOR A WHILE!' scrolling across the screen? My husband put that there because he got so stressed out the last time we had people over. He wants everything to be perfect. *I* don't worry about it—I know people aren't going to notice if the kitchen isn't sparkling; they just remember if they had a good time."

"I'm the total opposite—I want everything to be perfect and my husband doesn't care," Janice replied. "So we don't do Shabbat as often."

"You haven't made it a ritual. You have to just do it every week," Marie said emphatically. "Sometimes we order pizza, and we say the crust is the challah, and we light candles and do the blessing over the wine. Once in a while we remember that it's Friday night after we've already started eating, and Steve will go, 'Oh well,' and I'll say, 'No! Not "oh well"!' And I bring out the candles and the wine. It doesn't have to be hard. And the kids get so excited. I'll tell them on Friday mornings"— her voice dropped to a theatrical whisper— "'Cassie and Nate, it's Shabbat tonight!' And Cassie will run around shrieking, 'Shabbat, Shabbat, Shabbat!' They love it!"

Janice said, "One time, before I decided to convert, I brought up to Jon that we need to do Shabbat every week, and he said, 'Why? *You're* not Jewish.'" She shot us a look of outrage. "I said, 'No, but my *children* are Jewish!' Unbelievable! Because if he's going to say that, then fine, I can just take the kids to church with me this Sunday! How about *that*?"

"Why do you think he said that?" I asked.

"Because he was being lazy." Janice explained that since she had begun the process of converting to Judaism, he had become more interested in Jewish rituals. "He grew up Orthodox, and he thought Shabbat was basically a bunch of meaningless technicalities—you wash your hands a certain way, you say certain things. But now because he's doing it with me, he's starting to see it as more spiritual. We're learning the reasons behind the rituals."

The challah had risen. Marie went upstairs to tend to three-year-old Nate, who had woken up from his nap, and Janice and I divided the dough into five balls and worked them into long snakes. I showed her how to braid five strands into one loaf, which I had learned recently from Amanda, a Christian woman who was raising Jewish children.

Amanda prided herself on her bread-baking expertise and felt that making challah was a way for her to connect to Jewish tradition while she remained deeply committed to her own blend of Catholic and Episcopalian Christianity. She and her husband belonged to a church social group for Episcopalian-Jewish intermarried couples. When I interviewed her about her experiences in her interfaith marriage, I happened to mention that my recent attempts to bake challah had ended in miserable failure, so she offered to teach me to do it well. Amanda also invited Teresa, a Christian woman who worked at her church and was engaged to marry a Jewish man. The three of us, along with Amanda's and my young children, gathered around the kitchen island to mix and knead and wait.

Amanda had started several loaves in advance so that Teresa and I could see how they were supposed to look at different stages of the process. One braided loaf was ready to go into the oven, another rested under a towel as it rose, a lump of dough was waiting to be divided and braided, and raw ingredients were ready to be measured and mixed in large bowls. Teresa and I each mixed our own dough, and Amanda coached us through kneading and turning it until it was finally smooth enough to rise. "Keep going," she told me when I prematurely claimed to have finished kneading. When the first loaf came out of the oven, Amanda and her kindergarten-aged daughter sang the *ha-motzi* song (the Jewish blessing for bread) in English and Hebrew and we ate the hot bread with some salmon salad, chèvre, and pear slices for lunch.

While we ate and waited for the remaining dough to rise, Teresa told us about her upcoming wedding. She described her fiancé's Jewish friends' and relatives' reactions to her entry into their family. Her deep connection to Christianity was not what her fiancé's family had hoped for. Her own family was very committed to the church, and she had left law school to work in church ministry. She did not plan to convert to Judaism, and her fiancé did not expect her to, but his friends and family had been quietly waiting for her to change her mind. Her new job at the church, she told us, seemed to disappoint them. One of his friends commented, "Now she'll never want to convert!" Despite his strong Jewish upbringing, complete with Jewish day-school attendance, Teresa's fiancé did not share their attitude toward conversion. That morning, when she told him that she was going to learn to make challah, he had said, "Oh, you don't have to do that!" as if she were troubling herself out of a misplaced sense of obligation.

Centered on domestic ritual items like the Jewish sabbath bread, rich with the symbolism of family and tradition, these stories suggest that the women believed that religious and ethnic tradition was passed on in their families primarily through religious and familial experience. They drew their children into the process of mixing, kneading, braiding, and baking the challah that they would bless and eat at their family's Shabbat dinner. Even though the women had not been raised in this tradition, they emphasized the sensory and spiritual experiences of repetitive ritual and prayer as they strove to pass it on to their children and to live it themselves.

Women's role in Jewish continuity has been an important theme for American and western European Jews since at least the mid-nineteenth century. American Jews characterized Jewish women's efforts to shape their children's moral and emotional attachments to Judaism as vitally important in preventing their assimilation into American culture. Faced with competition from Christian holidays, mid-twentieth-century Jewish homemaking manuals advised Jewish mothers to found and reinforce children's love for Jewish holidays beginning in early childhood in order to ensure their continuing loyalty to Judaism. Miriam Isaacs and Trude Weiss Rosmarin's *What Every Jewish Woman Should Know* (1941) advised, "If ever lavishness in gifts is appropriate it is on Hanukkah. Jewish children should be showered with gifts, Hanukkah gifts, as a perhaps primitive but most effective means of making them immune against envy of the Christian children and their Christmas presents" (qtd. in Joselit 1994, 72, 235). The *Guide for the Jewish Homemaker* also made clear women's power to create a Jewish home: "For even before you open the door of the Jewish home, you see the mezuzah, a reminder that the home is intended to be a sanctuary, and that the job of its presiding genius, the wife and mother, is essentially a spiritual one" (Levi and Kaplan [1959] 1964, xvi). These ideas had had currency for at least a century in the United States and beyond (see also Greenberg 1981; Kitov 2000; Radcliffe 1991). German Jewish women in the mid-nineteenth century were also responsible for the "informal transmission of religious feelings and identification through observance in the home" (Kaplan 1991, 205f). A large body of Jewish sociological and educational research explores how formative Jewish experiences in childhood and adolescence affect a Jew's affiliation with Jewish institutions or sense of "Jewish identity" as an adult (for example, Beck 2005; Cohen 2005). Anthropologists working in both Jewish and non-Jewish communities have studied the ways in which women wield power in their families and their communities by presiding over meal preparation (Counihan 1988; Sered 1992). Women participating in the Mothers Circle were learning to assume the role of Jewish mothers in ensuring their children's love of Judaism, even though the women themselves were not Jewish.

The women's stories also reveal a complicated relationship to religious authority, which they both respected and ignored. Religious authority is found not in texts but in ritual itself and its power to evoke feelings and a sense of connection to generations of ancestors and God. Such feelings of connection are central to the ethnic familialist approach. While ethnic familialists' reliance upon non-Jewish wives and mothers to enact these Jewish practices does not align with Jewish norms, it does reflect streams of American discourses about gender roles that encourage women to see themselves as taking care of men's spirituality, a view inherited from nineteenth-century Victorian middle-class gender ideology. In this view, men worked outside the home and relied on women to uphold "piety, purity, submissiveness, and domesticity" on their behalf. "Religion belonged to women by divine right, a gift of God and nature," and with their special talent women were to improve men and the world (Welter 1966, 152). As Jewish women assimilated into Christian middle-class societies, they adopted this role (Hyman 1991, 1995).

Ethnic familialism depends heavily on women's religious leadership, whether the women are Jewish or not. Yet among my informants, the men's spoken and unspoken awkwardness about Hebrew names, lack of Jewish knowledge, and distaste for Christian holiday symbols were as much a part of ethnic familialism as Shabbat celebrations and challah baking were. This model of intermarried family life involved a visceral kind of religious experience that was tightly bound up with family, ethnicity, and ambivalence. The experiential approach of ethnic familialism takes some of the same cultural threads that universalist individualism uses, but it weaves them into a different cloth. Ethnic familialist parents do not necessarily teach their children the values and history of multiple religions so that children can make rational, informed choices. Instead, they consciously inculcate Judaism into their lives in order to make it "what you are." Both perspectives embody a deeply American tension between individual and community.

Redrawing Boundaries

The women I've described both absorbed and resisted gendered expectations about their religious leadership. They worked for Jewish continuity but reserved the right to make their own judgments as well. For a mix of reasons that are not fully recognized by Jewish public leaders and institutions, they created Jewish families with religious activity that partly resisted and partly accommodated the discourse of Jewish media and official pronouncements. The women led their families' religious practices and understandings in strategic ways that met their own needs while responding to the claims of public leaders and sometimes even keeping their own rabbis at arm's length.

Teresa and Amanda held strongly to their Christian faith, but both felt a responsibility to the Jewish people to make sure their own children knew (or would know) their Jewish heritage out of a sense of appreciation rather than obligation. Amanda taught Judaism, along with Christianity, to her three children. She enrolled them in Jewish religious school, insisted on family synagogue attendance, and planned for their *b'nai mitzvah* (the plural form of bar or bat mitzvah). Yet she admitted to being less than forthright with the rabbi of their synagogue about the fact that the children were learning about more than Judaism. That level of detail, she felt, was none of his business, especially because she suspected that he would use it to judge their Jewish commitment as deficient.

Amanda did not expect her children to make an informed choice about religion. She saw Judaism and Christianity as inherent in them, not as a choice. She said that she prepared her children for encounters with people who disagreed with their family's understanding of its religious identity. "I tell my kids, people are going to say you can't be both [Jewish and Christian]. Jewish people are going to say that; Christian people are going to say that. That's okay. I'll just say they're going to say that you can't be both. That's okay. You can't make everyone happy. What are you going to do?" Amanda described the world that the children had been born into as simply including different Jews who have different definitions of Jewishness. In this respect, her view reflects universalist individualism's way of resolving disagreement with religious norms by redefining religious boundaries to be more inclusive.

Amanda also felt responsible for mentoring her husband in Judaism. She described her role as caretaker of her family's "spirituality," with her own relationship with God serving as a wellspring for her entire family. She felt that she possessed more insight into her husband's latent desire for such a relationship than he did, pointing out that "he's Jewish, kind of agnostic-bordering-atheist, and he decided to marry this very religious or spiritual Christian." In her eyes, by choosing to marry a woman who was so different from himself on the surface, her husband had revealed that he wanted religious experience in his life, even though his behavior suggested that he was not especially interested in it. Although he did not accompany her to church, she said, "He wants me to go to temple when they go to temple. And I usually do, and I mainly do it for him because he's not there yet, and I do it for them [the children] because they need to be supported in their Judaism." At the Dovetail conference, family members described supporting one another equally in their respective religious efforts. Amanda's family, in contrast, depended upon her to support religious practices that might not be carried out otherwise.

Amanda remained anchored in Christianity but did not begrudge her husband his need to see his children as Jewish. She urged more Jewish observance in their household, despite her own religious difference, feeling that her children deserved to experience Judaism.

> I said to [my husband], "Honey, we can't not do this; this is too beautiful for them [to miss out on]; it's too old and long and rich and beautiful. We can't not do that. . . ."
>
> But he is a sexist, a little bit. It's his son he wants to be bar mitzvahed. He doesn't care if his daughter is bat mitzvahed. So that's when I said, "We're not doing that. We're not having a son do it but not our daughter.

I mean, that's just not—" and he's like "But the males have been doing
it for thousands of years." And I said, "Good. We had infant baptisms for
thousands of years; we didn't do that with our children."

While she encouraged her husband's efforts to perform Jewish traditions, she
also felt that it was her role to instruct and correct him: performing tradition in
a thoughtless, rote manner disrespected the tradition as well as its adherents.
In Amanda's view, all of her children, boys and girls, deserved to experience
the fullness of their traditions as a source of emotional and spiritual strength.
To ensure such an experience, she shaped the family's religious practices and
interpreted their meaning, sometimes correcting and teaching her husband
when she disagreed with his understanding of them.

Amanda felt that she had greater spiritual understanding than her husband did, particularly in her sense of the artificiality of religious boundaries. To
Amanda, having children of a different religion from her own was not a problem as long as her children found religious meaning. But there was a twinge of
ambivalence in the sense of personal fulfillment that she derived from taking
on a leadership role in her family's Jewish life.

I would be sobbing crying if any of our children were ordained a rabbi. I
would be so happy. And there would only be one little thing in the back
of my mind: that they weren't choosing my tradition. That would make
me a little sad, but it would make me mostly happy that they had chosen
a life of—they had turned toward the power of the divine. The belief in
the divine in people's lives. That would make me happy. It's choosing the
positive, in my view. And everybody gets there in different ways. So that's
why I can be married to a Jewish person. It doesn't matter to me.

Amanda's ambivalence coexisted with her view of her role in her family's religious life: she was the person who facilitated the development of each member's
spiritual life as he or she moved toward maturity. Fishman (2004) addresses
her interviewees' complex feelings about having different religions within the
same household in a quite different way, focusing more on guilt, resentment,
and deprivation than on the more positive outlook that Amanda reported (157).
Certainly, different families may experience this situation in different ways.
However, the emphasis on guilt, resentment, and deprivation reflects the longstanding focus in intermarriage discourse on the pathologies of intermarried
couples (see chapter 1). It is fairer to our informants to recognize that these
negative feelings are not the only or necessary interpretations or experiences
of intermarried religious life. Such generalizations may seem natural when they
are taken from summaries of large amounts of interview data, particularly when
the generalizations fit into existing cultural narratives about intermarriage, but
these summaries are taken out of the context of individual subjects' lives.

Ethnography focused on the stories and experiences of individuals is a necessary, even corrective, supplement to social analysis of broader patterns. Amanda's story provides a deeper context in which to understand how inter-married couples might experience tensions and contradictions in both positive and negative ways. In her view, the divine transcended particular religious ritu-als and symbols, which universalist individualist discourses also emphasize. For her husband, the symbols and rituals themselves were important but lacked the content that Amanda saw as so vital. Within the same family, the visceral con-nection of the Jew to the Jewish people coexisted with more easily articulated intellectual and emotional connections.

Women, Men, and Spirituality

My women informants often talked about both Jewish and Christian "spirituality"—their personal, emotional responses to religious rituals and prayers—more easily and readily than their husbands did. At a Mothers Circle "Couples' *Havdalah*" (the brief ceremony marking the end of Shabbat on Satur-day evening) and discussion over desserts and wine, this difference was clear. On a warm spring evening, several intermarried couples, three Mothers Circle leaders, two of the leaders' husbands who were also Jewish educators, and the Mothers Circle rabbi stood in a wide circle on the patio of Joe and Denise's home. Two couples gingerly held ritual objects—a braided candle, a spice box, and a cup of wine—with which the Jewish men and non-Jewish women appeared to be equally unfamiliar. Joe and another Jewish educator spent five minutes tuning their banjo and guitar while everyone waited. When they were satisfied with their sound, they played a contemporary Jewish melody while the rabbi read the blessings in English and Hebrew from a handout. The educators sang along quietly, and the intermarried couples stood awkwardly silent.

At the ceremony's conclusion, the rabbi directed us to choose our desserts and carry them into the next room. When all were seated in a circle, he said, "I would like each of us to talk about our spiritual journeys. What has that been like in the context of your relationship with your spouse?"

For a few seconds, there was silence as everyone glanced around nervously. That each member of the circle had had a spiritual journey and that he or she could articulate its qualities appeared quite uncertain. Then one leader's hus-band, Sam, volunteered. Sam and his wife, Rachel, described a long period of being uninvolved with Judaism early in their marriage. Their interest in Juda-ism was revived when their first son was born, reflecting the typical growth of interest in religion as the life course progresses. They had debated whether to circumcise him and had settled on doing it in the hospital. But Rachel's father begged them to have a bris and offered to pay for it. Rachel had been raised Orthodox and later rejected Orthodoxy because she felt that it had focused only on boys and treated girls as an afterthought. The birth of the couple's children as well as Rachel's brother's conversion to Christianity (because of his Christian wife) spurred Rachel and Sam to embrace Reform Judaism, which they saw as an egalitarian alternative.

The rabbi pointed to Daniel, who was sitting next to Rachel, prompting him and his wife, Lydia, to speak next. Daniel and Lydia explained that Lydia was Catholic and was considering conversion to Judaism. They were going to raise their child in Judaism so he would have "one coherent identity." They had met adults without one religious identity and said that these people seemed to be confused, a fate that they hoped their child would avoid. Daniel and Lydia apparently were familiar with the claim that mixing religions led to confusion. Dovetail conference participants resisted this claim forcefully, but this couple had evidently accepted it.

Next came Mike and Karen. Like all the other couples present, they planned to raise their child as a Jew. Karen had been raised in Catholicism, and she had found it "rigid, strict, and not appealing. It turned me off from religion." She had no immediate plans to convert to Judaism, saying that, to her, being Jewish was more like being Italian than spiritual. Her involvement in Judaism extended to making hamantaschen and giving her son "strong traditions," which she emphasized were most important to her. Mike said very little.

Alan and Barbara spoke next. Raised Episcopalian, Barbara said that her feelings about religion were the opposite of Karen's. She loved Jewish "prayers and spirituality" but was not interested in the "cultural stuff." "The havdalah prayers really touched me," she said. Like Karen, she also had no plans to convert to Judaism, but her parents were learning about Judaism along with her. Like Mike, Alan said little.

The rabbi asked the women to reflect on their relationship to the Jewish community. The women offered their thoughts on what they wanted for themselves and their children: a sense of cultural belonging and tradition, spirituality, belief in God. Their husbands, in contrast, sheepishly articulated their Jewish experiences in stereotyped ways: they went to summer camp, had bar mitzvahs, and never thought about what they meant. As the women described attending support groups and classes to learn the basics of Judaism and work through difficulties with their own religious backgrounds, extended family members, and the wider Jewish community, the men seemed to fade into the background.

When the discussion concluded, the rabbi offered humble and heartfelt thanks to the women: "On behalf of the Jewish people, I want to thank you for what you are doing for us."

The contrast between the women's intentionality and the men's apparent passivity was striking. The Mothers Circle women often mentioned that their husbands seemed to hope that Jewishness would be transmitted to their children with no sustained ritual practice on their part, and they even resisted their wives' ritual efforts. The men relied on their non-Jewish wives to perpetuate Judaism in their families and apparently did not question whether their children were "really" Jewish. Did this apparent passivity reflect their actual thoughts and feelings about their own and their family's Jewishness? It is hard to tell. The women's open discussion of their own thoughts and feelings was undoubtedly made easier by the social construction of spirituality as a woman's domain. As Amanda's comments suggest, women saw themselves as the caretakers of men's religious lives and experiences. The men were not necessarily absent from their own religious lives—historian Keren McGinity (in a forthcoming book) has interviewed intermarried Jewish men who did speak at length about their experiences with intermarriage and spirituality—but it might not have felt natural for them to discuss it openly in this setting.

A Reform rabbi told me in an interview that when he began a men's Torah study group, he found that the men with whom he studied were professionally successful and highly competent in most areas of their lives yet were intimidated by their lack of familiarity with Jewish texts and traditions. Their unfamiliarity with these difficult texts, which they felt that they should already understand simply because they were Jews with bar mitzvah training, made them uncomfortable and filled them with anxiety about appearing incompetent. But even if it was difficult for the men to articulate fully why being Jewish mattered to them, their attendance at the Torah study group suggested that it nonetheless did matter.

Although the men at the havdalah service were not necessarily part of any such study group, the Mothers Circle rabbi's description of his interactions with them suggests that similar gendered anxieties about competence were at work. These observations are consistent with some of my informants' stories. For example, Marie described her husband's anxiety about impressing Shabbat guests, while she relaxed and enjoyed their company. Alicia implied that her husband worried about feeling incompetent because he didn't know his own Hebrew name, while she was learning about Judaism from the ground up. The women didn't experience the same anxieties because they were in their own realm of the domestic and religious. Moreover, being from non-Jewish backgrounds, they were not expected to know anything about Judaism. The men, in contrast, contended with accusations of betrayal and assimilation set forth in intermarriage discourse. For those who really did lack Jewish education, this combination could very well have instilled anxiety.

But was it always just anxiety? Some Jews wanted their children to be aware of their Jewishness but not to the extent that it made them seem different from other Americans. There was a fine line between being just Jewish enough and being too Jewish. One Jewish man I interviewed, Dave, described the discomfort he felt when his young son demonstrated Jewish knowledge that he had gathered at his Jewish preschool, knowledge unfamiliar to Dave himself. "I felt an obligation to add more Jews because 6 million were lost in the Holocaust," Dave said. "So we're raising our son Jewish, and he attends the Jewish day school just because it's convenient and has the best services for him, but now he's becoming too religious. It's awkward for us when he sings Hebrew songs that we have never heard of or non-Jewish friends are over and he is doing religious Jewish things that they don't understand and we can't explain. I would like him to be more mainstream." Dave also explained that he was very sensitive to antisemitism, and he and his wife separately described having conflicts over the presence of a Christmas tree in their home. Dave and his family worked to balance their expressions of and loyalty to Judaism with their desire to fit seamlessly into their American surroundings.

While the men maintained their connection to Judaism through inarticulate emotion, their wives connected to it emotionally as well as through the ideas of universalism and individualism. The Mothers Circle rabbi articulated these ideas for the group, saying that Judaism is committed to the idea of "one humanity under one God." This was a universalist Judaism, involving the beliefs that Judaism is open to all members of a Jewish family even if not all the members are Jews; that Jewish practice should come from the heart rather than from laws; and that such practice should be meaningful to the individual. This universalist Judaism echoes some aspects of the Dovetail conference discussions but diverges in its emphasis on the unity of the family and Jewish identity for the children and family. By espousing this view, the rabbi gave the non-Jewish women a language with which to perpetuate Judaism on behalf of their entire families because he saw Jewish norms as inclusive of them and their children.

The rabbi's way of understanding Jewish norms is just one of several converging cultural and religious patterns that encourage non-Jewish women to take on Jewish leadership roles within their families. The Mothers Circle invoked powerful and remarkably resilient gender roles and traditions from Judaism as well as American culture. Its curriculum helped many of the women, and perhaps their husbands as well, to feel comfortable with their religious leadership in their families and helped the Jewish institutions that supported the Mothers Circle financially and rhetorically to see themselves as perpetuating Jewish continuity.

Read against the backdrop of American religious history, the shift of religious authority toward women in intermarried, Jewish-identified families extends an existing cultural trajectory. In American religion, women have always constituted the majority of participants and been at the center of religious practices. Recent studies such as the Pew Forum on Religion and Public

Life's (2009b) survey have found that this pattern continues. Yet despite their enthusiasm for and commitment to religion, women have not historically had much official power in it. As historian Ann Braude argues, "The willingness of women to participate in the institution that enforces their subordination and provides the cosmological justification for it requires explanation, but women have done more than participate. They have embraced the churches and the belief systems they teach, finding special meaning there for their lives as women and defending them against a variety of threats from without" (Braude 1997, 90–91). As agents of Jewish continuity, the Mothers Circle women serve the interests of religious institutions that do not reward them with official power within the religions' authority structures, just as other American women have done.

The Mothers Circle women do not seek official power within the religious community, though. Their interest lies in their families' religious experiences. The Jewish rituals that ethnic familialism emphasizes and that the women especially enjoy are domestic. The wives, as homemakers, are comfortable with the domestic and spiritual realms, see them as complementary, and feel that women are naturally more spiritually attuned than men are. Yet in an obvious departure from Jewish tradition, many ethnic familialist, non-Jewish women assume responsibility for the Jewish domestic realm without actually becoming Jewish themselves.

Gendered patterns distinguish universalist individualist and ethnic familialist discourses. Each set hinges on its interpretation of gender roles. Whereas ethnic familialists tended to follow traditional gendered patterns, universalist individualists chose a more consciously plotted course. Jude and Tabitha felt that living their two religions was a shared household responsibility, as did Mary Heléne Rosenbaum and Ned Rosenbaum in *Celebrating Our Differences* ([1994] 1999). Jude commented that he had to be more active in practicing and teaching his children about Judaism because Tabitha remained committed to Catholicism. If he'd married a Jew, he said, he would have been "lazy," presumably because he could have assumed that Jewishness would automatically be conferred upon his children but also because he could have expected his Jewish wife to manage the children's religious education and observance. Because his actual wife practiced Catholicism with their children, he had to take responsibility for practicing Judaism with them.

Jude's comments cut in two opposing directions: on one side, he took an egalitarian view of religious responsibilities in the household; on the other side, his wife made him do so. By insisting on "fairness" to both religious traditions, universalist individualism demands more religious participation from men. Yet Jude's comments suggest that he would have found ethnic familialism equally attractive if his wife had been willing to give up Christianity. The universalist individualist women to whom I spoke insisted on having two equal religions in their marriage, taking pride in being "prophetic outcasts" who took an unconventional and unpopular road. Likewise, their pride in their egalitarianism points to what they purposely rejected: the traditional gender role in which the woman runs the domestic-religious realm on behalf of the entire family. Universalist individualism requires family members to integrate their religious lives as individuals rather than their expecting the wife and mother of the family to do it for them.

The rhetoric of fairness attracts Americans who are steeped in a culture that emphasizes egalitarianism, yet Hochschild ([1989] 2003) documents tension in couples whose egalitarian practices outpaced husbands' beliefs. These men claimed to believe in egalitarianism but evinced awkwardness about it because they actually preferred a more traditional household arrangement. Because the gendered division of labor opposes the American cultural value of fairness, marriages that rely on assumed traditionalist roles either come to understand themselves as fair or experience an imbalance in what Hochschild calls an "economy of gratitude." Hochschild documents a great deal of conflict when spouses disagreed about the amount of gratitude they owed to or expected from each other. Her women informants often felt more grateful to their husbands than vice versa because they felt that the stakes for women in marriage were higher than for men. Divorce would leave the women and their children in an economically precarious situation while it would be unlikely to have this effect on their husbands (19, 212–217). Perhaps recognizing the potential for such imbalance in marriages like Sandy's, the Mothers Circle rabbi urged the women's husbands to recognize the importance of their wives' "gift" to them and the Jewish people of raising their children as Jews. He said that in the Fathers Circle, where these Jewish husbands met a few times a year, the men did express their gratitude. Several women whom I interviewed, however, felt resentment rather than gratitude. Some non-Jewish wives were very bitter about having given up celebrating Christmas with decorations and festivities in order to participate in a Jewish community that they felt rejected them. They believed that their husbands did not recognize the sacrifices that they were making.

The role of nostalgia and childhood experiences in shaping adults' religious inclinations only complicated many couples' economies of gratitude, particularly concerning Christmas celebrations. Although Mothers Circle alumna Elaine and most of her compatriots had agreed to raise their children as Jews, many were troubled by the idea that their husbands' fear of assimilation outweighed the women's own deeply held attachments from childhood. As Elaine put it, "The Christmas tree is a problem for a lot of women. They still want to have it, and even though they are totally committed to raising the children as Jews and have become very knowledgeable about Judaism, their husbands still won't let them have the Christmas tree." These adults' visceral experience of the Christmas tree's meanings demonstrated the power of their childhood religious experiences, the same power that Isaacs and Weiss Rosmarin urged their mid-twentieth-century readers of *What Every Jewish Woman Should Know* to invoke in their childrearing practices. The Christmas tree's presence or absence was a jolt, a rupture between the childhood of each parent and the present reality of an interfaith-Jewish child whose upbringing would differ from that of both parents. "I really wanted to raise my kids Catholic," said Elaine. "My reasons were aesthetic or nostalgic; it was what I grew up with and what I knew. My husband wanted them to be Jewish, but he couldn't say why. He couldn't answer one question about Judaism; all he knew was that he loved Camp Barney [a Jewish summer camp near Atlanta]." For the women, the men's veto of the Christmas tree also violated the premise of a marriage based on fairness and mutual respect, an assumption deeply embedded in universalist individualist discourses.

Christmas trees and religious life-cycle ceremonies, as two centers of discomfort in interfaith families' lives, raise intermarried spouses' consciousness of these ruptures with the past and assumptions about fairness. "Some women do feel like they are losing something" by raising their children as Jews, said Elaine. However, some non-Jewish women, such as Mothers Circle alumna Bonnie, said unsentimentally that children need not relive their parents' childhoods. She explicitly rejected the nostalgic frame in favor of individuality seated in a strong connection to family: "I have a wonderful memory of Christmas, when I was about seven or eight, where I was with my parents, grandparents, and siblings, and they opened the door to the living room where there was the tree and all the Santa Claus stuff. It was a powerful memory, and my son will never have one like that. But he is not me; he's his own person, and he will have his own powerful memories." Other Jewish-Christian couples preserved the Christmas experience in the homes of Christian relatives, where they would "help Grandma celebrate her holiday" by having a festive meal and opening presents or by having the Christmas tree in their homes but marking it off as "not about Jesus" or "just for Mom," as recommended by Jewish outreach educators. Some gave up Christmas entirely.

However the women understood the economy of gratitude and notions of fairness in their own particular situations, their default role as formers of religious identity gave them a great deal of power over their families' experience of Judaism. Through their own efforts and over their husbands' resistance, they shaped their families' practices and habits. Despite dominant cultural narratives about the decline of Judaism because of intermarriage, the informants' stories show not simple decline but complex and contradictory change.

The discourse of ethnic familialism embodies contradictions between American, Protestant Christian, and traditional Jewish thought. Ethnic familialists chose to practice Judaism, a minority religion in the United States that makes particularistic demands on its adherents, while simultaneously ignoring its centuries-long norm of endogamy. They did so instead of adopting universalist individualism, whose emphasis on personal satisfaction offers a more straightforward and less dissonant way to organize individual religious practice. In the ethnic familialist approach to intermarriage, families create a Jewish-identified lifeworld in which the straightforward mixing of Judaism with Christianity is forbidden. Yet Christianity did enter these households within carefully marked boundaries, as when a mother said that her children manifested her Christian inner spirituality through the external form of Judaism or when a family decorated a Christmas tree that was "just for Mom," not for the entire family. They verbally quarantined this Christian symbol's power in the household in order to dispel any suspicions about the family's religious allegiance.

At the same time, by valuing religious experience through ritual, whose practice is often spearheaded by Christian or secular non-Jewish women, this ethnic familialist solution to the problem of religious mixing leaves room for ambiguity. While universalist individualists personalized religion according to their conscious choices, ethnic familialists such as Janice, Marie, and Amanda "made it their own" simply by performing Jewish rituals, experiencing them without intellectualizing their meaning. Non-Jewish and converted Jewish ethnic familialist women initiated the observance of Jewish ritual often entirely on their own, without help from their Jewish husbands. The non-Jewish women thus legitimized themselves as Jews, even if only subjectively, on behalf of their entire families and despite the differences between their own religious upbringings and the Jewish one that they taught their children. As many of my women informants demonstrated, ethnic familialists adopted Jewish rituals centered on children, home, and food to anchor their participation in Judaism.

Conscious of Jewish discourses that insist on marriage and mutual obligation between Jews, as well as American ones emphasizing autonomy and tolerance, my informants who used ethnic familialist discourses lived with dissonance and ambivalence. They managed a subcurrent of anxiety that never quite subsided as they attempted to merge American, Protestant, and Jewish cultural values in their lives. Rather than dismissing the traditional Jewish emphasis on endogamy as ill-founded and outdated, as universalist individualists did, ethnic familialists took it to heart, compensating for their portrayal as "bad Jews" in normative Jewish discourses on intermarriage by taking on Jewish ritual practices and setting religious boundaries within the family that situated them as otherwise normative Jewish families.

Ethnic familialists remained attached to religious norms and boundaries even as they recast and sometimes ignored them for their own purposes. They internalized religious norms as part of their deepest sense of themselves as individuals so that betrayal of these norms was betrayal of themselves. My Jewish informants' opposition to having Christmas trees in their homes arose not from Jewish legal prohibitions but from fears that having the Christmas tree would somehow make them less Jewish. Universalist individualists found it easy to explain why they could and should celebrate multiple religious holidays at once. But such explanations fell flat for ethnic familialists because they were acting out religious emotions and norms that they had internalized through early religious experiences. Women played a central role in perpetuating this internalization of religious norms even when they were situated outside the boundaries of the religious institutions that embody and safeguard these norms. Like universalist individualists, they rewrote boundaries but did so in a different gender frame, demonstrating how central gender is to religious experience.

Ethnic familialist intermarried Jewish men found themselves in a strange position. Their marriages occupied unnamed space within Jewish understandings of kinship, even as the men dedicated themselves to ensuring that their children would identify with Judaism. Ethnic familialists experienced greater conflict among the claims of modernity, individualism, and peoplehood than universalist individualists did. Their fragmentation of values, desires, and experiences could be called postmodern, but my informants did not necessarily see such fragmentation as desirable. Some elements of the American Jewish community, such as the previously secular recruits to Orthodox Jewish communities whom sociologists Lynn Davidman (1991) and Debra Renee Kaufman (1991) describe, desire a "return" to wholeness of experience and self-concept. The women in those studies chose to commit themselves to Orthodox Judaism as a response to feeling unmoored in the secular world, where they perceived everything to be a matter of personal choice. Being grounded in marriage, family, and relationship with God, particularly in the context of a Jewish community to which they felt a visceral connection, helped them to feel more secure. In the case of my intermarried informants, non-Jewish wives made the choice to support their families' tricky balance of nostalgia, race, and religion.

As a group, non-Jewish intermarried women held some power to help shape the composition of the Jewish people itself, not with the traditional textual sources of authority that rabbis use but with culture and patterns that continue through mimesis and emotion. Through their participation in the Mothers Circle, the women learned about Jewish traditions and found themselves teaching their husbands what they had learned so that they informally performed the teaching work that religious institutions and leaders also do (see also Thompson 2013). Depending on how their families understood the nature of religious identity and belonging, Jewish men such as Jude and non-Jewish women such as Sandy found themselves in unanticipated leadership roles. Taking on these roles was their way of responding to the cultural contradictions amid which they lived—the familiar gender roles that some of them rejected, Jewish discourses about assimilation and resistance, and American notions of morality as resistance of an oppressive majority. Navigating the marriage of conflicting cultural and religious values required creativity and commitment even as it created challenges.

4

Translating Jewish Experience

Jewish outreach professionals, the religious experts who specialize in programming for Jews who do not affiliate formally with Jewish institutions, face the same tensions of universalism, individualism, ethnicity, and family that intermarried couples do. But as representatives of the subset of Jewish institutions that actively reach out to these couples, they also participate in—or actively resist—deeply entrenched ideas about categorical difference between Jews and non-Jews. Some of the professionals I interviewed explained their interest in embracing intermarried couples in terms that invoked dominant cultural narratives that equate intermarriage with assimilation, relying on the vaguely defined, monolithic concepts of Jewish continuity and the Jewish people. A minority advocated for including intermarried couples in Jewish communities without regard for the claims of Jewish law, but many expressed discomfort with that idea, evidently hoping that the couples would join Jewish institutions on the institutions' preferred terms. These religious experts took approaches to intermarried couples that tended to be strategic and goal-oriented, while avoiding questions about the content of Jewishness itself.

Some rabbis and Jewish educators combined universalist individualist and ethnic familialist language in their public self-representations to intermarried couples. In the short term, they wanted to secure the couples' participation in and affiliation with Jewish organizations. In the long term, they wanted to ensure Jewish continuity, broadly understood to mean the continued existence of the Jewish people as a distinct group. This latter goal drove outreach efforts, yet debate had been going on for decades over whether such continuity efforts should emphasize individuals' choice to be Jewish or their kinship obligation to other Jews. The outreach events that I attended, with their public use of individualist universalist language and their private, more informal use of ethnic familialist language, reflected this tension.

Intertwining Languages

The language of universalist individualism, honoring the autonomy of persons and the unity of humanity, coexisted with family-centered language at an outreach event I attended in Atlanta in February 2007. Its facilitator, Rabbi G, as I will call him, had retired from leadership of his Reform congregation but continued to work closely with the Mothers Circle. He led a panel discussion called "Raising Your Children As Jews When You Are Not Jewish," featuring four of the circle's alumnae. In 2002, these women had taken part in an eight-month, sixteen-session pilot Mothers Circle course in Atlanta that had covered the basic how-to's of having a Jewish home and included "ask the rabbi" sessions, havdalah and Shabbat services, and Fathers Circle programs. In the Fathers Circle sessions the women's husbands had gathered more informally and less frequently to socialize with each other, the rabbi, and other Jewish educators and affirm their appreciation of their wives' efforts in the Mothers Circle.

Several Jewish educators and representatives from Jewish organizations were present at the outreach event to promote their offerings. A staff member at a local Reform day school handed out literature in hopes of enrolling the children of intermarried couples. A program officer from the Jewish Outreach Institute (JOI) had flown in from New York. Mothers Circle leaders from Atlanta were on hand. About twenty-five people, more women than men, sat in the audience, including married couples with young children as well as couples who had not yet married but were exploring how to join two religions.

The audience members varied in how self-conscious they were about their choices and possibilities. One intermarried man told me that he had come to the event because he was concerned about his infant son's eventually choosing something other than Judaism. He said that he wanted to know how to prevent that from happening. Like many of my informants, he implied that he had internalized the association of intermarriage with assimilation and that he hoped to situate himself within normative American Judaism by securing his son's identity as a Jew. A woman sitting nearby, amused but not judgmental, pointed out the irony of his concern, saying that when he was a child his parents probably had thought something similar about preventing him from intermarrying. Conversations among audience members began and ended as parents attended to their young children's needs for attention and trips to the bathroom.

Eventually, the four panelists joined Rabbi G on a dais. The women all appeared to be white, middle class, and in their thirties or early forties. Rabbi

G asked questions that addressed the concerns of non-Jews, especially women, who were married to Jews, as the panel's title suggested. The discussion among the panelists reflected some of the concerns raised by the non-Jewish women whom I introduced in chapter 3: feelings of alienation or exclusion, concerns about relationships with their own family members, their husbands' involvement in the families' religious activities. At first, the panelists' remarks seemed to paint a familiar picture of categorical difference between Jews and non-Jews. But as the women continued to describe their experiences and feelings, the portrait grew murky.

"What has been your experience coming into the Jewish community, and what were your reactions to it?" Rabbi G asked.

Two of the women described negative experiences. "My husband's family had reservations about his dating a non-Jew. I didn't like feeling like an outsider. Once I felt that way, I kept looking for more evidence or confirmation that that's how they felt about me," said Elaine. A Catholic from the Midwest, she said that she had never known any Jews before meeting her husband. She had had little context in which to interpret her in-laws' reception of her.

Katherine, who also was raised Catholic, said that her family resisted the introduction of a Jew into their family. "My parents were less accepting than my husband's were. His weren't completely accepting either at first. Our parents had stereotyped views of each other."

But two of the women said that they had had positive experiences. "I always felt welcomed," said Bonnie of her Jewish in-laws.

Ann, who said that she was raised Baptist, Presbyterian, and "sorta secular," agreed. "My husband's family accepted me with open arms. I had an easier time because his sister had already intermarried. My first experience with the Jewish community has been the Mothers Circle, and it is wonderful!"

"No two cases are alike," commented Rabbi G. "Ann, why is it wonderful?"

"People are so appreciative that we non-Jewish women are raising our kids Jewish. The mother sets the tone in the home for the religious experience and upbringing, and we are creating new Jewish experiences," said Ann.

"A non-Jewish mother or spouse sometimes brings more Jewishness into the home than would be the case with a Jewish-Jewish couple," observed Rabbi G.

Bonnie agreed. "My husband is more involved than he would be otherwise because I'm not Jewish. I can't raise the kids Jewish all on my own. Our Jewish friends are impressed that it's not a hassle for me to get him to go to the synagogue with us. They call me up to ask Jewish questions—I don't always know the answers, but they ask."

"You are becoming like a human Jew Google," Rabbi G quipped. "Are there stereotypes or stumbling blocks you have encountered coming into the Jewish community?"

"Once my mom sent an email to several family members and she wrote 'G-d' [the spelling of "God" used by some Jews to show reverence toward God's name] instead of 'God,'" said Elaine. "My aunt asked why she wrote that, and my mom said it was out of respect for our Jewish family members. So my aunt said, 'I didn't know Jews didn't believe in God!'" The audience laughed.

Rabbi G continued with an open-ended question that both emphasized his respect for the women's individual choices and allowed the women to tell their own stories: "How did you come to make the decision to be at least co-responsible for raising Jewish children?"

Katherine recounted a shift from a universalist individualist perspective to a more ethnic familialist one:

> I've been married for twenty years. When my husband and I got married—we were living in New York then—we had both a rabbi and a priest for our interfaith wedding ceremony. We planned to raise our children in both religions. We thought of ourselves as smart and urban and marveled at how rich our lives would be! But when our older son was in kindergarten, he said, "I feel more Jewish than Christian." And I was struggling with my own religion as well, so I moved away from it and toward Judaism. My journey has evolved. Our whole family considers ourselves Jewish now, and our home has become more Jewish than anything my husband knew growing up.

Even as Katherine and her husband attempted to instill a dual religious identity in their son, he felt himself to be Jewish at a very young age. Her son's experience of himself as Jewish aligned with her own struggle, together moving the family to create a different familial religious practice and self-understanding. Universalist individualist and ethnic familialist perspectives were part of a continuum within which individuals and families could shift and move.

Ann's story was different. "We decided to raise the children Jewish when we were seriously dating. My experience with my husband's family was that they had strong traditions, and I felt that whatever traditions my family would practice, I wanted them to be strong. Also, my husband's father is a Holocaust survivor, and I wanted to add to the Jewish population, not take away from it. My own background was not strongly religious, so I wasn't losing anything—my family celebrated the major holidays, but secularly, not religiously."

Bonnie said, "My husband's family wasn't religious—"

"They're H2O Jews—Holidays, 2 Only," Rabbi G joked.

"—and Christianity never resonated with me," Bonnie continued. "The idea that you had to take 'Jesus as savior' on faith alone didn't make sense. I like that Judaism is based on what you do rather than only belief. That makes more sense to me. I was trying to be sensitive with my own family so that it would be clear I hadn't actually converted to Judaism, but then my father thought I already was Jewish, so I don't know what I was trying to hide or be careful about."

With these comments, the women expressed differing theories about fairness: to the Jewish people, their own families, their spouses, and their children. From a universalist individualist perspective, fairness starts from the individual and proceeds outward to the community. The individual determines what is authentic and how to live his or her life with integrity based on what he or she discerns through reason, choice, and struggle. The individual must decide how to enact his or her heritage in the context of what he or she has determined is right for him or her. From an ethnic familialist perspective, fairness starts from one's relationships to family, history, and community as well as the individual. Katherine and her family began with an idea that a dual-religion household would be fairest to all members of the family. Her son's feeling of being more Jewish than Christian propelled all of them toward a greater connection with Judaism, demonstrating the mutual influence of choice and emotion. In contrast, Ann understood fairness to her husband's family and the Jewish people to require that she and her husband raise Jewish children in order to increase the Jewish population. But her own desire for "strong traditions" in her family supported this choice. What was fair to her husband, his family, and the Jewish people was also fair to her, though for different reasons. In another vein, the carefulness around Jewish-Christian boundaries that Bonnie thought was fair to her family of origin turned out to be quite different from their view of it.

"Is there anything you feel that you've lost by agreeing to raise the kids Jewish?" Rabbi G asked.

Katherine replied, "It's an extension of my own religion—Jesus celebrated Passover—so no." Her comment suggested another understanding of fairness as the identification of areas of agreement within a family. Finding the similarities between Judaism and Christianity could be a way of honoring both spouses' heritages so that neither had to feel that he or she was losing something valuable.

Ann had a different view. "I thought I was losing something until I started making it my own rather than thinking about what I grew up with." Several other Mothers Circle women, some of whom had converted to Judaism and some of whom had not, had told me of the importance of making Judaism and Jewishness their own, which meant finding Jewish practices and meanings that were special to them personally. In doing so, they could see themselves as having chosen to participate in Jewish families for their own reasons.

"Everyone's spiritual journey is completely unique," said Rabbi G, employing universalist individualist language that suggested that each person could find a unique but equally valid way to participate in religious life. "There is no one story that everyone will share. And not to sound like I think you should convert or should already have converted, because people should only convert if they feel profoundly and deeply that they should do it, but what has prevented you from converting?"

"I don't know," said Bonnie.

"I don't feel a personal connection to Judaism," said Elaine. "I didn't receive a welcome in the beginning, and I'm a stubborn person. Plus, there are the language and cultural barriers."

Katherine said, "I am on a journey toward that step. But it has taken twenty years."

Ann said, "I am just starting to learn what Judaism is about."

"What traditions have become your favorites?" asked Rabbi G.

Bonnie said, "Shabbat." All the other women nodded and smiled knowingly. They clearly knew that Bonnie would say Shabbat was her favorite. "It's the best way to end the week. I am making my own challah every Friday morning!"

Elaine said, "I like the home-based stuff. I never liked going to church, so I like this much better."

Katherine said, "It just makes more sense that it should be home-based."

Rabbi G agreed. "Shabbat is a relief from the rat race."

Katherine turned to the audience and said, "I want to point out that the Mothers Circle has no agenda. There is no pressure to convert."

The women's descriptions of their religious lives sounded as if many of them already had become Jewish in every way except for actual conversion. Did a categorical difference between Jews and non-Jews exist even when the non-Jews were living Jewish lives and leading Jewish families? Did categorical difference still exist after someone's conversion to Judaism, or did that difference vanish once the conversion was complete? Would it have been as easy for the women to "make Judaism their own" without the "home-based stuff"? As American women, their predisposition to take on religious household labor may have made "making Judaism their own" easier. Even so, what was the difference between that and conversion?

"My mother-in-law sent me an article from *Reform Judaism* magazine from a year or two ago honoring non-Jewish women who raise Jewish kids. It made me think that I was really accepted now," said Bonnie.

"The Reform movement has recognized them for decades," acknowledged Rabbi G. "It does no good to hide your head in the sand about it."

Audience members had been invited to write questions for the panelists on index cards, which were collected and handed to Rabbi G several times during the evening. The questions provide some insight into what the audience's concerns were, which might have differed from the panelists' predictions.

Rabbi G read the first question: "What has been your most overwhelming experience with raising Jewish children?"

Bonnie answered, "When we adopted our son. We were there for his birth and took him home from the hospital, and then we had to convert him. There was a bris, a baby naming, and the *mikveh* [immersion required by Jewish law for conversion to Judaism]. It felt like there were so many different things we had to do, and my parents were in town. Then, when he was two years old, he went in the mikveh with his father. He didn't like being dunked under the water, but he had to be three times, and when he came up the last time, the rabbi and the cantor started singing a wonderful song, I don't know what it was, and there was this naked little kid and it was very powerful. I tear up just thinking about it."

Ann said that she had had no overwhelming experiences yet.

Elaine said, "A close friend was killed in a car wreck, and I chose her name as the basis of my child's Hebrew name. I was kind of amazed that I was able to come up with the Hebrew name."

Katherine said, "Getting the date of my son's bar mitzvah was overwhelming!"

The rabbi read the next question: "'What is your favorite holiday?' We did that one already. Next one: 'Are the Jewish spouses involved in the activities of the Mothers Circle?'[1] I can answer that one. The daddies have meaningful interactions there, too. They say their wives have done so much for them and their faith." By using language such as *daddies* instead of *men*, Rabbi G emphasized parental roles. The Mothers Circle facilitators also used this language, referring to group members as *moms* but rarely as *women*, thus highlighting family ties over adults' chosen beliefs. Jewish law or other forms of obligation between Jews did not enter the conversation, other than in Ann's comment about her wish to add to the Jewish population because of her father-in-law's survival of the Holocaust.

Rabbi G concluded the event by expressing his gratitude to non-Jewish women who raise their children as Jews because "they are doing something so important for Judaism."

The panelists' discussion implied that the perceived peril addressed by Jewish continuity efforts largely had been solved because these non-Jewish women were showing that they could raise their children as Jews. No one spoke about whether the children would remain Jews as adults or raise their own children as Jews. It was unclear whether this was because the panelists felt sure that the children would continue to be Jewish because they had been raised that way, because they felt that the children could ultimately choose their own religious paths for themselves when they were adults, or because it simply didn't occur to them to wonder about it. The panel discussion's configurations of ethnic familialist and universalist individualist ideas enabled a version of Jewish continuity, even as the panelists sidestepped the issue of what kind of Jewishness would be continued.

Switching Languages, Marking Boundaries

At a national conference in 2007 held by the Jewish Outreach Institute in Washington, D.C., I observed a reiteration of the Atlanta panel discussion. However, the conversations at this conference used universalist individualist and ethnic familialist languages differently from those at the panel discussion in Atlanta. Here, participants switched between the two languages as a way of translating their experiences for one another. The ways in which discussions and questions were framed revealed more than their actual content did.

Founded in 1988, JOI creates and promotes outreach programming and is funded by a number of philanthropies and Jewish community organizations. Jewish educators turn to JOI for help in creating "opportunities for including the intermarried in the Jewish community" (Jewish Outreach Institute 2008). JOI promotes the idea of welcoming people into Jewish communities regardless of their individual religious affiliations and emphasizes the inclusion of intermarried Jews as well as converts and non-white Jews, who experience exclusion based on social prejudices rather than Jewish law. By deemphasizing traditional views of intermarriage and Jewishness by matrilineal descent or conversion, the rabbis and Jewish educators involved with JOI say that they are recognizing the reality of contemporary Jews' lives. JOI's website explains it this way: "The fact is, less than half of all Jews—intermarried or otherwise—are actually participating in Jewish institutions. In order to bridge the growing divide between the minority of Jews engaged with the organized community and the majority who are not, JOI advocates the creation of programs and events where the two can meet on neutral ground. Instead of asking people to cross our threshold we must go out and meet them first, to welcome them in" (Jewish Outreach Institute 2008). The organization has responded to a change in how many Jews view Jewishness in a way that it hopes will enable Jewish institutions to survive. But others in the Jewish community have resisted, saying that changing institutions to mirror the views of secular Jews undermines the integrity of the community as a whole.

The "neutral ground" that JOI seeks to create depends on scientific research and strategies. At the organization's 2007 national conference in Washington, D.C., its leader, Rabbi Kerry Olitzky, said that JOI was working to "grow the [big] tent through the methodology of outreach." Framing outreach as a methodology made it seem reproducible with reliable results, similar to a scientific experiment. By 2007, the organization was attracting growing interest: whereas a year and a half earlier, its conference in Atlanta had drawn 125 people, this one had generated a waiting list beyond the 250 participants it could accommodate. Attendees had traveled from as far away as Australia. The agenda of the conference was to showcase "Big Tent Judaism, . . . an approach to Jewish community that takes its lead from the values and vision of our Biblical forbearers Abraham and Sarah's tent, which was open on four sides to welcome all who approach. Individuals and organizations that practice a Big Tent Judaism seek to engage, support and advocate for all those who would cast their lot with the Jewish people, regardless of prior knowledge or background" (Jewish Outreach Institute 2008). To illustrate, a gospel-style choir from an African American synagogue called Congregation Temple Beth'El in Philadelphia performed, and the stories of converts and the intermarried were featured throughout the conference. The programming emphasized the variety of individuals included in Big Tent Judaism.

Early in the conference, Rabbi G hosted a panel discussion with the same Mothers Circle alumnae who had participated in the one in Atlanta. The Atlanta session had appeared to focus on marketing the Mothers Circle program to potential participants, but the purpose of the panel at the JOI conference was to market it to outreach professionals. The audience was far larger than the one in Atlanta had been.

"Mothers Circle undergirds and exemplifies what Big Tent Judaism is all about," Rabbi G began, "and Mothers Circle deepens the engagement of the families with synagogues, allowing them to become access points." Reflecting on more than thirty-five years as a rabbi, he said, "Of all the work that I've done, none has been more sacred to me than what the Mothers Circle has done and continues to do." Turning to the panelists, he asked, "What has been your reception into and experience with the Jewish community?"

Katherine elaborated on the story she had told at the Atlanta panel discussion. She commented that she and her future husband had struggled to find a rabbi to perform their dual-faith wedding ceremony, even when they had looked in neighboring states. Because they had initially intended to raise their children in both Catholicism and Judaism, their two sons had each had a bris and a baptism. Her Jewish mother- and father-in-law had always been "generous and supporting" and had even attended the children's baptisms.

Bonnie told a somewhat different story from the one she had shared in Atlanta. "My in-laws were not delighted that I was older, divorced, and not Jewish, but we eventually forged a good relationship. Recently my mother-in-law said to me, 'There is something I have wanted to say to you for a long time. We are so sorry about the way our relationship got started when you and Michael started dating. You are a wonderful daughter-in-law.' I almost fell out of my chair! So in our relationship now, I just let her be who she is and she lets me be who I am. And now I've been taking Jewish classes for about seven years, and my in-laws can't believe how much Jewish stuff I do!"

"That is what it's all about," Rabbi G agreed. "We let you be who you are." Letting people be who they are was the implicit principle of JOI's Big Tent Judaism as well. Both Rabbi G and Bonnie highlighted the value of recognizing individuals' autonomy, choice, and inherent uniqueness, reflecting universalist individualist language.

Ann had agreed to raise her children, now four and six years old, as Jews. "One of the reasons I chose to raise my children Jewish was how open they [Jewish people] were to me. Even my husband's Orthodox relatives were open. When I didn't know what was going on, they taught me the different customs and explained things."

"What led you to decide to bring up Jewish kids?" Rabbi G asked the other panelists.

Katherine answered, "It was a long process because we expected to raise them in both. My feelings changed about my religion for a variety of reasons. I did more learning about Judaism over time, and Mothers Circle helped open it up. Your husband may be Jewish, but he doesn't necessarily have the background or knowledge about how to celebrate the holidays or even [practice Judaism] on a daily basis. Children need to hear that we want them to make the world better here and now. I was raised in a very strong Catholic family. For a variety of reasons, I have moved away from that, and I was searching and searching. My involvement in the synagogue over the last ten years helped me decide to convert. Judaism is how I want to live my life."

Ann added, "I wanted to raise my children in a home that had a strong religious identity. I saw that in his family. My husband's father is a Holocaust survivor, so that went into it, too."

"What keeps you doing this?" Rabbi G asked.

"The tradition. The memories," she replied. "My husband's relatives have so many memories of all the holidays. I have to admit, the last few weeks, it felt like a marathon. My children learned so many Jewish values from the holidays. They've had a blast!"

"What has been your husband's role?" Rabbi G asked.

Ann said, "Hebrew pronunciation. And I ask my husband when I'm preparing for a holiday, 'How did you do it?' And he remembers maybe a third of how they did it. But we always incorporate that into our practice."

"The wife is the one who carries the spiritual piece," Bonnie said. "But I'm not the Jew! Every time I tell my husband we're going to the temple, he's been right there. Mothers Circle gave us a place to bring the Judaism into my home. It's really created like a hav—is it *havurah* [circle of friends]?—for us." She laughed. "I was making challah the other day, and I called Rachel [a Mothers Circle leader] and said"—she assumed a terrified voice and facial expression—"'It's not going to rise!' And Rachel told me she makes hers in a bread machine."

Rachel added, "Sometimes the husbands are more ambivalent, and it takes the women to bring them back to Judaism. So I think the Mothers Circle empowers these women to go home and say, 'We're a Jewish family, and this is what we're doing.'"

"I had never seriously considered converting," Bonnie said, laughing again, "because I didn't want to disappoint my aunts, who were very Christian, wonderfully so! And my mother had just died. But my father thinks I'm Jewish already! He said, 'Well, now that you're a Jew . . .' so all that worry was for naught!"

Ann agreed. "Mothers Circle enabled me to do the synagogue shopping that my husband neglected to do. I asked him a number of times to choose a synagogue for our family, and he kept never getting around to it, so once I had taken part in Mothers Circle, I felt like I knew enough to choose one on my own."

Rachel turned to the audience to reflect on being a Mothers Circle facilitator. "If you tear your clothes and mourn when people intermarry—well, that strategy isn't working, and I wanted to know if there were other ways of dealing with intermarriage. The moms in the Mothers Circle bring so much joy to our people. They are really a blessing to us." Engaging her fellow Jewish outreach workers, she shifted the dialogue from the universalist individualist register to the ethnic familialist one, as if she were talking to members of her own family, not to a gathering of autonomous, rational choosers.

The rabbi turned to the panelists and said, "There's no way we can ever thank you enough for what you are doing for our people." With this comment he used both languages, universalist individualism and ethnic familialism, to bridge the gap between Jews and non-Jews. He recognized the women's choice to raise Jewish children as well as the import of their choice for the goal of Jewish continuity.

Audience members began to stand up and pass around a microphone into which they asked their questions. Whereas the audience questions in Atlanta had reflected personal concerns such as "overwhelming experiences," these questions reflected audience members' concerns as educators and religious experts. First came a pragmatic question: "What makes it so accessible?" one woman asked.

Rachel said, "The Mothers Circle is free. There's no cost. And we have multiple locations, so it's convenient."

Bonnie added, "And there's no push to convert."

"That's right," Katherine affirmed. "No judgment whatsoever." For decades, Jewish institutions, leaders, and extended family members had used the strategy of pressuring non-Jewish spouses to convert to Judaism with varying success. The audience members here would have been familiar with such pressure, whether or not they exerted it themselves. Whether conversion was the proper goal of outreach remained a matter of debate.

Katherine continued explaining why the Mothers Circle felt so accessible. "And the support the women give each other. We're all there for the same reasons. We all have the same fears."

Another audience member asked, "How do you handle comments that your children aren't Jewish?" This question assumed that because the women were not Jewish, most of their children would be Jewish by patrilineal descent and thus not recognized by Conservative or Orthodox rabbis and their communities (see chapter 1). Some of their children had undergone conversions; but because many of them were Reform conversions, their validity under Jewish law still would have been disputed. The legitimacy of the children's Jewishness may have been more of a concern for Jewish religious experts than for the families themselves, however, because the children's status affected whether and how the religious experts could work with them. For example, children who are considered not to be Jewish according to rabbinic law generally would not be eligible to celebrate a bar or bat mitzvah in a Conservative or Orthodox synagogue. Thus, a child's Jewish status was directly relevant to the work of many Jewish educators and rabbis.

Bonnie said, "I don't really get those questions. My child was converted. I wanted to have all the ritual aspects of conversion for him, so he went to the mikveh, had a bris. But a friend of mine was talking about someone else once, and she made some comments that implied that the person wasn't *really* Jewish. Then she realized who she was talking to, and sort of made a left turn and tried to make it sound otherwise. But it's like racism—you don't always know what people are saying about you. All you can do is live your own life and not worry about what other people think of your choices."

Bonnie's response to this question highlights an important difference between the conversations that Jewish institutional leaders have about intermarriage and the actual experiences of intermarried couples. The audience member's question about the children's Jewishness anticipated the topic of similar conversations that would be held more privately during the conference. The status of children who were not born to Jewish mothers and who had undergone either non-Orthodox conversions or no conversion at all was a concern for the institutions and their leaders. But the couples themselves tended to avoid settings in which these concerns dominated and instead sought communities in which they were accepted and felt comfortable. In most cases, the communities with which they affiliated defined Jewishness in ways that aligned with the couples' own self-definitions—for example, many chose to affiliate with Reform congregations that accepted patrilineal descent or with a community of liberal Jewish friends. In such settings, questions about their children's Jewishness were unlikely to arise.

Another audience member asked, "What do your parents or family think about this?" This question suggested a sense that some audience members expected non-Jews to view Jewishness as foreign and perhaps undesirable, given the long history of Christian anti-Judaism. More immediately, it reframed the women's experiences in ethnic familialist language, perhaps as a way of translating the women's more universalist and individualist self-understandings into an orientation more familiar to the Jewish educators. As Rachel's comments directed toward the audience had suggested, the audience was accustomed to understanding the dynamics of intermarriage in the context of the Jewish people more generally, not on the basis of individuals' experience of intermarriage. The question of how non-Jewish family members regarded the women's choices suggests that the questioner approached the non-Jews' experiences with assumptions rooted in Jewish history as well as curiosity and empathy. Conversion from Christianity to Judaism or Christians' participation in Jewish practices was not tolerated by Christian authorities for significant periods of Jewish-Christian history. Awareness of this history could foster an assumption that contemporary Christians might be hostile to their family members' Judaizing. But the question also suggests that the questioner could be attempting to imagine how she would feel if one of her Jewish relatives married a Christian and began actively celebrating Christian holidays while holding Jewish celebrations at arm's length. Would it be possible to experience such a change in a positive, welcoming way?

Katherine described her family's holiday celebrations as inclusive while also protecting Jewishness by setting particular boundaries. "We always include our Christian family in our holiday celebrations. My father respects it, but he does wish it was a different way. We go to their house for Christmas; Santa doesn't come. I don't miss anything about my past religious life per se—it's more the traditions, Christmas and Easter. We go help my mother celebrate Christmas and Easter. We are creating traditions for our own children, and they are Jewish. I keep saying, 'Now that my children are Jewish,' and that's wrong because they were Jewish the day they were born!"

Using an ethnic familialist frame for this situation, as the questioner did, allows us to recognize that while the strategy of participating within certain boundaries does help the intermarried couple maintain its Jewish self-concept, it also changes their family's experience of the celebration. When Katherine's father "wishes that it were a different way," he recognizes that part of his family does not share his perspective on the holiday, whether that entails full-fledged belief in the holiday's religious elements or simply unselfconscious participation in it. Reframing the holiday's meaning for some of the participants changes it for all of the participants. Wide differences among family members' beliefs about and experiences of holidays might have been present even if the entire family followed the same religion. But boundary setting calls attention to differences within a family.

Exogamous families could also avoid calling attention to differences by expanding their frame of reference. Bonnie answered the question of her family's response to her Jewish choices by saying, "I think my father and my family are glad that I have a spiritual path. I do have a friend who has sent me books about Jesus, and I have had straight-on conversations with her about belief." By describing her religious choices as a "spiritual path," Bonnie and her family framed their different religious choices as part of the same continuum, a universalizing move that highlighted the essential similarity and equivalent value of spiritual paths generally. In contrast, the friend who tried to steer Bonnie toward Jesus failed to recognize the more universalizing approach that Bonnie and her family took toward their religious choices.

The next audience member's question sought to capture the women's experiences as both outsiders and family members: "Now that you've been *mishpoche* [family] for so long, is there anything about the Jewish community that still mystifies you?" The Yiddish term *mishpoche* is significant here because it reaches beyond the nuclear family to encompass a broader kinship network, from blood relations to the entire Jewish people, depending on the context in which it's used. Thus, the questioner was highlighting the women's status as simultaneous insiders and outsiders.

Their answers suggest that they were not quite ready to see themselves as insiders. Bonnie said that she was still mystified by "Hebrew. Going to services. Everything."

Ann ventured, "When I went to my first synagogue service, I was almost in tears. That the traditions and the service keep going and going and going—" The audience roared with laughter, thinking that she was commenting on how long and boring the service was. But Ann was not trying to joke about the tedium of Jewish worship services. She waited a moment for the laughter to die down and then clarified, "It has kept going over all these years; it's amazing." She had been trying to convey her awe at the longevity of Jewish tradition.

The women on this panel approached their families' religious lives in a matter-of-fact way, and the audience in Atlanta, who were potential Mothers Circle members, had asked questions in order to understand how they could incorporate the Mothers Circle insights into their own lives. At that event, the panelists' comments had suggested that they felt that Jewishness had become relatively accessible to them, similar to the universalist individualist sentiments in which religious practices are open to all. By contrast, the audience at the JOI conference was still attempting to understand the women's place within Judaism and the Jewish people.

Institutionalizing Jewishness

Later that evening, an energetic keynote speaker, a member of a prominent philanthropic Jewish family, took the stage to argue that the insider-outsider distinction that he sensed in Jewish communities should be erased. He indirectly raised questions about the goals of Jewish institutions when they did outreach: were they really invested in bringing new members into their communities; and if so, for what purpose? These were questions that conference participants were willing to address in private conversation but less so in public.

The speaker described his experiences: he had married a Catholic woman with whom he had had four children, and they had joined a synagogue so that their children could attend religious school. A rabbi welcomed them into his congregation, telling the family, "Yes, we want you to be part of us." The speaker told the audience, "I was really lucky," but admitted, "I think part of that was because [of his famous family name]."

The audience laughed uproariously and applauded, perhaps surprised that he would so openly recognize that a synagogue leader would consider him a desirable member because of his financial resources. But they misunderstood his meaning, just as they had mistaken Ann's meaning about the longevity of Jewish traditions.

"The fact that I didn't think that was funny, and you all thought that was funny—" The audience burst into laughter again. The speaker continued earnestly:

> It really makes a statement about where we are today. [When the rabbi accepted us,] I didn't think I was being welcomed because of my last name. I thought I was being welcomed because these men and women understood what was supposed to happen when someone says, "I want to be part of my heritage, and my wife wants to be part of my heritage." I didn't realize that they may be looking for a check, or they may be looking for an identification with an important Jewish family. I just thought they cared about my children and bringing more people into the Jewish world. And I found that that's not always the case.

The speaker sensed that becoming an insider in Jewish institutions was not necessarily a function of "what's in your heart" (in the words of the Mothers Circle leader Rachel) but of the financial and social capital that one could contribute. His assessment was evidently familiar to the audience, as their laughter demonstrated. But he was challenging them to force their institutions to change.

The speaker went on to discuss the prevalence of outreach in Jewish communal organizations. "In most of the Jewish world, in my experience, it's sort of like being in a Samuel Beckett play. 'Outreach! Outreach! Yes! Let's go! Here it comes!' And it's sort of weird, because nothing really happens." The audience laughed again as he explained that many of the institutions interested in outreach failed to change despite their avowed interest in it. Implicitly, he was arguing that institutions' outreach efforts centered more on their interest in sustaining themselves in their present forms. They sought engagement with intermarried couples insofar as increased membership could serve institutional goals rather than the larger goals of the Jewish people.

The speaker urged those present to recognize the value in the methodology that JOI was providing at this conference. "I genuinely believe that our best days are ahead of us if we open our doors and we don't create a litmus test. I passionately believe that [when we] . . . make our communities the strongest communities, the most intellectual communities, the most creative communities—those that are the most full of meaning are those that are open and allow everybody to come in—people will genuinely want to become Jewish." For him, the concept of Big Tent Judaism meant that people could self-identify as Jews and that their participation and recognition in Jewish communities would not be subject to a threshold. Recognizing Jewishness as a choice meant foregrounding personal and shared meaning, while it also clearly avoided issues of personal status and the boundaries created by Jewish law.

Despite this rhetoric of openness, not everyone at the conference was convinced. Later, in a breakout group for a different session of the conference, a small group of participants mused about the limits of openness.

"We had a situation where a synagogue employee wanted the rabbis to perform an interfaith wedding ceremony. But our community doesn't allow that, and we can't provide that. We feel like we need to be able to refer them somewhere where they can get their needs met, so they don't feel alienated from Judaism entirely," said Aliza, a nondenominational Jewish educator.

"Let's be real. We're not doing this just so people don't feel alienated," said Andrea, another Jewish educator. "We have to admit that it's not all about being nice. There's a selfish reason too. We want there to be Jews in the world! We are all about growing Jewish children."

"Yes, there's the continuity aspect of outreach," said Jon, a Conservative rabbi. "That's what it's all about."

"We don't want to die," said Aliza earnestly. She had deeply internalized the demographic decline narrative that Jewish media had conveyed for decades. Like other informants, she seemed to fear the potential obliteration of the Jewish people through assimilation as deeply as the prospect of her own death as an individual. The keynote speaker had asserted that American Judaism could enjoy a vibrant renaissance if only it could move past the politics of personal status, but the religious experts did not agree with such a move.

"But how do you communicate boundaries without being judgmental?" asked Jon. "We're hearing this message that there should be no litmus test and anyone who says they're Jewish should be considered Jewish. But there's only so far the boundary extends, and only so far I can go." Referring to the gospel-style choir that had performed earlier that evening, he said, "They should have explained who the people in the choir were and what the story with that syna-gogue was. I would not consider them Jewish. They started out in the fifties with a charismatic leader who was reading the scriptures and thought they led her to Judaism, and she brought people with her. She had a church to start with and then they gradually went toward Judaism." In emphasizing that he would not consider this group Jewish, Jon brought the conversation back to a common trope in intermarriage discourse. The keynote speaker had emphasized that the politics of personal status were more likely to be harmful than helpful to the goal of continuing Judaism. But for Jon, the consequences of having a Jewish community in which members' status according to Jewish law was unclear or unacceptable were apparently worse.

This conversation suggests that, for some, the ideals of universalism and individualism were the public representation of an open, welcoming form of Jewishness, while more ambivalent ethnic familialist feelings lay beneath it. Having this conversation in an open session among hundreds of conference participants would have made the conference appear to be trumpeting the same negative messages about intermarriage that it decried. But the fact that it was not conveying these messages publicly did not mean that the ambivalence had subsided. Rather, the public message adapted to the American cultural context, framing Jewish community membership in a way that was thought to appeal to intermarried couples and strategically avoided the instrumentalizing language of conversion for the sake of Jewish continuity that often repelled intermarried couples from Jewish institutions. Notably, talk of conversion rarely appeared during this conference.

The next morning, I had a conversation over breakfast with Katherine, her husband, and their two middle-school-aged sons. I told her husband about the people I had met at the Dovetail conference who raised their children in both parents' religions. The older son looked up from the text message he was send-ing on his phone and said, "I think you should raise your kids in both religions and then let the kids decide when they are old enough." I asked him if he would want to have two religions until he decided. "Probably not," he said. "Most kids would probably choose nothing."

This comment struck me as deeply ironic. All around us, adults were investing a great deal of energy and anxiety into strategies to ensure that this young man and his peers would find Judaism irresistible and inevitable. Mean-while, this boy was pointing out candidly that religious choice meant not just choosing one or another religion but also the possibility of choosing none, as an increasing number of Americans are doing (Kosmin et al. 2009). Some of my adult informants who eventually did choose Judaism remembered hating Hebrew school as children, reflecting sociologist Richard Madsen's (2009) find-ing that Americans' religious choices are not necessarily static. Madsen found that, across religious groups, individuals' religious commitments shift over the life course and that the meanings that people attach to their religious practices also change. The vagaries of religious identification and experience in the contemporary United States presented the outreach workers with unenviable challenges.

Insiders, Outsiders, and Kinship

What would happen if Jewish communities had no litmus test for entry, as the keynote speaker had advocated? If there were no insiders or outsiders, could there still be boundaries marking Judaism as distinct from Christianity? Would the boundaries of Jewishness become irrelevant? The Mothers Circle in Atlanta, the model outreach strategy on exhibit at JOI's conference, had experimented with radical openness to non-Jewish women and their Jewish husbands. No litmus test determined whether anyone was "Jewish enough" to participate in the Mothers Circle. In fact, the only litmus test was whether someone might be *too* Jewish. As a woman from a non-Jewish background, I would have qualified for membership in the Mothers Circle in its earlier years. But because of the conditions of a grant that funded the Mothers Circle in Atlanta, women who had converted were ineligible to join, presumably because they were considered so committed to Judaism that they no longer required the support of such a group. In a clever workaround devised by one of the group's leaders, I was admitted as an alumna, not as a regular member. This "reverse litmus test" frustrated at least one in-married Jewish woman who wanted to participate in the outreach activities designated for intermarried couples. At an outreach event held by a separate but related Jewish organization in Atlanta, I heard this woman complain about being excluded from the opportunity to be coached in Jewish motherhood. It was unclear whether the grantmakers and program organizers simply had not considered including Jews along with non-Jews or whether they had assumed that the already-Jewish already knew how to "be Jewish" or had access to coaching from other sources. If nothing else, those who were already Jews were apparently deemed unlikely to defect to non-Jewishness.

The Mothers Circle leaders recognized that litmus tests arose in part from dissonant definitions of Jewishness among American Jewish communities: people recognized as Jews in one community might not be recognized as Jews in another, and non-Jews married to Jews might be welcomed as equal members of one Jewish community while their participation in Jewish ritual might be restricted in another. The Mothers Circle members and leaders handled this tension for the purposes of their group's activities by changing the "rules" of kinship to include non-Jewish wives and mothers. In this model, the *halakhic* (Jewish legal) definition of a Jew as someone who has a Jewish mother or who has converted according to Jewish law is rejected as outmoded and overly narrow in favor of a model based on choice and emotion—"what's in your heart." By adopting this alternative model, the Mothers Circle attempted to meet the needs of non-Jewish women to feel accepted by the Jewish community as well as the Jewish community's desire for more Jewish children.

Rachel explained:

> So "who is a Jew," to me, is what you're doing, it's your actions more than your lineage or your birth. That's my opinion. I know that's not the halakhic opinion. The halakhic opinion would be if you're born to a Jewish mother. . . . It does not matter to me at all if women convert . . . because I think you don't have to convert to be Jewish, but my husband thinks it's easier if you convert because there's no question. And there's some truth to that, but if [a] mother never converted and still raised her kids in Judaism, it makes absolutely no difference to me.

Rachel emphasized that intermarriage is now a given and that the kinship structure of Jewishness has to evolve to absorb non-Jews who are part of Jewish families:

> Like my rabbi says, biology is a stronger drive than theology. So people are going to intermarry, and it used to be the Jewish thing to do was just to write them off. But now that, especially in Atlanta, interfaith has a higher rate of marriage than in-faith marriage in the Jewish community—we feel those people can bring strength to our people, and the non-Jewish mothers that I work with make great Jewish moms even though they're not Jewish, and they sometimes do a better job of raising Jewish kids than Jewish moms do.

This model provides no clear way to tell where Jewishness begins and ends: if all the members of an interfaith family can be considered fully Jewish, are the Christian in-laws who participate in Jewish rituals also Jewish? If formal conversion continues to exist once the definition of Jewishness has been expanded past the traditional boundaries, does conversion take on some other meaning besides entry into the Jewish people? Rachel's viewpoint suggests that, for her, Jewish kinship is no longer standardized and non-Jews can hold different places in Jewish community and kinship depending on the community to which they belong.

As the Jewish community struggles to understand how to place non-Jews within its kinship structure, intermarried non-Jewish women do not passively accept that community's decisions about their status. Some resist pressure to formally convert to Judaism, still actively participating in Jewish family and community life but within the context of their own individual histories and experiences. Rachel explained that their resistance to conversion is rooted in respect for their own kin as well as, in some cases, their negative reception by Jews:

> Number one, they were treated badly and why would [they] want to join these people who are not nice to outsiders? And the second common thing is that a lot of the women don't want to hurt their own families of origin by leaving the faith that they were brought up in, and I've heard many women say, "I feel Jewish, I live Jewish, I'm raising a Jewish kid, but by actually converting, that's rejecting my own family." And some of them actually do convert years later when their parents are no longer living. I know several people in that scenario; . . . what better way to insult your mother or your father [than] by saying, "What you gave me I'm rejecting."

Rachel observed that the non-Jewish women's experiences with their Jewish in-laws and Jewish organizations were the basis for their feelings of kinship, or lack thereof, with the Jewish people. Yet even when such women rejected conversion to Judaism, they continued to serve as leaders of their families' Jewish homes, as I discussed in chapter 3.

Jewish religious experts used universalist individualist and ethnic familialist languages in different ways to translate Jews' and non-Jews' experiences. But as it did in Jewish media coverage (see chapter 1), utilitarian language featured prominently in such experts' discussions about intermarriage. Focusing on Jewish continuity, this language tended to underscore differences between Jews and non-Jews and downplay disagreements among Jews concerning definitions of Jewishness. In the absence of consensus on religious authority and what it means to be Jewish in a pluralistic, voluntaristic society, religious experts emphasized the importance of having Jewish children for the sake of Jewish continuity. Such discussion often focused on strategies for ensuring children's Jewishness but less often on the content of that Jewishness.

This strategic focus sometimes produced poignant results. Some religious experts had trouble comprehending non-Jewish women's expressions of deep spiritual stirrings as they taught Judaism to their children. The kind of creative solutions to conflicts between individualism and the desire for community that Shir Hadash exemplified, focusing on how to foster meaning-centered reflection among individuals in the context of moral community, were less common here because of an overdetermined emphasis on children's Jewish identification. But even as religious experts emphasized maintaining boundaries in order to avoid the loss of the Jewish people as a distinct group, the central questions remained. Who and what are the Jewish people? What is being maintained when the boundaries are kept whole?

Dominant cultural narratives about intermarriage obscure the ways in which people apply different languages in different circumstances to explain the meaning and significance of intermarriage. Institutions such as JOI attempt to provide creative resources for rabbis and Jewish educators that address the needs delineated by dominant cultural narratives—Jewish children for the sake of Jewish continuity—as well as the more existential, human needs of particular individuals. As the private conversations among JOI conference participants suggest, the ways in which such messages are received depend on the narratives that have already been internalized by the receivers.

5

Sovereign Selves
in a Fractured Community

Navigating the conflicting cultural and religious values and themes in discourses about intermarriage challenges religious experts as much as laypeople. In interviews and participant-observation with these experts—rabbis, Jewish educators, and other clergy—I discovered that their shared vocabulary of Jewish traditions and symbols obscured deep divisions. For some clergy, as for some laypeople, universalism and individualism expressed the ultimate truth of their religious convictions. Others saw the role of universalism and individualism as much more limited and focused instead on covenant and community. Matters grew more complicated as laypeople challenged the clergy's convictions with their own demands and claims. Many laypeople were unwilling to grant any particular religious authority to clergy beyond their ability to officiate at religious rituals such as weddings. Many rabbis struggled to understand their role as leaders among laypeople who regarded themselves as ultimately autonomous.

As rabbis grappled with these complicated matters, they sometimes aired contentious disagreements with one another in public, even though their private interactions with intermarried couples were often more compassionate, as I will discuss later in the chapter. Reconstructionist Rabbi R, one of thirteen rabbis I interviewed in Atlanta, was one of only a handful of rabbis in the city who officiated at interfaith wedding ceremonies. He explained that he found himself at odds with his Orthodox colleagues:

> This is going to be heretical, but it's on the record now: I so deeply hope that people can connect to Judaism, and I see the beauty in it, and it's the set of rituals and symbols and stories that inform who I am as a spiritual person. But I am okay, at the end of the day, if somebody is spiritually happy and that's not a Jewish home, for them. So if a child grows up as a result of an interfaith relationship, there certainly is a sadness. But I

don't see it as the same kind of loss, if they're a good person. And so, I feel like I could be perceived as—and I've been accused, actually; I've had an Orthodox rabbi accuse—that I'm helping destroy the Jewish people by doing interfaith ceremonies. A very public thing, and I very publicly responded back to him. I said, "No, you've given up on the people that I work with. And so I'm not destroying what you've already let go of."

Some of the voices in discourses on intermarriage would agree with Rabbi R's detractor that rabbinic officiation at interfaith weddings undermines the Jewish people. For ethnic familialists, however, rabbinic officiation is one way in which they can align their lives with normative Judaism despite their intermarriage. Narrowly focused discourses about intermarriage and Jewish continuity obscured the rabbis' broader disagreements and agreements with one another and with laypeople.

The reasoning behind the rabbis' viewpoints and their personal experiences with intermarried couples were often missing from public discussion. Private discussion was evidently lacking as well. One Reform rabbi in Atlanta told me that local rabbis did not discuss intermarriage in any sustained, formal way or circulate any official information about their approaches to it. They relied on the grapevine for information about which of their colleagues would officiate at wedding ceremonies for intermarrying couples.

If the rabbis had discussed their views with one another, they would have seen clearly that they understood the stakes of intermarriage in drastically different ways. Even though discourses about intermarriage often rehearsed the claim that rabbinic officiation at interfaith wedding ceremonies was harmful to the Jewish people, the Orthodox rabbis I interviewed framed their stance on intermarriage and inclusiveness differently from how Rabbi R portrayed it. In their eyes, intermarriage endangered Jews' ability to continue to serve God by observing Jewish law with integrity as a group. For the more liberal rabbis, the Jewish mission could be upheld by a broader contingent because Judaism was a rich set of "rituals and symbols and stories" that helped to define people's emotional lives. For these rabbis, both Jews and non-Jews could use and appreciate this set of symbols for positive and affirming ends. While the mixing of Judaism and Christianity in the way that some Dovetail conference participants advocated was clearly out of bounds for the rabbis, there could be room for inclusion of non-Jews in Jewish communities.

My analysis of these rabbis' contrasting views is based upon interviews with four Orthodox, four Conservative, one Reconstructionist, and four Reform rabbis in the Atlanta area; two educators who worked with the Mothers Circle; and several rabbis and educators outside the Atlanta area. I also observed a clergy panel discussion at the Dovetail conference. Because I promised my informants anonymity (as far as possible), I identify them only by their movement affiliation and a randomly selected initial. In the interviews, the rabbis described their interactions with intermarried couples concerning life-cycle rituals, such as weddings and baby namings, and their perspectives on Jewishness more generally. In my observations, I witnessed rabbis and Jewish educators interacting with each other and with intermarried people around the topic of intermarriage. I asked the rabbis about their experiences, the sources that helped them in their work with intermarried couples in everyday life, and what *Jewish continuity* meant to them. While the rabbis used a common vocabulary to articulate their views on intermarriage—*God, the Jewish people*, and *covenant*, for example—their shared vocabulary did not reflect a shared understanding of the meaning of these terms or of the goal of Jewish continuity.

Embracing Individualism

The views of clergy who participated in a panel discussion at the Dovetail conference contrasted sharply with those of most of the rabbis I interviewed in Atlanta. The Dovetail panelists argued that universalism and individualism benefited intermarried couples, their children, and ultimately the entire religious community. For example, Rabbi P, one of the Dovetail panelists, said that the idea that God has both "essence" and "attributes" informed his approach to interfaith marriage. In this view, while only one God exists, different people perceive different attributes of God. Similarly, said the rabbi, religions channel generically human experiences through religiously specific symbols. For instance, agony—the suffering of slavery and death—and ecstasy, or redemption, are represented through the religious symbols of matzah and the cross. Even though religious symbols express these experiences in particular ways for their audiences, he said, we should recognize that these experiences transcend religious particularity. Rabbi P's explanation echoed universalist claims of truths that extended across all religions, affirming the views expressed by the lay conference participants. Repeating the individualistic themes of earlier discussions, a priest on the panel, Father S, offered what he said was a "realistic" approach to intermarriage, saying that he preferred to "meet folks where they are, not where they should be." He had performed about a thousand Catholic-Jewish weddings along with a smaller number of Catholic-Muslim and Catholic-Hindu ones. In preparation for such weddings, Father S counseled the engaged interfaith couples to help them discern their beliefs—a task, he said, that endogamous couples never had to face.

Such universalism and individualism could be difficult to reconcile with the requirements and logics of religious institutions. Father S noted that not all priests were as open to intermarriage as he was. Even though Vatican II had, he said, "technically" eased the process of intermarriage, some dioceses, churches, and priests remained unaware that the church allowed interfaith marriage and were unfamiliar with the dispensations that made it possible. Rabbi P agreed with Father S's "realism," saying that Jewish organizations' and clergy's disapproval of intermarriage could not stop Jews from intermarrying. "To think otherwise is a rabbinical power trip," he declared. Worse, Jewish institutions' official opposition to intermarriage prevented rabbis from interacting with intermarrying couples as effectively as they otherwise might, he said. For example, congregational rabbis often were not allowed to perform interfaith weddings, even though some were willing. This situation led to "maverick" rabbis who could be hired to officiate at interfaith weddings but did not offer counseling to help the intermarrying couple identify and understand their religious values. Again, Rabbi P's views coincided neatly with claims that laypeople had made in their own discussion groups. He appeared to agree with them that clergy and institutions opposed to intermarriage were interested primarily in their own power. Father S and Rabbi P had to reconcile their understandings of universalism and individualism with their religious institutions' traditions and habits, as did the laypeople with whom they worked.

Rabbi P also agreed in large part with Dovetail's teenage panelists and adults about the cosmopolitan and individualistic purposes of religious education, offering an institutional critique. Official opposition to intermarriage hinders religious education of children in synagogues, Rabbi P said, because it obscures the true purposes of religious education. As an associate rabbi at a synagogue, he had overheard a religious-school teacher tell a group of third graders that "they needed to have a Jewish identity so that they would not marry non-Jews when they grew up." This was a "religious abomination," he asserted: children should be educated for religious values, drawing on both parents' religions so that they would be "enlightened," not dedicated to their single religion out of "ignorance." Departing from the views of some lay conference participants, however, Rabbi P repeated the advice of many Jewish outreach workers that parents should raise children in only one religion to ensure a coherent religious identity.

Coming from a distinctly different institutional context, a Congregationalist minister on the panel reported that her church had no official barriers to intermarriage. This institutional freedom allowed her to focus on "creative rethinking" of community and religious expression, continuing Christianity and Judaism not through "preservation" and "enforcement" but through "creative exploration and heart." Like the laypeople who had spoken earlier in the day, the minister saw spiritual meaning as the opposite of the "old, irrelevant boxes" of ethnic and religious identity.

Though these religious leaders differed somewhat in their approaches to intermarriage, they agreed that institutional disapproval was harmful to inter-married couples and their children and to clergy members' relationship with them. The leaders' discussion emphasized how clergy members could help identify and meet the needs of intermarried couples discerning their personal beliefs. These emphases aligned well with the priorities of participants in this conference. In other contexts, these clergy members may have handled discussions of intermarriage somewhat differently. The same messages delivered in the same way might not have worked as well in conversations with congregants and other clergy or in the context of their communities' historical and theological self-definitions and shared practices. These considerations were left out of this discussion.

Competing Visions of Jewishness

Rabbis who distanced themselves from intermarriage and refused to officiate at interfaith weddings spoke about these issues differently, prioritizing contexts and conversations that the Dovetail conference clergy left out of their remarks. The Dovetail panelists seemed to be holding a debate with intermarriage discourses with which they assumed their audience would be familiar. The rabbis whom I interviewed individually in offices, synagogue conference rooms, or coffee shops spoke on a more personal level, recounting experiences and narrating beliefs that had shaped their approaches to intermarriage. Even when these rabbis felt that Jewish sources and traditions made clear that intermarriage was not an authentic or legitimate expression of Jewishness, they said that they did not condemn or reject intermarried couples as individuals when meeting them face to face. While my intermarried informants understood Jewishness in the context of their individual and familial commitments, these rabbis and Jewish educators interacted with and thought about intermarried couples in a broader context of covenant and community.

As both individual rabbis and representatives of Jewish institutions, my rabbinic informants defined Jewishness and determined its ritual applications. Some rabbis felt that they had to resist the encroachment of individualism and insist upon the inviolability of Jewish communal boundaries. Others felt that Jewish institutions had to acknowledge the legitimacy of individuals' own judgments and perspectives. The rabbis' contrasting perspectives highlight conflict among Jewish leaders concerning non-Orthodox denominations' disagreement with Orthodox understandings of Jewish law and covenant. They also demonstrate that the tensions of universalist individualism and ethnic familialism existed in rabbis' deliberations as well as in those of intermarried couples.

These tensions were most clearly manifested in the rabbis' understand-ings of the term *Jewish continuity*, which I asked each of them to define. Self-help books written by rabbis on intermarriage suggest a range of approaches to intermarriage and Jewish continuity, from the intermarriage-negative vol-umes *It All Begins with a Date* (Silverstein 1995a) and *Preserving Jewishness in Your Family after Intermarriage Has Occurred* (Silverstein 1995b) to the intermarriage-positive guidebook *Making a Successful Jewish Interfaith Marriage* (Olitzky with Littman 2003). In some cases, *continuity* means preventing intermarriage or treating it as a type of family malady; in other cases, it entails emphasizing Judaism regardless of the religious backgrounds of the individuals in the fam-ily. The ways in which the rabbis I interviewed conceived of the boundaries of Jewish community helped them to define Jewish continuity. In some Jewish communities, Jewish law set the rules. Non-Jews were not included in Jewish ritual because they were not members of the covenant that Jews share. Ortho-dox communities hold that the Torah was revealed by God at Mount Sinai and that the Jewish people are responsible for living up to God's commandments, as set out in the Torah and later interpreted within the appropriate rabbinic framework. The meaning of the *mitzvot* (commandments) is to be found in their observance, writes Orthodox rabbi Norman Lamm (1966). The Torah is both of God and godly. To observe mitzvot, whether ritual or ethical, is to prac-tice holiness, in Lamm's view. To study and observe Torah, especially mitz-vot that do not have clear "rational or ethical or nationalistic" significance, is to experience communion with God. As a "chosen" people, Lamm explains, Jews are to separate themselves from non-Jews, observe Jewish law in order to cultivate holiness individually and collectively, and teach it via example to the other nations of the world (110–112). According to several of my Orthodox informants, the Jewish people's role is to live out God's will in order to show other peoples how to be in communion with God.

In communities that adhere more loosely to Jewish law, rabbis often deter-mine the boundaries between Jews and non-Jews on an individualized and informal basis. They decide how to accommodate non-Jewish partners, spouses, or parents of Jewish congregation members at life-cycle ceremonies. This more haphazard approach reflects the view that God is comfortable with Jews' having a high degree of personal autonomy. In this view, the Jewish people maintain a permanent covenantal relationship with God, as set out in and through the Torah. This relationship is not necessarily an exclusive "chosen" status separate from other peoples, and its manifestation in daily life can change in response to historical context. Personal meaning and choice are accorded a legitimate place in Jews' relationship to God, given their prominence in contemporary Ameri-can culture. Reform and Reconstructionist theologies assume that Jews have personal autonomy. Reform Judaism casts the observance of individual mitzvot as a matter of choice. Individual Jews may determine their own observance depending on whether they find a particular *mitzvah* (commandment) to be a meaningful way to connect to God and community (Borowitz 1983, 267–272; Borowitz 1984). Reconstructionist Judaism sees itself as post-halakhic, meaning that while it honors the tradition that Jewish law embodies, it emphasizes the autonomy of individuals in understanding the relationship of Jewish teachings to particular circumstances of their own lives (Alpert and Staub 1985, 31–32). Conservative Judaism finds itself in an awkward intermediate position in that it officially regards Jewish law as binding, but many individual Conservative Jews exercise a high degree of personal autonomy (Borowitz 1983, 262–263). Lay autonomy is evidenced not least by an increasing intermarriage rate among Conservative Jews (Fishkoff 2005; Tigay 2006). In this sense, Conservative lay-people's views align with the official philosophy of the Reform movement, which holds that personal autonomy is perfectly compatible with non-halakhic practice (Borowitz 1983). Rabbi Neil Gillman, a faculty member at the (Conservative) Jewish Theological Seminary of America, argued at the 2007 United Synagogue of Conservative Judaism Biennial Convention that because of this divide between rabbis' and laypeople's views of the authority of Jewish law, the Conservative movement should stop considering itself a halakhic movement (Fishkoff 2005; Tigay 2006). Conservative rabbis' challenge, then, is to reconcile their commitment to Jewish law and a relatively traditional sense of Jewish mission with their congregants' commitment to religious personal autonomy. With these different assumptions about Jewishness, the rabbis I interviewed came to some similar conclusions in practice. But despite their shared vocabulary and, in some cases, practical approaches, their understandings of intermarriage and Jewishness varied widely.

Religious Mixing

Despite their divergent assumptions about Jewishness, all of my rabbinic informants agreed that Jewish continuity required that Jewish and Christian religious practices remain distinct and separate. Their resistance to religious mixing placed them squarely among normative religious voices in the Jewish discourses about intermarriage. Many of the rabbis felt that mixing religions would be worse than losing Jews to Christianity altogether. This resistance to religious mixing resonates with a long history of church suppression of Christians' "Judaizing," as well as each religion's intense concern about religious boundaries (Adelman 1991; Baron 1957; Fishberg [1911] 2006; Katz [1973] 1998; Maitland 1898; Scheindlin 1998). My intermarried informants also expressed this worry, fearing that admitting Christmas trees or Easter baskets into their homes would render them less Jewish. The rabbis I interviewed said that they would prefer intermarried couples to choose Christianity for their children rather than to raise them in both Judaism and Christianity.

In contrast, Christian denominations generally oppose intermarriage less stringently than most rabbis do. Roman Catholic canon law restricts clergy from performing religious wedding ceremonies jointly with clergy of different religions and establishes official procedures for intermarriage that resemble in many respects what liberal rabbis have set up in more informal, local ways. Both Protestants and Catholics express concern for the religious upbringing of children of intermarriage, focusing on the importance of building a "Christian home" (Evangelical Presbyterian Church n.d.). Some evangelicals urge one another to avoid marriages in which spouses are "unequally yoked," a reference to Paul's admonition against being "yoked" to "unbelievers" (2 Corinthians 6:14ff). With Vatican II, the leadership in the Catholic Church relaxed its emphasis on spousal conversion; and the same is true in Reconstructionist and Reform Judaism, which now allow patrilineal descent. Hence, the idea that spouses can belong to separate religions has become more prevalent (Rose 2001).

The importance of avoiding religious mixing prompted Conservative Rabbi E to change his views on conversion to Judaism. Whereas in the past he had expected prospective converts to meet high standards of spiritual commitment to Judaism, he later came to accept less spiritually committed intermarried non-Jews as candidates for conversion for the sake of rooting out Christian influences in the family. He explained:

> Most of the people that I deal with anyway are very passionate about the conversion, but those that are maybe lukewarm, I will say to them, "Is there going to be anything Christian in the home?" The answer is no.
>
> "If you don't want Christmas, if you're not going to have a Christmas tree, and you're not going to have an Easter egg roll, and you're not going to have any of that kind of stuff, but it's basically going to be a home with a menorah and the mezuzah on the door and so forth, even though you yourself are not passionately into Judaism. [If] you don't drive Hebrew school carpool, but you're not going out of your way to do very much," I said, "I will convert you."
>
> . . . The reason is very simple. My concern is the children. If the children are raised in an environment where both parents are Jewish—even though one is not enthusiastic about it—it doesn't matter. At least those kids are going to be Jewish. I've come to understand I want to save the next generation, and I can do that by not having the standard as demanding as I might have had before.

Clearly, for Rabbi E, this passive Jewishness was an unwelcome compromise. But in his view, families who raised children in both Christianity and Judaism nearly guaranteed that their children would not choose to remain Jewish throughout their lives. His comments suggested that he feared that Christianity was simply a more attractive option for children who could choose it, echoing the fears about assimilation that Jews had voiced for at least two hundred years. Rabbi E's lenient conversion policy was his way of reaching beyond despair to secure future generations' loyalty to Judaism.

In cases in which intermarried couples rejected the idea of the non-Jewish member's conversion to Judaism, Rabbi E suspected that they would only confuse their children. His stance echoed the "discord approach" that Marshall Sklare had described in 1970, only altered to focus on the children rather than the marriage:

> [If an intermarried couple has] the foolishness to tell me what they're going to do is expose their children to both religions, then I tell them that they're very foolish parents, and that this is terrible, terrible parenting, and that what they are doing is telling their child that on Monday they're a vegetarian; on Tuesday they're a carnivore; on Wednesday they're a vegetarian; on Thursday they're a carnivore. I said, "You're dealing with two contradictory concepts, and what you are forcing the child to do is pick not a religion but a parent."

Many of the rabbis I interviewed cast the dangers of mixing Judaism and Christianity as pragmatic psychological concerns: children might not know who they are; they might be confused. Conservative Rabbi L added to this observation that children raised in both religions could choose one parent's religion as a way of hurting the other parent. The discord that these rabbis described could go in many directions within such families.

Rabbi E added that he strongly disagreed with parents who opted to raise their children in both Judaism and Christianity because they believed that they owed their children the opportunity to choose a religion rather than "imposing" one on them. "I said, 'You impose politics on your child. You impose values on your child. . . . You impose everything else on your children, so all of a sudden religion you're not going to impose on them.' I said, 'That's nonsense.'" Rabbi E was more comfortable, though disappointed, when a child of intermarried parents was being raised as a Christian rather than as "both," even though a child who was "both" might still have some allegiance to Judaism. For him and many of my other rabbinic informants, the mixing of Christianity and Judaism within the individual child, the home, and the Jewish people was the most disturbing part of intermarriage.

The problem of mixing "two contradictory concepts" recalls the Mothers Circle women's conversation with Joe about their husbands' apparently inexplicable opposition to having Christmas trees in their homes. By choosing intermarriage under the framework of personal autonomy, these husbands had committed themselves to living under "two contradictory concepts." The rabbis themselves remained within only a Jewish framework, but to them as well as to the intermarried husbands, mixing religions in the home felt like a slippery slope: Christianity might prove too attractive to resist, or Christian relatives might successfully proselytize within the family. The boundaries of Judaism could only become blurrier if they admitted people who held dual allegiances to Judaism and Christianity. While the rabbis did not appear to be afraid that Jews would begin worshipping Jesus, they did worry that dual allegiances would contribute to greater confusion about what is Jewish and what is not. The boundaries clearly mattered, as did their clarity.

For all of the rabbis, Jewish continuity depended upon Jews' devotion to Judaism alone. Contradicting universalist individualist claims about fairness to both spouses' backgrounds, Reform Rabbi M asserted that religious membership was more than just heritage. For him, as for many of the other rabbis, it was a commitment to a holistic framework for living. Rabbi M saw religious membership as rooted in personal meaning and expressed through symbols and rituals. Thus, intermarried couples who raised their children as both Christian and Jewish because they saw them as half Jewish and half Christian, according to the folk understanding of kinship, were attempting something that was impossible. Rabbi M said, "I have a mother, and I have a father. I'm not half a woman. I don't know what a half of a Jew is. If you have a Jewish father and a mother who's Christian, then there's a choice. I don't think 'both' works." While choice plays into the Reform understanding of Jewishness, Rabbi M wanted people to make the choice to be part of a Jewish community. Mixing Judaism and Christianity evaded commitment to the Jewish framework and betrayed its authenticity.

Similarly, Reform Rabbi Maurice Davis points out in his article "Why I Won't Perform an Intermarriage" that while the integrity of Jewish law per se is not a Reform rabbi's concern, authenticity is—meaning concern for the integrity of the religious community's symbols and the common history that the symbols evoke (Davis 1988, 20). Rabbi M said that intermarrying or already intermarried couples who wish to practice both Christianity and Judaism must consider what it means to participate in a religious community in the first place. If the intermarrying couple believes that Rabbi M's refusal to officiate at their wedding or other interfaith ceremonies represents his rejection or condemnation of the couple, then the couple is interpreting it in the wrong frame of reference. When a couple decides to marry across religious boundaries, the couple steps into a secular American framework. His job, he said, is to point out that the Jewish and secular frameworks are separate, which is different from condemnation or rejection.

Rabbi M recognized that, in some cases, intermarried couples try to do "both" to satisfy their parents. But, he argued, to be a serious and authentic member of a religious community, a person must seek out meaning and not just perform religious practices out of filial loyalty. In this respect, he agreed with the clergy at the Dovetail conference who insisted on the importance of counseling intermarrying couples to help them discern their beliefs. But Rabbi M's argument extended well past the concerns of the spouses-to-be. He believed that trying to satisfy parents is not an authentic or responsible way to connect to Judaism: "For folks that are looking to rent a rabbi, I'm not really interested. If they are interested in developing a relationship and figuring out where we're going to journey and what path to choose, I'm in. But I think to be authentic also means that Jewish tradition isn't just hoops to jump through. It means something. Symbolic language matters, and most of us don't know how to read symbolic language." Symbolic language requires the individual to take responsibility for interpreting it and using it with integrity. Because this language in Judaism so heavily emphasizes covenant, said Rabbi M, choosing symbols without attention to their covenantal context is an inauthentic use of them. In his reading, choice plays an important part in religious practice, but it must be constrained by tradition as well as active participation in the religious community and acceptance of its norms.

These rabbis' arguments against religious mixing used some of the same elements of ethnic familialism and universalist individualism that intermarried couples used in constructing their family practices. For Rabbi M, preserving heritage was pointless without an active personal choice to find meaning in that heritage. In contrast, Rabbi E saw personal meaning as potentially expendable if it meant that *Jewish* heritage would be preserved and respected. What differed significantly from the laypeople's claims was the rabbis' emphasis on community boundaries and the integrity of contemporary practice with historic tradition.

The Meaning of Membership

For the rabbis, these considerations of heritage and its meaning translated into practical questions about community membership and practices. All of those I interviewed clearly distinguished between Jews, as participants in the particular Jewish covenant with God, and non-Jews, who could be wonderful people but were not part of that particular covenant. Reform Rabbi M said that he explained this separation to a couple who had approached him about officiating at a "baby naming" as a Jewish counterpart to a planned baptism in a church for the same child. "There's no such thing, really, as a baby naming," he told me. "For me, it's entering a child into the covenant, and once you enter a child into the Jewish covenant, you're making a commitment to have a particular kind of relationship with this community and with God." Rabbi M read the attempt to straddle boundaries and holistic frameworks as misguided at best. Covenant could not be negotiated according to personal preferences; it required a commitment to people and traditions beyond the self.

At the same time, some rabbis felt that Jewish communal boundaries could be redefined to enable non-Jews to participate without being part of the Jewish covenant. Reconstructionist Rabbi R approached the inclusion of diverse members of his congregation from several angles at once. Rabbi R, who led the LGBT congregation I've already described, used universalist individualist language to talk about his way of including non-Jews while avoiding mixing religions. Many members chose to belong to his congregation because they felt that it honored their right to private judgment and their experiences as individuals without pressing upon them a normative vision of Jewishness that left them feeling inadequate.

Rabbi R took an individualized view of religion, framing his synagogue community as having room for members of all stripes, with distinctions among them carefully balanced between honoring Jewish tradition and honoring individuals. He maintained distinctions between Jews and non-Jews in synagogue ritual, creating opportunities for non-Jewish members to participate in rituals that were not linked to the particular relationship of the Jewish people to Torah. He felt that it was appropriate and honest to acknowledge non-Jews as such rather than have them participate equally as if they were Jews. The rabbi described a blessing for parents of b'nai mitzvah, which he had created to include a special group *aliyah* (the honor of being called up to the Torah as it is read during services) for each of three groups: children as "partners in creation," Jewish adults as "partners in Torah," and non-Jews as "partners in creating Jewish community." In this way, he expanded the boundaries of the community to include non-Jewish members but preserved the exclusivity of the particular Jewish covenant with God. He told me that the non-Jewish members had said that they had found great personal meaning in this public acknowledgment of their part in the community.

At the beginning of his rabbinic career, Rabbi R decided to officiate at interfaith wedding ceremonies: "I felt like, in my heart, I felt it was the right thing to do." He explained that he had relied on "instinct" to make this decision because the issue had been pressed upon him earlier than he had anticipated: he had received the request before he had even started his first job. His approach to intermarriage welcomed non-Jews without pressuring them to eventually convert to Judaism, honoring them as persons rather than treating them as outsiders. He described his conversation with an intermarrying couple who had come to his office just before my interview with him. They had hoped that he would officiate at their wedding, but they were afraid that he would condemn them, turn them away, or pressure the non-Jewish partner to convert. Rabbi R said that he had told them, "'Look, I'm a rabbi, but I'm a spiritual leader, and I want to connect with the human being that is sitting in front of me.' And so, to not welcome or to, like, act from this fear that Jewish people aren't going to survive totally diminishes the humanity of the other person." Rabbi R's sense of what was most important in his approach to intermarried couples contrasted sharply with that of Rabbi E, who believed that maintaining clear boundaries was the best way to ensure the well-being of both Judaism and individual Jews, given what he understood to be long odds against the survival of Jews as a distinct people. Rabbi R saw such boundary setting as a contradiction to equally important Jewish values related to honoring and caring for individuals, regardless of their religious membership.

Reform Rabbi G also officiated at interfaith weddings and spoke of welcoming non-Jews as members of the "universal human family." He saw his approach as rooted in the Bible, noting that above the door of his synagogue was displayed "a quote from Isaiah: 'my house shall be called the house of prayer for all peoples.' I take that very, very literally." Emphasizing the unity of all humanity, he avoided strong distinctions between Jews and non-Jews and thus did not see conversion as an outright necessity for intermarried couples. "I think the only thing [conversion] does, it formalizes in the mind of . . . the person undergoing that it's something they feel they need to do." For him, conversion was a concrete manifestation of a newly Jewish heart formed by a deeply personal spiritual transformation. Beyond simply participating in Jewish community with one's Jewish family, becoming Jewish entailed a sense of owning the particular symbolic language and covenant of Judaism.

For Rabbi R, and for most of the rabbis I interviewed, conversion to Judaism was to be undertaken only out of deep personal commitment, not because of factors such as concern for family unity or the continuity of the Jewish people. According to the Orthodox rabbis I interviewed, this approach largely agrees with Jewish law regarding conversion. But it is at odds with some aspects of intermarriage discourse that emphasize conversion of non-Jewish spouses in intermarried couples, such as the Conservative movement's 2005 document making conversion of non-Jewish spouses a priority (Edelstein 2005). Some of my intermarried informants agreed with the rabbis' view of conversion but for different reasons, feeling that pressure to convert was illegitimate because it did not acknowledge them as individuals. Likewise, Rabbi R said, "If there's an attachment to someone becoming Jewish, then you aren't encountering them as a human being. So from a Buberian perspective, you're actually seeing a more utilitarian side, . . . and so to me [welcoming intermarried couples with the hope of conversion] is slightly a sham." Rather than emphasizing formal membership in Judaism as an overriding concern for his community members, Rabbi R hoped that each individual would find the path to being a good person that was right for him or her, an approach to religious meaning shared by the "moderately affiliated" American Jewish informants of Cohen and Eisen (2000) and the Americans with various religious attachments interviewed by Bellah et al. (1985).

While Rabbi R saw Judaism as one important spiritual path, he recognized others as valid as well. His approach to conversion aligned with his sense of his community's boundaries. He saw conversion to Judaism as necessary if non-Jews wished to participate in the covenant between God and the Jewish people but not if they simply wanted to be part of his community. When people approached him about conversion, he told them, "I think you're fine just the way that you are, and I have no investment in you becoming Jewish. My only investment is you find a path that makes more sense to you." In this respect, traditional Jewish attitudes toward conversion align with a more modern American emphasis on personal meaning, and both of these conflict with the emphasis on conversion found in the continuity-focused perspective that Rabbi E articulated.

The continuity discourse, in which conversion takes on a more instrumental meaning, was familiar to Rabbi R and to the interfaith couples with whom he worked. He described having heard "chauvinist" messages during his own youth that held up Judaism as the best, if not the only, way to live. This assertion was given as a reason to avoid intermarriage. Rabbi R explained that in the traditional Jewish household in which he grew up, "I . . . [had] lots of pressure to only have Jewish partners, . . . that I was going to dishonor the memories of all of the Holocaust victims if I did x, y, or z. Those weren't messages that were going to keep me Jewish. Luckily, I got enough of the other positive messages that did hook me, but I floated away for a little while too because of our community's . . . disgusting, gross messages." Non-Jewish partners of Jews heard these messages, too, he said: "Non-Jewish people who come into our community are made to feel like they are an enemy, or at very best that we have to put up with them." He described an interfaith couple in which one partner was a seemingly unflappable military man: "I thought literally he was going to cry because of how he'd been treated." The man was "shocked" when Rabbi R told him, "I just want to connect to you as a person."

Several other rabbis told me that they did not believe that rabbis still rejected intermarried couples, and one Orthodox rabbi felt that the tide had turned so completely in favor of welcoming the intermarried that no one was even trying to make a case for endogamy anymore. However, Rabbi R's stories of couples with whom he had met and the accounts of many of the intermarried couples I interviewed suggest the opposite. Rabbi R said that, in the past nine years, he had experienced twelve to fifteen situations much like the one I've just described. This gap in rabbis' perceptions may have had to do with their different sets of experiences in daily life and how they perceived discourses on intermarriage.

When working with interfaith couples and non-Jews in his community, Rabbi R kept anti-intermarriage messages in mind, hoping to compensate by being especially welcoming to non-Jews. He felt this responsibility because of the painful rejections many of them had experienced, but he also relied on his understanding of Jewish values: "I know it's not a Jewish value to humiliate people. The Talmud says humiliating somebody is like murdering them. So what makes it okay in these instances?" When he talked with non-Jews, Rabbi R emphasized that he was "an ambassador . . . for and to the Jewish community. And so I'm, like, 'Let me welcome you. Let me explain to you how this community works. And at this point, you've probably experienced a little bit of the nuttiness, and I hope that I can help you see that as endearing rather than offensive.'" He felt that the negative messages not only harmed individuals but also undercut the purported goal of Jewish continuity: "Our fear and our elitism make us show the worst of our tradition and not the best. Ultimately, I think that's a failing solution for how we're going to handle continuity from here on out." Rabbi R's approach to intermarriage required a balance between caring for individual persons and respecting Jewish tradition and values.

Few, if any, of the rabbis I interviewed would have characterized themselves as insensitive to individuals. In distinguishing between Jews and non-Jews for the purposes of leading their communities and helping individuals and couples, rabbis drew on divergent understandings of Jewishness and the purposes of boundaries. The privilege of membership in the Jewish covenant came with the responsibility to respect Judaism's integrity, they agreed, but they understood this integrity in different ways.

Covenant and Authority

In interviews, rabbis frequently used the language of covenant, which did not appear in the panel discussions that I observed. These rabbis integrated their understanding of Jews' relationship with God with their communities' needs and the actual intermarried Jews who sought their guidance or assistance. Rabbis who chose to officiate at intermarriages saw personal autonomy as clearly reconcilable with an authentic understanding of Judaism. Those who flatly opposed intermarriage and would not accommodate it in any way similarly held their own clear understandings of Judaism's boundaries. But those in the middle, whose opposition to intermarriage collided with many laypeople's limited interest in rabbinic authority, faced difficult challenges both in practical terms and in definitions of Jewish continuity. Divergent understandings of Jewishness challenged rabbis' communications with one another as well as with laypeople.

Rabbi R felt that, as a Jewish leader, he was responsible for honoring both the Jewish people's particular relationship with God and the value of individual persons, Jewish or not. "I'm from a movement that believes that Judaism continues to evolve," he explained. "I'm hoping [what] continues is the flourishing of a Jewish vision and ideal of a just world." In his view, Jewish continuity lay in Jews' continued practice of "social justice." He said, "I'm just as concerned about peoplehood continuing as the next rabbi [is]; I just so think that they're doing it wrong." He constructed his understanding of social justice from a combination of his own instincts and experiences and Jewish textual sources:

> [In the Torah] you have these texts of unity [with outsiders] and these texts of separation [from outsiders]. So, I'm an out gay rabbi. I understand what it feels like to be separated. So, that's where, I mean it comes from instinct. It really comes from this place of both saying . . . I am valid, and that nobody can give me that validity, and nobody can take it away. And I had to get to that point. And so, that voice is the inner voice that informs me; . . . it's the small, still voice that our text talks about [see 1 Kings 19:11–12].
>
> So for me, there's always this inner godly piece that connects with the external godly piece of the text. And . . . there's a dialogue. Text is less important to me than probably [it is to] a lot of other rabbis because I don't see the text as God speaking. I really see the text as humanity's struggle to hear God's voice.

Rabbi R's view of Judaism focused particularly on ideals and values that could be translated into action by Jews and non-Jews alike. Authenticity and validity were located within the individual, and individuals pursued relationships with God in ways that resonated with their own instincts and experiences.

Of the thirteen Atlanta rabbis I interviewed, Rabbi R and Reform Rabbi G, who spoke of the "universal human family," along with two other Reform rabbis, were the most willing to accommodate intermarriage. These four rabbis officiated at interfaith weddings, though they did not co-officiate with Christian clergy. They distinguished between Jews and non-Jews for ritual purposes, doing so in the most welcoming ways they could. An intermediate, more moderate group of rabbis included one traditionalist Reform rabbi and four Conservative rabbis (ranging from self-described "liberal" to "Conservadox"), who did not officiate at interfaith weddings. The Conservative rabbis were in this group because, as my Conservative informants told me, the Rabbinical Assembly did not permit its members to officiate at interfaith weddings. This policy aligned with the rabbis' own views. The Reform movement's rabbinical organization, the Central Conference of American Rabbis, opposed rabbinic officiation but permitted individual rabbis to come to their own decisions about it, according to a 1909 decision affirmed in 1973 (McGinity 2009, 127).

Reform Rabbi M had decided against officiating because he felt it was inconsistent with his responsibility to the Jewish people and their particular covenant with God. He was careful to add that this decision did not constitute rejection or condemnation of intermarried people as individuals:

> Some people say it is [rejection], but I want folks to understand that Jewish liturgy and Christian liturgy, there's integrity to it and there's authenticity to it. Nobody in the Catholic Church, for example, or in the Jewish community wants me as a rabbi to go to a church as a guest and receive communion. . . . So when I use our liturgy, even as a Reform rabbi, where I might make certain modifications, reforms, the liturgy is designed for folks who engage in a particular covenant with the Jewish people and with God within the Jewish framework, and that's the part that I don't feel like I can participate in or officiate.

Rabbi M framed the issue of officiating at an intermarriage as being about symbolism and boundaries. Because he represented both the Jewish community and Judaism in his capacity as a rabbi, he did not want to give the impression that Jewish boundaries were completely porous. In other words, he wanted to preserve the exclusivity of the Jewish covenant with God. Another Reform rabbi, who did officiate at intermarriages, was similarly concerned with boundaries, specifying that any weddings at which he officiated had to be strictly Jewish and could not involve participation from Christian clergy or mention Jesus.

In "Why I Won't Perform an Intermarriage," Reform rabbi Maurice Davis (1988) explains his refusal to officiate in a similar way. The Jewish wedding ceremony assumes that the bride and groom are both Jews and that their commitment to one another takes place in the context of "the faith of Moses and of Israel." But in an intermarriage, either the non-Jewish partner or the rabbi has to "pretend" that the situation is otherwise, which would be "inauthentic." Further, Davis believes that his resistance helps to channel more non-Jewish partners of Jews toward conversion to Judaism, which he sees as a desirable end (20–21). Rabbi M and Rabbi Davis both made a simultaneously pragmatic and symbolic argument against officiating at an intermarriage. As Rabbi M explained, "it's more than me officiating, and I'm not responsible only to the couple. I'm responsible to the covenant with the Jewish people and with God. And that's what makes it that much harder for me. . . . I am responsible for the individuals as well, and nobody likes to be told no; . . . in our world that's just rejection or condemnation. But if anybody ever sits with me, they're not going to ever hear that unless they have decided beforehand." All the rabbis I interviewed shared concern for setting the boundaries of the community and its practices. While some intermarried couples may have been able to understand or sympathize with Rabbi M's distinction, many of my intermarried informants did not. Because rabbis had refused to officiate at their weddings, they were sure that they would be rejected and shunned by Conservative and Orthodox rabbis and their congregations.

Like Rabbi M, some rabbis turned this judgment back on the couples themselves. One Conservative rabbi said, "People come in, they have a chip on their shoulder, somebody blinked at them, and they say, 'Oh, they shunned me.' Nobody shunned you." An Orthodox rabbi said, "People with psychological issues, or any issue, when they don't feel like they're a part of things, they project that onto the people who are there." While the rabbis felt that they were welcoming as a rule, they saw that couples sometimes perceived them to be unwelcoming because they had delineated the boundaries of the religious community.

The couples and the rabbis appeared to have different ideas of what it meant to be welcomed. The rabbis felt that it was not only within their purview but actually their job to set and gently enforce the community's boundaries, allowing laypeople to make their own judgments about whether they wanted to participate in the community. But in some cases, the laypeople seemed to feel that it was unreasonable for the rabbis to set any limits on their religious lives and participation. These couples felt that *welcoming* should mean "no strings attached," an approach similar to Rabbi R's and to the Jewish Outreach Institute's. For example, JOI's mission statement discusses engaging intermarried couples but never mentions conversion. This suggests a religious framework that does not distinguish between the covenant of the Jewish people and the individualism of American culture. Especially for people attempting to practice both Judaism and Christianity, whether as religion or heritage in their families, American and Jewish frameworks were not separate.

All of my rabbinic informants felt that the Jewish framework—covenant—entailed mutual responsibilities with and toward other Jews. For the Orthodox rabbis I interviewed, Jewish law formed the basis of these responsibilities: observing Jewish law enacts the responsibilities and privileges of this covenant with other Jews, constantly and consistently. While Rabbi M resisted the authority of Jewish law, saying that "as a Reform Jew, as a Reform rabbi, there are times when I will challenge [it]," he agreed that Jews were mutually bound by their covenant. Rabbi M argued that intermarriage was wrong not because it was against Jewish law but because it stepped outside the "covenantal relationships" between Jews. He was concerned with the integrity of the symbols and narratives of the Jewish people rather than of Jewish law. Intermarried couples could adopt this symbolic language, but only if they chose to operate within the system and agreed not to mix it with others.

The Conservative rabbis I interviewed managed the gap between their own philosophies and their congregants' needs or wishes in different ways. The most liberal of them, Rabbi J, proactively sought congregants' ideas on how to "embrace" intermarried couples in congregational life while remaining within the bounds of Jewish law. He attempted to meet intermarried congregants' felt needs to affirm their membership among the Jewish people through Jewish ritual; but like Rabbi M, he resisted their requests to change Jewish ritual to suit their personal wishes. For example, a Jewish woman married to a non-Jewish man wanted Rabbi J to officiate at a naming ceremony for her infant son, whom she chose not to circumcise. Jewish law requires circumcision as part of entering a male Jew into the covenant, either as an infant or as a convert, and the custom of doing a naming ceremony for female Jewish infants is a recent, extra-halakhic practice. Jewish law does not forbid it; it is simply not addressed. Rabbi J said that he ultimately would like to help the woman affirm her own and her son's Jewishness, but he was unable to do so publicly and was uncomfortable doing so privately in his office. He did not feel able to officiate at a ritual that did not exist in Jewish tradition instead of performing the appropriate existing ritual. While Jewish law made the limits clear to Rabbi J, that clarity did not prevent intermarried Jews from asking him to officiate at rituals beyond his limits.

Conservative rabbis K and L did not report any such requests from intermarried Jews, but they also did not describe themselves as embracing intermarried couples. Rabbi L's approach was to lead his congregation in an egalitarian but otherwise traditional observance of Judaism, making clear distinctions between Jews and non-Jews in ritual. He did not feel that outreach was part of his work, though he did work with candidates for conversion: "We try to create a place in which the non-Jewish spouse wants to come over naturally, experiences and grows into the feeling of [being Jewish]—from a short sojourn into a dwelling." In this view, conversion of the non-Jewish spouse would be the ideal end, but Rabbi L did not push for it because he felt it was pointless from a pragmatic standpoint. Likewise, he did not feel that preaching against intermarriage was a useful expenditure of energy:

> I don't preach anti-intermarriage ever. I don't ever. What's the point? I counsel, I work with people, it's a personal thing. What am I going to stand up and say, "Rabbi's against intermarriage," right? I mean, give me a break. This is a stupid sermon topic. Anybody who it actually applies to, you only run the risk of alienating them, and everyone else, it's like apple pie. Who could be against it? Who could be against "Marry Jewish and raise a Jewish family"? That's like, you know, I'm for lower taxes, too.

Rabbi L's refusal to embrace intermarriage may have freed him from some of the entreaties that Rabbi J received from his congregants. Nevertheless, he felt that pushing for conversion and preaching against intermarriage were pointless because both efforts would only fail when confronted by laypeople's claims of personal autonomy.

Viewing Judaism as a choice, Rabbi L acknowledged that the relationship between the mission of the Jewish people and individuals' ability to choose whether to be obligated to carry it out was still unclear: "In some future day, what defines the idealized future Jewishly is that all the nations of the world will recognize God." Jews were to achieve this universalistic goal in a particularistic way. "And don't we believe that, at least for the Jewish people, any who really want to join them, that Judaism actually offers a way to do your small part to make that reality come true? To make a world [in] which all recognize the kingship of God and the ethical imperative that that implies." He hoped to inspire people to take part in this mission but said that the Jewish community was not sure how the social fact of personal autonomy fit with this mission.

This lack of clarity may be the reason that so many of the rabbis in this middle category focused only on the practical aspects of intermarriage: not only were they relevant to Judaism, but they could be handled easily. The individualism of Jews who insisted on religious personal autonomy ultimately implied universalism, a lack of substantive difference between Jewishness and any other religious identification. The challenge for Rabbi L and other Conservative rabbis was to translate this particularistic Jewish mission into laypeople's language of personal autonomy and universalism.

For Conservative Rabbi E, the murkiness of a Jewishness always determined by choice, even as it was also "what you are," evoked a sense of hopelessness and betrayal. "There are [intermarried Jews] that just disappear, and it breaks my heart. Breaks my heart. You pour so much into people. You have thousands of years of tradition behind every one of these children and every one of these young adults, and then they go to college. They fall in love, I don't want to say [with] the wrong person, but they fall in love with somebody that doesn't share their same spiritual history and vision, and thousands of years are done. That's how fragile it is." According to Rabbi E, the universalistic Jewish mission that Rabbi L articulated was impossible to carry out without the corresponding particularism of Jewish in-marriage.

Rabbi E felt that personal autonomy had already overwhelmingly won over loyalty to Judaism. With a sad nostalgia, he told me the following anecdote to demonstrate that there was no going back to the days when people were loyal to Judaism:

> A fairly traditional couple from the synagogue . . . caught me at the beginning of services a couple of years ago. Their son went to day school and yeshiva and everything and was living with a non-Jewish woman, and it was a serious relationship, though marriage was not imminent. What they said to me was that, had they belonged to the synagogue when their son was younger and [he] would have been exposed to me, I would have redirected his life, given him the proper priorities, and they said, "He

wouldn't be with that shiksa." That was the line: "wouldn't be with that shiksa."

I looked at them, and I said to them, "Let me explain something to you. In the early days of the synagogue, I taught every bar and bat mitzvah. I went to their birthday parties. I took the kids to Six Flags. I did everything with them, and today 50 percent of the weddings I can participate [in] and . . . perform, 50 percent I cannot go to." I said, "So sociology is bigger than all of us," and that's an anecdote to explain the reality of our world.

Rabbi E did not believe that sociology should be more powerful than covenant, but he felt that it was the reality that mattered to intermarried Jews. Yet the parents of intermarried or interdating Jews also misunderstood the problem: they blamed themselves or the lack of proper childhood influences for these relationships. In reality, Rabbi E said, there was nothing they could have done differently.

The parents' and the rabbi's efforts made no difference, Rabbi E explained, because Jews who intermarried were basically speaking a different language. When he discussed with such couples why intermarriage was wrong, "I try to explain it to them in their terms." The argument that the Torah prohibits intermarriage was not "going to wash with these couples" because, if it did, they would not have been interested in intermarrying in the first place. Instead, he attempted to evoke feelings of loyalty to family or the Jewish people by conveying to the couple that their children probably would not have an enduring Jewish identity. The statistics on intermarriage that have featured so prominently in intermarriage discourse were a key part of his argument. If Jews were a majority of the population, he explained, children of intermarriage would absorb Jewishness from their surroundings and would be likely to identify with Judaism throughout their lives. If that were the case, then he might not oppose intermarriage as strongly. But "where we are now, clearly the statistics are that when there's an intermarriage, the chances are . . . one out of ten, maybe, that the kids will be Jewish. So that's the way I try to explain it to them, also without being nasty, and I always offer to counsel and to help and so forth." Using the language of personal autonomy rather than the language of innate, immutable Jewishness, Rabbi E hoped that his pragmatic approach would make an impression on the couples.

Even though Rabbi E had devised strategies to dissuade Jews from marrying non-Jews or to encourage conversion when the couples were determined to marry anyway, he conveyed deep sadness and frustration at the changes in the American Jewish population that, he said, have fractured the wholeness of the community. "There is a great effort underway now by federations and others to try and bring in interfaith couples, take them on trips to Israel, do outreach, . . . if not [to] get the non-Jewish partner to convert, to at least get a guarantee in some fashion that the children will be raised as Jews." He felt that these efforts were unlikely to yield the desired results and questioned whether money should be spent "to bring people back who have betrayed, have done something that clearly puts them outside the pale of the future." Referring to intermarrying Jews as "converts," Rabbi E equated intermarriage with conversion to Christianity. Yet he acknowledged that contemporary intermarriage might hold different meanings than it had in the past:

> What is different about this generation of converts from [converts in] the past is that in the past when people used to convert, very often it was to spite their parents; they hated their religion and this was their path to get out. . . . Marrying somebody not Jewish, the blonde goddess. . . . Today there's no anger necessarily or no spite or no nastiness. . . . Their religion has become America. It's not their own religion. . . . I mean to me, it's just the fact that there's no loyalty anymore in anything. It's got nothing to do with religion alone. It's with sports, it's with politics, it's everything. Everybody's just into whatever they want to do.

Rabbi E was trapped between his deep desire to continue the Jewish people's existence free of Christian influence and the apparent inevitability of American cultural norms, which he believed inspired self-focus to the point of disloyalty. His view corresponded to sociological research on the decline of American communal life in general (Bellah et al. 1985, 1991; Putnam 2000). Despite clear connections between the phenomenon of intermarriage and broader American cultural trends, he was unwilling to deal with the language of personal autonomy with which other Conservative rabbis struggled because, to him, it was so far outside of, even a betrayal of, his understanding of Judaism as the covenant relationship of a people who have a particular mission.

Orthodox rabbis sidestepped some of the issues created by the centrality of personal autonomy because they used a frame emphasizing the obligations of Jews to God and each other. Like Rabbi E and other rabbinic informants, Orthodox informants felt that no Jewish people could exist without the Jews' covenant with God and the attendant obligations that Jews owe to God. Rabbi E seemed to assume that these obligations existed but felt that the language of personal autonomy was so overwhelmingly strong in the people with whom he worked that it was hopeless to even bring up these obligations to God with them. In contrast, my Orthodox informants made Jews' obligations to God and each other the centerpiece of their approach to intermarried couples.

Embracing "What You Are"

Orthodox Rabbi Z hoped to inspire less-observant Jews to embrace their mission as part of God's chosen people. He explained his understanding of Jews' mission as being "to serve non-Jews" and, in doing so, to serve "God's purpose." After having tried and failed twice to form "a world where there would be a spiritual brotherhood of man, so to speak, and people would recognize God and live well," he explained, "God shifted gears and said, 'Okay, one exemplar nation will be the teachers, and [it will undertake] a different way of going about educating people.'" God selected the Jewish people to teach others, Rabbi Z said. In order to carry out this mission, "each individual has to maintain their own holiness, their own connection to God; that's the first step in maintaining nationhood." When Jews maintain holiness by observing Jewish law, they serve as an example to other nations. "So we fail in that mission when each individual is not connected and each individual is not learned, educated, and engaged in daily Jewish life." Individual Jews' actions affected the ability of the entire Jewish people to meet its obligations to God. The language of personal autonomy was conspicuously absent from this formulation, as was hopelessness or worry about speaking to less observant Jews "in their terms." The relevant terms, for Rabbi Z, were the obligations of the Jewish people to God and the world.

Orthodox Rabbi X articulated the Jewish mission similarly but used the language of "family." The Jewish people, he said, was "a family that's devoted exclusively to testifying that there is a creator of the universe." By observing Jewish law, people fulfilled their role of demonstrating "what it's like to be in a close, intimate relationship with the Creator of the universe." Rabbi X believed that Jews must focus on their mission and that non-Jews, who do not share this mission, should "watch us, learn from us, be inspired by us." This mission was the basis of his outreach to nonobservant Jews. Observing Jewish law for self-satisfaction or only for the sake of other religious Jews was wrong, he said. Rather, outreach to non-observant Jews to help them become more observant and connected to their Jewish heritage was work toward testifying to the Creator. "What it is to be a Jew is to be responsible for the whole world, and we're only Jewish for the world, and we're not chosen elevated over the world; we're chosen to bear responsibility for the world. And if we can't impact the world, we have no reason to exist."

Aside from Rabbi R, who emphasized social justice work as the focus of Jewish continuity, the Orthodox rabbis I interviewed were the only ones to focus on this Jewish mission in response to my question about the meaning of *Jewish continuity*. Rabbi X elaborated: "It's like we're brought into being only because there's a God, and the world itself was created only to know God. . . . Other than that, I think the continuity discussion is a joke. It's a waste of time—who the hell cares if there are Jews in the room; let's just be good people." He shared the concern frequently aired in continuity discourse that intermarriage and loosening religious boundaries could lead to a shrinking Jewish population. But that discourse often shied away from discussing theological matters, instead focusing on assimilation itself. In contrast, Rabbi X clearly articulated intermarriage as a threat to Jews' mission, saying that it would "dilute our message" and "dilute our identity."

Some Orthodox rabbis did outreach to unaffiliated Jews because they felt it was their duty to the Jewish people and to God to bring other Jews closer to Jewish observance. Creating a fully Jewishly identified family was part of that aim because the nuclear family was a microcosm of the global Jewish family. Intermarriage, like low affiliation with Jewish organizations, was a symptom of the failure of an earlier generation of Jews to inculcate Jewishness in their children. Parents had to demonstrate what it meant to be Jewish to their children, or they would have no right to expect that their children would understand themselves as Jews or marry other Jews, said a third Orthodox rabbi, Rabbi Y:

> The problem . . . is if you allow [intermarried couples to participate publicly in Jewish life], then are you somehow, some way, covertly encouraging [intermarriage]? . . . So if you make it so comfortable, then the next generation of this one says, "Okay, no, no, no, Mom and Dad, I won't do it." The next generation says, "What's the reason?"
>
> And so you have the four children at the seder [the Passover ritual meal]. Right, you know that. So they represent four generations. *Chacham* is the first generation that came in the old country, and they knew exactly what was right, what was wrong.
>
> What's next? The *rashah*. Rashah is not evil in that sense; he just doesn't know. Rashah says, "Why this, why that?" It was never taught because the first generation came, they were so keen on earning a living they didn't have time to teach.
>
> The next child is the *tam*. The simple one. The simple one remembers the grandfather and then is confused. Granddad was religious, but Dad is not. "What's going on? What's happening? Who am I?"
>
> The fourth generation . . . can't even ask the question. Can't even ask. You know the *sh'ayno yodea lishoal*? Can't even ask, "What is this, what's going on?"
>
> So the same issue is, you and I are talking now, and so we have a common language. Do we not? There's a common language, a common value system. Down the line, there may not be. I'm not talking about your children, I'm talking about for people that have a common language like us down the line. So that's the fear. So the fear is if you're going to make it so easy, not for conversion but acceptance without conversion, then what?

This interpretation of the four sons in the Passover seder derives from Samson Raphael Hirsch, the founder of modern Orthodoxy in nineteenth-century Germany. His point was, according to Elie Wiesel in *A Passover Haggadah* (1993), that "there is regression and loss. The more removed each generation is from Sinai, the less it knows, the more complacent it becomes." Rabbi Y used this story to point out that the current widespread nonobservance of Jewish law was not due to Jews' purposeful resistance but to ignorance. Thus, outreach and education could overcome this ignorance and bring Jews back to religious observance. But his observation that Jews' common language was gradually eroding could be applied not just to the gap between observant and nonobservant Jews but even to rabbis who used the same Jewish vocabulary to convey widely varying meanings.

The proper way to work with intermarried Jews was under the umbrella of more general outreach, the Orthodox rabbis told me. In other words, intermarried Jews were not a distinct group but part of a broader collection of Jews who did not observe Jewish law. This might seem like splitting hairs to people who see intermarried and unaffiliated Jews as essentially the same group, but framing the situation in this way mattered to my Orthodox informants because the distinction reflected the boundaries around acceptable Jewish behaviors. Thus, Rabbi Z argued that unaffiliated Jews, whom he said surveys described as "happy to be Jewish," were unaffiliated with Jewish institutions only because they had not found satisfactory ways into the Jewish community. They also misunderstood synagogues, expecting to find spiritual fulfillment in them when really Jewish spirituality was centered in the home. It happened that many of the unaffiliated Jews were indeed intermarried, but Rabbi Z and Rabbi X saw their ignorance of Judaism, not spite toward their Jewish heritage, as the cause of intermarriage. Thus, the two rabbis focused on outreach to the unaffiliated as a remedy for the heart of the problem of nonobservant Jews.

In their outreach work, these Orthodox rabbis consciously resisted "welcoming" the intermarried. Non-Orthodox groups sometimes emphasize welcoming non-Jewish partners of Jews into the Jewish community with the hope that a warm reception will persuade the non-Jew eventually to convert. The Union for Reform Judaism (2005) describes this commitment on its website: "Asking someone you care about to consider conversion is simply an invitation. It is not coercion or pressure. It is an expression of valuing the individual and a desire to share a tradition that you consider precious." Rabbis X, Y, and Z saw welcoming, even with the ulterior motive of seeking conversions, as completely wrong-headed and likely to worsen the problem of intermarriage. Rabbi Z said, "Recognition of a couple that [is] intermarried is fine. I mean, it's reality." But he distinguished between recognition and acceptance, saying that acceptance was essentially "promoting" intermarriage: "As soon as you talk about interfaith dating positively, and how to get along while you're dating, and determining if you're going to get married, that tells me you're promoting—at least accepting—intermarriage, and that is such a disaster in our community." In other words, treating intermarriage as a social fact to be approached pragmatically would ultimately be a self-fulfilling prophecy. As the community worked to become more welcoming, it would only increase the number of intermarriages because people would feel comfortable with intermarriage. According to this logic, the increase in intermarriage would inhibit the Jewish people's ability to fulfill its mission to be a holy nation because it would no longer be a separate people that could model a close relationship with God through an observant life. Actively contributing to this increase would amount to betraying God, in Rabbi Z's view.

Orthodox rabbis X, Y, and Z said that they addressed issues caused by intermarriage in individual people's lives on a case-by-case basis, welcoming individual intermarried Jews into their communities if those Jews were sincerely interested in learning about Judaism and becoming more observant. However, they would not publicly discuss intermarriage in welcoming terms because they felt that this could lessen the stigma that they felt intermarriage deserved. This delicate balance was lost on many of the intermarried couples that these rabbis might have worked with, as Rabbi X acknowledged:

> We do have an image problem out there. The problem is that many couples who are involved in a proposed intermarriage have some voice in their head that's condemning them. Somebody in their family, could be their parents, are condemning them, and therefore the level of guilt they have with that voice is such that they expect the Orthodox guy to come down hard on them. So they already know what we're going to say. Most of the time the traditional relative in a Jewish family does such a horrible job in representing the three-dimensional approach of an Orthodox cleric that [the intermarried Jew doesn't] even get to the Orthodox guy. They assume that I am their aunt times ten, I'm absolutely the wrath of God will be brought upon you; that kind of thing, and I'm going to sit there and talk to them about you're going to go to hell if you marry this girl. That's what they think I'm going to say, which I'll never say.

Between couples' family experiences and the public rhetoric in intermarriage discourse, many of these couples reflexively avoided Orthodox rabbis and communities. The rabbis took issue with the couples' assumption that they would be unwelcome in Orthodox communities because, they argued, the couples did not understand the full context of their disapproval of intermarriage, just as Reform Rabbi M described concerning his experiences. But couples were unlikely to approach the rabbis for a fuller explanation of the condemning language they had heard in intermarriage discourse, particularly when they were starting with the assumption of personal autonomy rather than of obligation. In other words, if Orthodox rabbis could not or would not discuss their more nuanced view of intermarriage in public, how would intermarried couples know that this nuanced view existed?

Orthodox rabbis interested in outreach to the intermarried were in a bind. How could they reach intermarried Jews who remained scared of them because of the public face rabbis had to wear for the sake of discouraging further intermarriage? JOI avoids the entire question of discouraging further intermarriage, but to the Orthodox rabbis, this approach failed to convey the seriousness of the issue. Even worse, said Rabbi Z, more liberal outreach groups were spreading what he saw as misinformation about Jewish tradition—for instance, claiming that figures from the Bible, such as Joseph and Moses, could be understood as intermarried based on the text itself. Rabbi Z objected to such readings as "disingenuous" because they ignored later rabbinic interpretation of the texts. Biblical figures from before the revelation at Mount Sinai could not have intermarried, he explained, because they were Israelites, not Jews. Only after Jewish law was given at Mount Sinai could Jews be expected to follow Jewish law as such, although "based on the character of Joseph and Moses, it's really homiletically inconceivable" that they could have intermarried in the way that contemporary Jews understand intermarriage. Rabbi Z said that when he explains this to intermarried Jews, "their eyes are widened and they find it very interesting. It unfortunately, or fortunately, undermines the credibility of the sources" of the misinformation.

If my Orthodox rabbinic informants encountered an opportunity to teach intermarried couples about intermarriage, the "open agenda" was for conversion of the non-Jewish spouse to Judaism, with an explicit explanation of how the conversion would serve the Jewish people's mission. Rabbi X said:

> We actually believe, according to Jewish law, and we believe that Jewish law is an expression of God's will, so we actually believe that Jews should not be married to non-Jews. Particularly, our greatest concern of course is when a Jewish woman is married to a non-Jewish man, the children are Jewish, and therefore we have actual extant Jewish children at risk, so to speak, because they are the product of an intermarriage, and therefore we say that our goal would be to inspire the non-Jewish spouse to convert. Now we don't do this publicly because we don't want to destigmatize intermarriage. We don't want to tell people, "Go ahead and intermarry; later on we'll deal with your non-Jewish spouse," because the likelihood of that happening is relatively low. . . . So we're very overt about the fact that we don't believe that intermarriage is a good thing. On the other hand, we don't condemn them. We try to reserve judgment and not really make them feel immorally assessed. Most people didn't make a moral decision to intermarry against some moral standard, they just got intermarried.

He pointed out, however, that if the couple had not yet married, the more appropriate move was to end the relationship. Jewish law forbade conversion for the sake of marriage, but an existing marriage presented a different situation:

> The law says—it's a very clear, classic Mishnaic source—that one who converts for the sake of marriage is not allowed to marry that person they intended to marry. So the conversion is valid, but they're not allowed to marry them, they have to marry somebody else. . . . So generally we understand that when [an intermarried] couple had access to each other and were living fine with each other as man and wife, and have nothing to gain by him or her converting because they already have each other, they have children, they're accepted as Mr. and Mrs. So-and-so, so that's not considered a conversion for the sake of marriage because they're already married. Whereas if a couple comes and their parents are saying, "Rabbi, do something," or the groom doesn't want to oppose his parents and so he's coming as a last resort with his non-Jewish spouse and he wants you to convert [her], that's a different story.

These distinctions are not reflected in broader discourses, perhaps partly because of the Orthodox refusal to discuss intermarriage publicly except to forbid it and partly because these distinctions might not mean much outside the framework of Jewish law. In other words, if the audience listening to an argument about halakhic distinctions does not share the assumption that halakhah is authoritative and obligatory, it may not find these arguments at all persuasive.

While the rabbis used the same vocabulary to talk about intermarriage, this vocabulary did not reside in a shared framework. Intermarriage in a context of personal meaning and symbolism carries different consequences than it does in a context of obligations to God that must be fulfilled both individually and as a people. Rabbinic informants rarely cited specific Jewish texts as the basis for their thoughts about intermarriage; rather, they cited their own experiences and their individual moral compasses. Their views were shaped by both their sense that Judaism is "what you are" and their conscious, explicit commitment to covenant, beliefs, and practices. Their understandings of Jewishness were certainly more sophisticated than my intermarried informants', but the same conceptual tensions of universalist individualism and ethnic familialism were present in them. The tensions in these rabbis' comments demonstrate that even religious experts disagree about the meanings of monolithic terms such as *the Jewish people, Jewish identity*, and *Jewish continuity*. The intense focus on intermarriage in public discourse and the lack of personal interaction among rabbis with divergent views on the topic disguise this disagreement and tension.

6

Moving Forward, Inconclusively

The Crisis of Jewish Identity

In intermarriage discourse, Conservative Rabbi E, history professor Jack Wertheimer, and others have raised the question of whether Jewish institutions' limited financial and human resources ought to be directed toward outreach to intermarried couples when they could instead be directed toward endogamous couples (see, for example, Wertheimer 2001). They feel that intermarried Jews' marriage choices clearly show their lack of loyalty to Judaism. Yet the kinds of programming inspired by the perceived need for outreach attract endogamous, presumably "loyal" Jewish couples as well. Endogamous Jews who are similar to my intermarried informants welcome the programming directed at intermarried couples because it suits their needs. One Jewish woman named Karen, whom I met at an outreach event, was incensed at what she perceived as the outreach organization's assumption that endogamous Jewish families do not need guidance to create a Jewish home. As Karen's story suggests, the categories of *intermarried* and *endogamous* obscure the common needs and experiences of Jews in general.

"It's outrageous. We want to learn and do Shabbat activities, too, and we're not supposed to come because we're both Jewish!" Karen told me over her shoulder as she encouraged her toddler to imitate a Shabbat song leader's hand motions. Karen and her husband had brought their two small children to a Shabbat afternoon event for interfaith families at the Atlanta Jewish community center. As she filled out the sign-in sheet, Karen informed the event organizer, a veteran Jewish educator of interfaith families, in no uncertain terms that she was displeased. She did not begrudge interfaith families their event; it was just that she wanted to be included.

"We need to learn, too!" she insisted. As she vented to me, I nodded sympathetically. Although the loud music prevented us from having further conversation, I later heard her reiterate her frustration to other couples.

The theory behind such programming for intermarried Jews is that they need opportunities to learn the content and the choreography of Jewish practices as well as a chance to connect with other families like them. "Basic Judaism" courses are often filled by intermarrying couples, so much so that a few students in such courses who are not intermarried or intermarrying have told me that they feel awkward and out of place. The association between intermarriage and basic instruction in Judaism suggests an underlying assumption that intermarried couples need to learn how to participate in Jewish community.

Karen's feelings of exclusion from the opportunity for basic instruction in Judaism illustrate my contention that dominant cultural narratives about intermarriage draw a stark line between intermarried and endogamous couples. This boundary exists not only in talk; it is instituted in programming and takes shape in the lived experiences of both intermarried and endogamous Jews. Ultimately, this boundary obscures a more central, common issue: American Jews' experience of Jewishness is often self-contradictory.

Misleading discursive distinctions equate Jewish loyalty with endogamy and apostasy or indifference with intermarriage, emphasizing the difference between intermarried and endogamous Jews. But Steven Cohen and Arnold Eisen (2000) found that, like my intermarried informants, "moderately affiliated" Jews looked to the "sovereign self" as their religious authority. Both their informants and mine also spoke of their sense of Jewishness as being innate. Wertheimer (2001) has lamented what he sees as a lack of concern among individualistic intermarried Jews about the future of Judaism. But the language of individualism has so deeply penetrated American Jews' consciousness that, at least for non-Orthodox Jews, it is inextricable from their conceptions of their own Jewishness. This discursive division between intermarried and endogamous Jews does not reflect sociological reality.

Contrary to dominant cultural narratives, religious norms still exert some control over the actions of my intermarried Jewish informants—paradoxically, through the cultural idiom of individualism. The discourses on intermarriage that I have explored in this book suggest that intermarried Jews have rejected Judaism's basic premises of the authority of Jewish law and peoplehood. My fieldwork, however, shows that they have not rejected it but have revised it in complicated and often self-contradictory ways. My informants feel that they should conform to religious rules and traditions in their own ways, for reasons having to do with family and self rather than God. For them, religious tradition may hold the shape that it held in previous generations, but it is filled with a content that is drastically different: it now focuses on the self as the main arbiter of Jewishness, even when there is a heartfelt claim of deference to tradition.

In my research, intermarried couples as well as religious experts drew on universalist individualist and ethnic familialist discourses to frame their families' religious lives. These discourses departed from halakhic understandings of Jewishness and incorporated American cultural understandings of individualism, kinship, and religion. In the Mothers Circle, universalist individualism and ethnic familialism contributed to the goal of Jewish continuity; in the Dovetail context, they more often contributed to "tolerance" and "respect" within the family. While my intermarried informants experienced some clerical and communal disapproval of their marital choices, it did not prevent them from marrying whomever they chose. Yet religious institutions and norms continued to be relevant to their lives in that the couples continued to argue with them, as the Dovetail conference participants did when venting their frustration with the "old, irrelevant boxes" that they thought traditional ideas imposed upon them. They sought religious experiences and connections with religious communities but resisted norms with which they did not personally identify.

For universalist individualists, "what you choose" and "what's in your heart" were the determining idioms for religious experience. Having Jewishly identified children was a matter of personal choice and negotiation between spouses, perhaps out of allegiance to one spouse's heritage, perhaps out of religious conviction. In this view, Jewish traditionalists' claims that Jewishness must follow halakhic rules were irrelevant because these rules were externally imposed. As much as "what's in your heart" mattered to universalist individualists, they also relied on their claim to Jewish heritage. They understood this claim to be entirely legitimate and supported by the special understanding of it that they had as "prophetic outcasts." Universalist individualists strongly privileged personal autonomy and understood Jewishness through that lens.

Ethnic familialists valued personal autonomy, but their loyalty to the Jewish people was also important to them. They expressed this loyalty not as a set of religious beliefs but as an inchoate sense of "what you are." Their choices to raise Jewishly identified children were rooted in a felt need for their children to be Jews. Ethnic familialist intermarried Jews felt that if their children were to identify with Jesus and Christianity, the children would be foreign to them. Their self-definition as Jews and as Americans uneasily coexisted as they attempted to balance personal autonomy and mutual obligation.

Individuals internalized Jewishness, according to my ethnic familialist informants, through emotional attachments developed through religious experiences. For many, these experiences occurred in childhood, but for some of the Mothers Circle women, they also occurred through their own experiences as parents. These experiences led them to their own versions of Jewishness, even when they did not hold formal membership in the Jewish community. They found their way into these religious experiences using universalist individualist discourses that allowed them to participate in Jewish rituals without sharing Jewish beliefs, and some eventually came to experience these rituals in the more visceral sense that their husbands did.

Whether or not they could "make Judaism their own," the Mothers Circle women's universalist individualism enabled their husbands to contribute to the agenda of Jewish continuity. Relying on both universalist individualist and ethnic familialist discourses, the women developed their own way of understanding their participation in their Jewish families, one that emphasized religious similarities and women's religious leadership in the home. At the same time, their husbands often identified with Jewishness through ethnic familialism but were unable to articulate their attachments to Judaism in rational language. Because their Jewishness was primarily familial and ethnic, these men might not have been motivated or able to create the experiences needed to foster their children's emotional attachments to Judaism. But their wives took on this task themselves, making it possible for their children to experience a "Jewish home." Because American gender norms aligned with these couples' experiences of Jewishness, the non-Jewish women enabled their husbands' wish to create Jewish families and the rabbis' and Jewish educators' wish for Jewish continuity.

Despite the fears that many of my rabbinic informants expressed about the mixing of Judaism and Christianity in intermarriages, in some ways, they have found success in attracting intermarried Jews to Jewish institutions because of this mixing. Ethnic familialism and universalist individualism both may result in children who identify only as secular, with no particular or consistent religious background of their own. The American cultural values of individualism and egalitarianism opened a space for Christian women to intervene in ethnic and familial Jewishness so that these religious experiences could be created for their children. The Christian women served as catalysts for Jewish practice within their families and for their families' involvement with the Jewish community.

Adaptation to Modernity and Unintended Consequences

Sociologists have sought to understand contemporary religious life in the context of secularization. My fieldwork suggests that contemporary religious life is even more deeply complicated and self-contradictory than other studies of secularization in American religion have found. Other sociologists have identified clearly that religion provides important structure and meaning for contemporary Americans' lives. For example, in her qualitative study of secular Jewish women who joined Orthodox Jewish communities, Lynn Davidman (1991) asks why people who appear to be successful in the secular world might choose "traditional" religion: if secularization undermines religion's hold on people's minds and habits, why would people who are already highly secularized reverse course and become religious? She concludes that these women became Orthodox because they sought the structure and meaning that they felt this way of life could give them. Modernity, in Davidman's view, need not entail the decline of religion. Rather, the availability of religious choices and options could strengthen individuals' commitment to their choices.

Some of my intermarried informants, however, sought structure and meaning without regular ritual practices or clearly articulated beliefs, holding a tenuous attachment to religious communities and adherence to religious norms. These informants were completely ensconced in the modern world and had no desire to detach from it or to transform their lives. They wanted religion to enrich but not govern their lives, and they used religion to tell themselves and their children how they connected to their parents and to a larger story and community in the world. Religion served as an orientation: one Jewish informant told me that she wanted her children to understand their Jewishness as "one notch below that they're American." In some ways these informants appeared to be the kind of modern, rationalized individuals for whom religious authority has indeed declined, but they themselves resisted that notion. Rather than embracing only the secular, differentiated, rationalized world, they insisted on straddling secularity and religion. Like Davidman's informants, mine sought structure and meaning for their lives, which religion provided.

But whereas Davidman's informants sought meaning and structure by fully adopting the lifestyles of their communities, my informants insisted on religious autonomy. Even ethnic familialists, who were less vocal about the importance of autonomy, adapted tradition to suit themselves while claiming that they conformed to it, intermarrying but raising their children in Judaism. This way of perpetuating and experiencing Jewishness as a matter of limitless personal choice does not officially exist in Jewish law or traditional understandings of Jewishness. As a result, non-Jewish wives of Jewish men found themselves in a position that does not officially exist in Judaism: they were not Jews, but they were the mothers of children whom some considered to be Jewish, and they were sometimes part of Jewish communities.

As these individualistic patterns became established, rabbis, Jewish educators, and Jewish institutions responded with programs such as the Mothers Circle. Women in the Mothers Circle voluntarily, ambivalently, and fearfully stepped into a leadership role for their families' Jewish religious lives. They were sometimes worried about others' claims that they were illegitimate, angry about being judged, curious about Judaism, open to spiritual connection to it, and anxious and confused about their husbands' ambivalence. This set of emotions did not govern their entire lives; it emerged mostly in the context of life-cycle ceremonies and holidays that took place a few times a year. Some rabbis have called for a community-wide recognition of these women under the biblical category of *ger toshav*, meaning "a gentile who live[s] among the Jewish people, happy to be part of the Jewish world and supportive of the religious and social frames of Jewish life" (Greenberg 2001). However, this idea has not taken hold, perhaps because, as the Orthodox rabbis I interviewed said, recognition would imply approval. These women chose to raise their children as Jews, but the women themselves were invisible within the religious authority structures of Judaism. Yet they have been essential to the Jewish community's goal of continuity, as certain strands of discourses on intermarriage clearly recognize in their efforts to welcome and include these women.

The unintended consequence of training these women to create a Jewish home is that non-Jewish intermarried women in many ways have become more empowered than their Jewish husbands in their religious family lives and, by extension, in the religious communities of which they are not officially members. The traditional role of Jewish women as creators of children's emotional ties to Judaism implicitly gives them an informal religious authority. While this is not religious authority in the sense of involving direct control over others' actions (Chaves 1994), the ability to form a child's emotions and experiences, particularly on behalf of religion, is as much a kind of power as is the authority to administer sacraments or excommunicate (see Thompson 2013, for an extended discussion of this point). Women's informal authority in traditional Judaism complements men's more formal authority. But among my informants, this complementary system had become lopsided in response to American adaptations. Within these families, Jewish religious authority became the province of non-Jewish women, yet another form of Jewish adaptation to historical American Christian patterns: in this case, that of men's rejection of religious power and reliance on women to perform religious labor (Braude 1997).

Talking Authority

Among my informants, individuals embraced and rejected converging and contradictory cultural patterns in order to make sense of their own experiences and to formulate their own responses to discourses on intermarriage that embraced or condemned them. The universalist individualists, ethnic familialists, and rabbis with whom I spoke wove together elements of social and individual experience. They did so to form their own answers to questions about the meanings of having Jewishly identified children and carrying on Jewish tradition in ways that some other Jews do not recognize. The partial nature of each of the sources of religious authority allowed space for informants to articulate the boundaries between secular and religious that existed in their own experience. Universalist individualism and ethnic familialism invoke various kinds of religious authority: God, the individual and his or her authenticity, universalism, the family, or obligation. For my informants, God along with the individual and the family could together constitute religious authority rather than one of those elements alone.

Even the views of the non-Orthodox rabbis whom I interviewed held some ambiguity and ambivalence about religious authority, though less so than those of my lay informants. In discourses on intermarriage, participants assume that they are at least all arguing about one thing: Judaism. But they do not share an understanding of religious authority in Judaism, so they are not really discussing a common topic. According to Emile Durkheim ([1912] 1995), religion divides the world into opposite and separate categories of sacred and profane and defines a community based on that group's agreement about what is sacred and what is profane (34, 44). My rabbinic informants agreed on fundamental symbols and meanings in Judaism, but Orthodox and non-Orthodox rabbis used such drastically different frameworks of religious authority that the symbols were not performing the same functions. This use of common vocabulary without shared agreement about the symbols and meanings that such vocabulary conveys suggests that these discourses occur not within a single Jewish community but across different but overlapping ones.

Even though all of the rabbis I interviewed agreed that Jewish in-marriage was preferable to intermarriage, their worldviews were in deep conflict, reflecting the challenges presented to Jews by modernity itself. The Orthodox rabbis maintained their belief in the authority of Jewish law and the reality of the Jewish people's covenant with God. This view governed their approach to intermarriage so that they oriented every action toward bringing intermarried couples into closer connection with this perspective and the observant lifestyle that goes with it. They interpreted intermarriage as either a mistake made out of ignorance or a purposeful rejection of "what you are." "What you choose" was always subordinate to "what you are" because individual choice should always aim toward serving God and the world. In contrast, non-Orthodox rabbis struggled to articulate a view of religious authority that encompassed both personal autonomy, which they saw as a given in the modern world, and the mutual obligation of Jews to one another. They often had to rely on persuasion, hoping that intermarried Jews would choose Judaism, whether out of loyalty to "what they are" or as part of their personal spiritual journey. These rabbis regarded intermarriage as an unfortunate, ineluctable sociological fact but one that required a response to preserve Jewish tradition, at least to the extent of excluding Christianity. For this group, modernity and tradition constantly tested one another. The non-Orthodox informants recognized choice as ultimately central to modern religious experience, while the Orthodox rabbis aimed to help intermarried and/or nonobservant Jews recognize "what they are" and thereby to lead them to full observance.

The terms of modernity have mandated struggle over the definitions of Jewishness and Judaism. While secularization has deeply affected the religious lives of western Europeans and North Americans for several centuries, it has had special impact on the lives of Jews. Intermarriage has symbolized for Jews the tensions within the religious and secular elements of themselves; with one another as they attempt to balance autonomy and historic, sacred, mutual obligation; and between the Jewish people and Protestant Christian society. Whereas American Christians barely register the fact of Jewish-Christian intermarriage, American Jews regard it as a central problem. As the recent history of discourses on intermarriage shows, Jews have taken conflicting approaches to these tensions, emphasizing Jewish endogamy, ostracizing intermarried Jews, welcoming non-Jewish spouses into the Jewish community and/or seeking their conversion, and using statistical data to triangulate outreach efforts. But underlying all of these approaches, as my ethnographic research has shown, is a divide between competing responses to modernity.

Jews have been subject to the claims of modernity and American culture even as they have sought to reject or accommodate them. Attending to religious authority in this context raises questions about the modern western conception of religion itself. The definition of religion in sociological discourses and in American culture generally is based on a Protestant Christian model that emphasizes belief and private judgment. As my informants demonstrated, this model only partially fits the experience of non-Protestants. Even though Christianity shapes the terms of modernity and Protestantism shapes the definition of religion in modernity, neither has fully infiltrated the definition of Jewishness for modern Jews. My informants' experiences raise questions about whether non-Protestants must always shift their religious discourses and individual identifications and whether this Protestant religious definition even fits the lived experiences of Protestants themselves. In other words, they raise the question of whether the Protestant notion of modern religion is an ideology but not lived experience, much like the gap between ideology and experience I found in discourses on intermarriage.

The Protestant Christian cultural framework into which Jews have assimilated has vexed Judaism's adaptation to the American context. While Judaism traditionally has emphasized principles of mutual obligation, the Protestant cultural framework emphasizes autonomy. Despite cultural emphases, these values are necessarily held in tension in individual people's lives. While the majority of American Jews who affiliate with any movement choose ones that, either by default or in ideology, assume that individual Jews have the right to religious self-determination, normative Judaism still assumes that mutual obligation dominates Jews' moral responsibilities.

The issue of intermarriage crystallizes the problem of balancing autonomy and obligation, but discourses typically cast intermarriage as the problem itself rather than an extreme, if common, version of the problem of modernity for all American Jews. Endogamous Jews may have found a balance between autonomy and obligation that meets the norms of traditional Judaism, but endogamy may mask the same issue of ambivalent religious commitment that is more clearly visible in intermarried couples. By focusing on intermarriage rather than the larger issues of modernity and secularization that it represents, American Jews avoid grappling with the central issue that has plagued Jews since Emancipation: how to balance autonomy and obligation.

As people engage in discourses about intermarriage, they also engage in a proxy discourse about being religious and being Jewish in the modern world. Because intermarriage is a choice, whereas being a part of the modern world largely is not, discussion of the condition of being a Jew in this world rarely emerges openly. Rather, it is restricted to intellectual discourses that do not generally make their way into the popular and lay sphere. People can continue to argue about whether intermarriage is good or bad and what making the choice to intermarry means about one's commitment to Judaism, but having an argument about whether to be part of the modern world would not make sense to most people. Observant Jews frequently revisit the question of *how* to be part of the modern world by discussing the requirements of halakhic observance. But they do not argue about *whether* to be part of the modern world.

Discourses on intermarriage thus reflect disagreement and anxiety about the definition of Jewishness. These discourses occupy themselves with intermarriage because it is an issue about which there is still some illusion of control. Communities can set boundaries that exclude intermarriage and the intermarried, as my Orthodox rabbi informants explained. In contrast, the condition of modernity itself cannot be changed by discourse or persuasion. Discourses about intermarriage serve as a proxy or outlet for discussion of the anxieties about the decline of religious authority and the ambiguity of religion in the modern western world.

Race, Religion, and Experience

The fact of intermarriage raises questions about what Judaism is, but the framing of intermarriage as a problem of individual Jews diverts attention from this basic issue. American Jews desire the continued existence of Judaism and mutual recognition among Jews, but arriving at a shared understanding of what is being continued is significantly complicated by the complex interplay of

American and Jewish concepts and definitions of religion, race, and ethnicity. In the struggle for détente in this debate, each side repeatedly draws lines in the sand, trying to mark the outermost boundaries of tolerance for non-Jews within Judaism and of deviance from an ideal of Judaism. A holistic Jewishness is nostalgically imagined as past generations' experience. Anthropologist Barbara Myerhoff's *Number Our Days* (1978) describes this holistic sense in her informants, old Jews who represented to her a past in which Jewishness was authentic and organic; after their deaths, they believed, only a pale reflection, "American temple Judaism," would be left in its stead. Myerhoff repeatedly mentions her informants' "neglectful" children, one man's description of her as a "shiksa," the way in which he prefaced his comments with phrases such as "you wouldn't know about this, but . . ." to communicate a sense that this holism has been lost to later generations of Jews. Myerhoff discusses the breakdown of the autonomous Jewish community in which her informants grew up: the "old people" in *Number Our Days* were dysfunctionally interdependent because they were displaced from this organic world into one in which their children no longer understood *yiddishkeit* (Jewishness).

This supposed holism of experience has been transposed into an American language offering only partial categories. All of the categories of analysis—ethnicity, religion, nation, race, culture—which discourses on intermarriage use to talk about both intermarriage and Judaism fall short because none captures the holistic sense of "what you are" that the ethnic familialists described. While the language of modern America calls Judaism a religion, in the lived experience of actual Jews and the non-Jews who marry some of them, Judaism is also kinship, blood, relatedness, looking alike, genes. But despite the physically grounded way in which some Jews think of their relatedness, the language of racial identity also fails to fully capture their experience. My intermarried informants assumed their Jewishness to be innate, but they also wanted the religious aspects of Jewishness to be present in their lives. Lacking a clear language to describe these complex feelings, American Jews grasp at many different ways of defining Jewishness, and they often come into conflict over their definitions. Those at the periphery of Jewishness—converts, Jews by patrilineal descent, non-Jews married to Jews—find themselves mired in this uneasiness about the language and definition of Jewishness.

The languages of race and ethnicity have been bound to sociological descriptions of assimilation of minority groups. A double process of assimilation and integration is at work for some minority cultures in the United States so that over time they become "white" and their difference is elided. Differences that were once cast as racial come to be viewed as ethnic, thus presenting a lower barrier to integration (Waters 1998). Yet racial views of Jewishness persist, however implicitly. Although most Jews say Judaism is a religion, many stereotypes about Jews focus on their supposed physical appearance (Fishman 2004, 110). In its Annual Survey of American Jewish Opinion, the American Jewish Committee (2000) asked responders to say whether opposing intermarriage between Jews and non-Jews was "racist." The language of race points to the problem of categorizing Judaism as a religion, defined in American culture as primarily a matter of individual belief, when many Jews feel it to be innate. Limiting marriage to those within the borders of a minority racial group for the sake of group survival is a language that has legitimacy in American culture. In contrast, Judaism as ethnicity may not merit a special moral status that allows it a legitimate aversion to intermarriage. The category of peoplehood does not exist in American culture, even though it is an important concept for Judaism. In American culture, it translates into food preferences and traditions that lack the weight of religious law or belief. But peoplehood does not translate into race either, so a genetic lineage argument for the Jewish people rings hollow. It also uncomfortably echoes antisemitic claims about Jews and ignores the fact that being white carries hard-won advantages in American society.

Sociological conceptions of ethnicity likewise fail to capture the deeply felt sense among my informants that individualism and Jewishness are not simply choices that they freely make, but are cultural values that are part of "what they are." Sociologist Richard Alba (2005) seems to see Jewish religion as a subset of ethnicity and identifies modern Jewish religious changes as part of the assimilation process. He notes that as Jews assimilated into American society, boundaries between Jews and non-Jews grew blurry due to the rapid increase in intermarriage, but Jews maintained connections to Jewish practices. Thus, religious practices change with ethnic assimilation. This conception of ethnicity can help explain social relationships between groups, but it contributes little to an understanding of how individuals experience these ethnic and religious changes and relationships. Somewhat closer to the individual level, Mary Waters's (1998) concept of symbolic ethnicity (drawing from Gans 1979) is more helpful in explaining some of my informants' experiences. Symbolic ethnicity entails belonging to an ethnic community but emphasizes individuals' choice to do so. However, the concept does not encompass my informants' sense that their religious belonging was not only a choice but a given. If religious or ethnic membership were really a free choice, my informants could have chosen to do the easy parts and ignore the difficult parts, but they did not. Their sense of "what you are" cannot be characterized simply as an instance of symbolic ethnicity or the biogenetic sense of Jewishness that Shelly Tenenbaum and Lynn Davidman's (2007) interviewees claimed to have. Putting up a Christmas tree, for example, did not change my informants' genetic makeup or ethnicity, but it did symbolize a choice that contradicted the mutual obligation framework of Judaism.

Genetics, ethnicity, race, and religion each offer only partial answers about the experience of Jewishness in my informants' lives. Ethnography has helped to reveal how people, as individuals within communities, experience Jewishness across all of these categories. My informants internalized a kind of religious authority, communicated by way of communal discourses that established norms, even though their individual experiences did not always directly reflect these norms. My informants interacted with these communal discourses through their choices about religious practices and affiliations and the ways in which they explained these choices. Communal discourses gradually take note of individuals' choices and respond so that there is multidirectional influence among individuals, families, communities, and their discourses. This influence was evident as my informants struggled to articulate why they had committed themselves to religious practices about which they were ambivalent. Even rabbis, who were religious authorities themselves, struggled with the meaning of Jewishness.

Contemporary discourses on intermarriage have successfully persuaded people to practice Judaism mainly when they adopt the language of choice. The language of choice is in some ways all that people have available to them: it is the American cultural idiom that allows people to depict themselves as individual agents, self-made to the core. This emphasis on choice allows people to put together contradictory religious elements in their lives: choice is what makes it coherent, as if choice can solve all contradictions.

But this language of choice does not acknowledge authority or binding mutual obligation or community. People do not necessarily understand or examine their every action or thought as a deliberated choice, especially in contexts as emotionally fraught as religion, family, and gender. The theory of secularization as a decline in the scope of religious authority implicitly suggests that choice is the alternative to an overarching "sacred canopy" of religious authority. At the same time, there is no way to avoid putting these contradictory systems together in lived experience because the language of choice organizes the modern world. Hence, ethnic familialist discourses contain much more ambivalence than universalist individualist ones do. Universalist individualist ones have embraced choice so that the contradictions are smoothed over. Ethnic familialist ones are ambivalent about choice, so they are faced with paradox. Choice is the most salient feature of religious experience in a secularized world only because it is privileged in the language of American culture, not because it fully represents what is most important about religious experience.

Based on my informants' experiences, I argue that as the traditional, supernatural sources of religious authority decline in favor of a more individualized authority, new and unconventional sources of religious authority develop within families and communities, broadening the ways in which people have access to religious authority. The rabbis in my study saw religious authority as located in both Jewish tradition and individuals' consciences. But if individual conscience and Jewish tradition hold equal weight, then the role and function of religious institutions and norms in Jewish communities are unclear. This arrangement would define Jewish community as the overlap of a group of individuals' consciences and commitments to Judaism. But in the discourses that I have described, there is little consensus on the definition of Judaism itself, though there is a shared vocabulary of Jewish concepts. The ideology of individualism supports my informants' idiosyncratic interpretations of tradition. Individuals may have autonomy to choose their religious membership, but without a shared understanding of that commitment, what is its content?

In ethnic familialism and universalist individualism, gender norms shape religious life more strongly than do religious norms. Even with the lopsided balance of religious authority within my informants' families, the non-Jewish women's efforts to "create Jewish homes" (in the language of the Mothers Circle) demonstrate that intermarriage does not automatically mean that these families are opting out of Jewish community. But at the same time, this form of Jewish living does not continue widely recognized forms of Jewish traditions; and despite their outreach efforts, Jewish educators and rabbis do see a need to set boundaries. I asked Rachel, a Mothers Circle leader, whether women in the group ought to be officially recognized as Jews without undergoing conversion, given their commitment to and practice of raising Jewish children. "That would be going too far," Rachel said. "There needs to be a formal commitment." Two Reform rabbis said that a "spiritual transformation" occurs in conversion that they see as necessary for official recognition of Jewishness. But an endogamous woman who was born Jewish objected to this idea, saying that it was "unfair" that she could be officially recognized as Jewish by accident of birth, regardless of her spiritual state, while people who were not born Jewish but were active participants in the Jewish community—indeed, were "Jewish in their hearts," as Rachel said—were denied this recognition. This language is contradictory and points to the problem of conflicting loci of religious authority: how can someone be Jewish in her heart but not Jewish because she has not made a formal commitment?

My informants' individualism innovated tradition. The people I interviewed followed traditional patterns in ways that make no sense in the patterns' original context. Their innovations could not rely on traditional interpretations of canonical textual sources of religious authority. Authoritative Jewish texts do not conceive of a non-Jewish woman in charge of a Jewish home. But since textual and clerical sources of religious authority have been upstaged by the individual's private judgment, non-Jewish women not only can but do run Jewish households. These women's new religious authority gradually becomes accepted so that the sources of religious authority expand to encompass previously unimagined options.

Individual experiences of religious membership and authority differ from their depiction in discourses and institutions. In studying religion as culture, this point is particularly salient. Although religious institutions are often taken to enshrine normative religious beliefs, individuals may experience such beliefs in unconventional and unexpected ways. My informants showed that individuals can maintain relationships with religious institutions while making choices at odds with the norms of those institutions. They also may create their own religious institutions to establish their own norms if they determine that existing institutions exclude them. Further, my rabbinic informants showed that discourses on intermarriage meant for public consumption differ substantially from the content of interactions between rabbis and individuals.

American cultural understandings of individualism provided cultural permission for my informants to intermarry in the first place, and religious voluntarism provided a cultural script that allowed them to assume that they could raise Jewish children in families that were not entirely Jewish. Universalist individualist discourses encouraged people to rely on their own judgment as the highest value, aligning with secularization theorists' view of the contraction of religious authority to a private individual sphere. But "tradition" compelled my Jewish male informants to insist, however ambivalently, on having Jewish children. Ethnic familialist discourses encouraged people to follow traditional patterns out of an assumption that this was what loyalty to Jewish tradition required. Yet both ethnic familialists and universalist individualists transformed assumed patterns by bringing to bear other sources of religious authority. For example, universalist individualists pointed to the "universal truths" of their beliefs, demonstrated by these beliefs' presence in multiple world religions, and ethnic familialists combined traditionalism with individualist interpretations. The combination of gender roles and individualism created new and unconventional kinds of religious authority that established important roles for non-Jewish women in religious communities of which they were not officially members. This development offers religious communities opportunities to grow while also raising questions about how these communities should, and do, define themselves. The stories of intermarried Jews and their non-Jewish spouses reveal Jews who do not make normative Jewish choices but are nevertheless serious about Jewishness in the ways in which they understand it.

Afterword

American Jews' engagement in discourse about intermarriage is a form of collective experience as Jews. Engaging in debate about intermarriage allows American Jews to behave as if we are one community despite our deep divergence over important theological and practical matters. Yet examination of this debate has shown that there is no consensus even about the definitions of its central terminology—Jewish continuity, for example. Lacking agreement on terms or outcome, we settle on debate itself as our way of being together.

Even if Jews regard arguing as a sport, arguing in circles for decades often signifies that something is going wrong. Worse, arguing in circles about people's lives adds to the burdens that such people carry every day. Although the intermarried couples I have described in this book chose to maintain and nourish their connections with Judaism, it would be no surprise to learn that other intermarried Jews have chosen to give up or further privatize their Jewishness rather than continue to endure a stigmatized status in Jewish public discourse. Although intermarried Jews may be welcome in particular Jewish institutions, such a welcome coexists with a vitriolic public debate of which intermarried Jews are well aware.

I began this research because I felt sad that people were being deeply misunderstood. Religious community shapes and touches our deepest being in unspoken and unspeakable ways. Across religious traditions, people who feel a conflict between who they are and who or what their religious communities and traditions expect of them have responded by fighting back, suppressing their "true" selves, or walking away. This is not just a Jewish issue. It is a Catholic issue, a Protestant issue, a Muslim issue. It is a human issue.

Out of my sadness, I hoped to help others understand my informants, to be fairer to them, and to render their stories with greater humanity than much of public discourse has allowed. In this way I hope to help readers experience my informants' lives as if they were actually spending time together as human beings rather than as subjects and objects of discourse.

Intermarriage discourse is a paltry substitute for actual experience with Jews whose commitments to Judaism differ from our own. Sustained argument over the topic of intermarriage gives us the illusion that we are a community because we believe ourselves to be fighting about the same thing. But if we look behind and beyond the immediate issue of intermarriage, what else are we fighting about? And what does that reveal about who we are? Is there some deeper connective tissue that holds us together as a community? If so, that connective tissue needs to be infused with energy, to be cared for and maintained. The negative energy generated by intermarriage discourse is harmful not just to intermarried couples but to all who participate in it. Our connective tissue suffers, becomes desiccated and flimsy.

Actual experience together *tells* us what binds us together, as sociologists have argued for decades. Robert Putnam, Robert Bellah and his colleagues, and others have recognized the dangers in Americans' withdrawal from civil society organizations in which they once mixed with people who were different from themselves and with whom they built the bonds, the social capital, that create and strengthen society. While I do not wish to suggest that all Jews should simply join existing Jewish institutions if such organizations do not meet their needs, I do think that collective experience among Jews of different stripes must take place. Jews across the world are finding it difficult, if not impossible, to articulate how they are one people. Again, this is not just a Jewish issue; it is a human issue. The globalizing of culture has disrupted the bonds of particular communities all over the world, and fear about retaining the authentic character, feeling, and experience of such cultures is real and widespread.

Culture must be lived in order to survive. This is where the opportunities are. Texts such as Robert Putnam's *Bowling Alone* (2000) challenge Americans to think about the social and emotional bonds forged through lived culture, community, and experience and the relational impoverishment that comes from globalized culture lived through media rather than personal contact (even as social media provide opportunities for other kinds of human connections). These are the same forces that are hurting intermarried people: discourses taking place through the media substitute for the kinds of social bonding that could be happening through communal interaction. If Reform and Orthodox communities rarely engage with one another except in their reading of opinion and news pieces about intermarriage in Jewish media and in their participation in flame wars in the online comment sections of such articles, no social bonding is likely to occur. No willingness to regard one another as part of the same lifeworld is likely either. That social distance only inspires Jews to continue fighting.

As a student and teacher of the topic of social experience, I suggest that in order for Jewish communities to be vibrant and to care for their connective tissue in ways that matter, in ways that are life-giving and life-affirming in their specific local contexts, Jews from varied backgrounds and with different commitments must personally connect with one another. Shared experience, lived in our present context, our local worlds, may allow Jews to develop a fuller understanding of what unites us as a people in a free society. These opportunities should *not* be in the context of dialogue, which is too prone to result in the repetition of statements of ideology. Such statements obviously matter to people, but the speakers understand their claims in the contexts of their own lived experiences, which are rarely communicated by or along with ideological statements. Instead, I urge the expansion of a more experience-focused approach that is already in practice in many respects. Communal service projects—helping to organize donations at food banks, for example—offer the opportunity to share with other Jews experiences that exemplify basic Jewish values. Such projects should be hands-on, they should meet real and basic needs in the community, and they should be done in small and diverse groups. They already take place under the auspices of college Hillel groups and American Jewish World Service, for example, and in some cases they are immersion experiences in which participants live and work together for a set period of time. What I am suggesting can be accomplished in less intensive ways as well.

When volunteers are working, they are too busy to argue, but they are building social capital by spending time together in common cause. As a teacher of service-learning courses for undergraduates, I have heard many students say that they developed a much deeper understanding of and appreciation for the people with whom they have shared such work. If Jews and Jewish institutions hope to build Jewish community in substantial ways, I urge them not just to offer but to normalize such service projects so that Jews from all different locations and contexts want to take this opportunity to be together as Jews. That experience can, I hope, reshape our rhetoric about one another and help us discover what, if anything, binds us to each other as Jews.

NOTES

INTRODUCTION

1. According to Hebrew Union College sociologist Bruce Phillips's calculations based on the National Jewish Population Study of 2000, 64 percent of American Jewish children are being raised in households with one Jewish parent and one non-Jewish parent. Personal communication, January 16, 2013.
2. This comment was made in response to my article on Interfaithfamily.com, "Because Their Children Are Jewish" (Thompson 2010).

CHAPTER 1 DEFINING JUDAISM BY DEBATING INTERMARRIAGE

1. For example, among the studies I describe are Kosmin et al. (1991), Tobin (1999), Tobin and Simon (1999), Fishman (2004), Phillips (2005), and Dashefsky and Heller (2008). Among the popular and self-help literature I describe are Hertzberg (1989), Kugel (1990), Lamm ([1980] 1991), Reuben (1992), Cantor (1994), Gordis (1994), McClain (1995), Silverstein (1995a, 1995b), Abramowitz and Silverman (1997), Dershowitz (1997), Luxner (1999), Jaffe (2000), Weiss and Block (2000), Friedman (2002), and Tugend (2003). Because discourses about intermarriage taking place in nonprint media, such as television, have been discussed by historians and sociologists such as Staub (2002), Fishman (2004), Goldstein (2006), and Berman (2009), I do not include them here.
2. For a discussion of the gender dynamics and assumptions behind the patrilineal descent discussion, see McGinity (2009, 174–175).
3. See ibid., chaps. 3 and 4, for an analysis of how exactly these factors affected Jewish women's intermarriages.

CHAPTER 2 AMERICAN CONTRADICTIONS: CONVERSATIONS ABOUT SELF AND COMMUNITY

1. Names have been changed.
2. In the 1990s, the recurring sketch "Coffee Talk" featured cast member Mike Myers as Linda Richman, a New York Jewish character based on his mother-in-law. The sketch frequently addressed Jewish-Christian relationships. One running joke was Richman's creative merger of the word Jew with Christian descriptors—for example, Episcopalian plus Jew to produce EpisciJew, Methodist plus Jew to produce Mooshew, Catholic plus Jew to produce Cashew (Witchel 2001).

CHAPTER 4 TRANSLATING JEWISH EXPERIENCE

1. This question came from me, so it may not be the best indicator of what the rest of the audience was thinking because I was there in my capacity as a researcher.

REFERENCES

Abramowitz, Yosef I., and Susan Silverman. 1997. *Jewish Family and Life: Traditions, Holidays, and Values for Today's Parents and Children.* New York: Golden Books.

Adelman, Howard. 1991. "Italian Jewish Women." In *Jewish Women in Historical Perspective*, edited by Judith R. Baskin, 135–158. Detroit: Wayne State University Press.

Alba, Richard. 2005. "Bright vs. Blurred Boundaries: Second-Generation Assimilation and Exclusion in France, Germany, and the United States." *Ethnic and Racial Studies* 28: 20–49.

Alpert, Rebecca T., and Jacob J. Staub. 1985. *Exploring Judaism: A Reconstructionist Approach.* Wyncote, Pa.: Reconstructionist.

American Academy of Child and Adolescent Psychiatry. 2011, March. *Facts for Families, No. 71: Multiracial Children.* http://www.aacap.org/galleries/FactsForFamilies/71_multira-cial_children.pdf. Accessed April 8, 2013.

American Jewish Committee. 2000. Annual Survey of American Jewish Opinion. http://www.ajc.org/site/apps/nlnet/content3.aspx?c=ijITI2PHKoG&b=846741&ct=1042043. Accessed April 8, 2013.

Appell, Victor, Arlene Chernow, Stephanie Fink, and Vicky Farhi. 2013. "Ask a Specialist." New York: Union for Reform Judaism. http://urj.org/cong/outreach/interfaith/?syspag e=article&item_id=78501. Accessed January 8, 2013.

Asad, Talal. 1993. *Genealogies of Religion: Discipline and Reasons of Power in Christianity and Islam.* Baltimore, Md.: Johns Hopkins University Press.

Baron, Salo W. 1957. *A Social and Religious History of the Jews.* Vols. 3, 4, 5, 9, 10. New York: Columbia University Press.

Barron, Milton L. 1946. "The Incidence of Jewish Intermarriage in Europe and America." *American Sociological Review* 11: 6–13.

Batnitzky, Leora. 2011. *How Judaism Became a Religion: An Introduction to Modern Jewish Thought.* Princeton, N.J.: Princeton University Press.

Beck, Pearl. 2005. *A Flame Still Burns: The Dimensions and Determinants of Jewish Identity among Young Adult Children of the Intermarried: Findings and Policy Implications.* New York: Jewish Outreach Institute. http://joi.org/flame/Children of Intermarriage Identity Study. pdf. Accessed April 8, 2013.

Beckerman, Gal. 2010, July 7. "New Study Finds That It's Not a Lack of Welcome That's Keeping the Intermarrieds Away." *Jewish Daily Forward.* http://forward.com/articles/129228/new-study-finds-that-it-s-not-a-lack-of-welcome/. Accessed April 8, 2013.

Bellah, Robert N. [1970] 1991. "Religious Evolution." In *Beyond Belief: Essays on Religion in a Post-Traditionalist World*, 20–50. Berkeley: University of California Press.

Bellah, Robert N., Richard Madsen, William M. Sullivan, Ann Swidler, and Steven M. Tipton. 1985. *Habits of the Heart: Individualism and Commitment in American Life*. New York: Harper and Row.

_____. 1991. *The Good Society*. New York: Knopf.

Berger, Peter L. 1998, August 26. "Protestantism and the Quest for Certainty." *Christian Century*, 782–796.

Berkman, Jacob. 2010, August 3. "Clinton-Mezvinsky Wedding Raises Questions about Intermarriage." Jewish Telegraphic Agency. http://www.jta.org/news/article/2010/08/03/2740329/mezvinsky-clinton-wedding-raises-questions-and-debate. Accessed April 8, 2013.

Berman, Lila Corwin. 2009. *Speaking of Jews: Rabbis, Intellectuals, and the Creation of an American Public Identity*. Berkeley: University of California Press.

_____. 2010. "Blame, Boundaries, and Birthrights: Jewish Intermarriage in Midcentury America." In *Boundaries of Jewish Identity*, edited by Susan A. Glenn and Naomi B. Sokoloff, 91–109. Seattle: University of Washington Press.

Berman, Louis A. 1968. *Jews and Intermarriage: A Study in Personality and Culture*. Cranbury, NJ: Thomas Yoseloff.

Borowitz, Eugene B. 1983. "The Crux of Liberal Jewish Thought: Personal Autonomy." In *Choices in Modern Jewish Thought: A Partisan Guide*, 243–272. New York: Behrman House.

_____. 1984. "The Autonomous Jewish Self." *Modern Judaism* 4: 39–56.

Braude, Ann. 1997. "Women's History *Is* American Religious History." In *Retelling U.S. Religious History*, edited by Thomas A. Tweed, 87–107. Berkeley: University of California Press.

Cantor, Norman F. 1994. *The Sacred Chain: A History of the Jews*. New York: HarperCollins.

Casanova, José. 1994. *Public Religions in the Modern World*. Chicago: University of Chicago Press.

"Catholics on the Move; Non-religious on the Rise." 2009, March 5. American Religious Identification Survey 2008. http://commons.trincoll.edu/aris/2009/03/05/catholics_on_the_move_non-religious_on_the_rise/. Accessed April 8, 2013.

Central Conference of American Rabbis. 1983, October. "Patrilineal and Matrilineal Descent." *Contemporary American Reform Responsa*. http://ccarnet.org/responsa/carr-61–68/. Accessed April 10, 2013.

Chaves, Mark. 1994. "Secularization as Declining Religious Authority." *Social Forces* 73: 749–774.

Cohen, Henry. [1962] 1974. "Jewish Life and Thought in an Academic Community." In *The Jew in American Society*, edited by Marshall Sklare, 289–301. New York: Behrman House.

Cohen, Shaye J. D. 1999. *The Beginnings of Jewishness: Boundaries, Varieties, Uncertainties*. Berkeley: University of California Press.

Cohen, Steven M. 1988. *Unity and Polarization in Judaism Today: The Attitudes of American and Israeli Jews*. New York: American Jewish Committee. http://www.bjpa.org/Publications/details.cfm?PublicationID=314. Accessed April 8, 2013.

_____. 2005. "Engaging the Next Generation of American Jews: Distinguishing the In-married, Inter-married, and Non-married." *Journal of Jewish Communal Service* 81: 43–52.

_____. 2006, November. *A Tale of Two Jewries: The "Inconvenient Truth" for American Jews*. New York: Jewish Life Network/Steinhardt Foundation. http://www.jewishlife.org/pdf/steven_cohen_paper.pdf. Accessed April 8, 2013.

Cohen, Steven M., and Arnold M. Eisen. 2000. *The Jew Within: Self, Family and Community in America*. Bloomington: Indiana University Press.

Cohen, Steven M., and Judith Veinstein. 2010. *Recruiting Jewish Campers: A Study of the Midwestern Market*. New York: Foundation for Jewish Camp. http://www.jewishcamp.org/sites/default/files/u5/NEW%20Midwest_Research_Report_FINAL.pdf. Accessed April 8, 2013.

Council of Jewish Federations and Welfare Funds. 1973. *Intermarriage: Facts for Planning*. New York: Council of Jewish Federations and Welfare Funds.

Counihan, Carole M. 1988. "Female Identity, Food, and Power in Contemporary Florence." *Anthropological Quarterly* 61: 51–62.

Cowan, Paul, with Rachel Cowan. 1987. *Mixed Blessings: Overcoming the Stumbling Blocks in an Interfaith Marriage*. New York: Penguin.

Cross, F. L., and E. A. Livingstone. 2005a. "Jews, Christian Attitudes To." In *The Oxford Dictionary of the Christian Church*, 881–882. 3rd rev. ed. New York: Oxford University Press.

_____. 2005b. "Protestantism." In *The Oxford Dictionary of the Christian Church*, 1348–1349. 3rd rev. ed. New York: Oxford University Press.

DaCosta, Kimberly McClain. 2007. *Making Multiracials: State, Family, and Market in the Redrawing of the Color Line*. Stanford, Calif.: Stanford University Press.

Dahlstrom, Daniel. 2006. "Moses Mendelssohn," *Stanford Encyclopedia of Philosophy*, edited by Edward N. Zalta. Stanford, Calif.: Stanford University. http://plato.stanford.edu/entries/mendelssohn/. Accessed April 8, 2013.

Dashefsky, Arnold, with Zachary I. Heller. 2008. *Intermarriage and Jewish Journeys in the United States*. Newton Center, Mass: Hebrew College, National Center for Jewish Policy Studies.

Dashefsky, Arnold, Ira M. Sheskin, and Ron Miller. 2012. "Intermarriage Data." *FAQs on American Jews*, table 2. Storrs: University of Connecticut, Mandell L. Berman Institute, North American Jewish Data Bank. http://www.jewishdatabank.org/FAQs/FAQs_Table2_Intermarriage.pdf. Accessed April 8, 2013.

Davidman, Lynn. 1991. *Tradition in a Rootless World: Women Turn to Orthodox Judaism*. Berkeley: University of California Press.

Davis, Maurice. 1988, January–February. "Why I Won't Perform an Intermarriage." *Moment*, 20–21.

Dershowitz, Alan M. 1997. *The Vanishing American Jew: In Search of Jewish Identity for the Next Century*. Boston: Little, Brown.

Dollinger, Marc. 2000. *Quest for Inclusion: Jews and Liberalism in Modern America*. Princeton, N.J.: Princeton University Press.

Drachsler, Julius. 1920. *Democracy and Assimilation: The Blending of Immigrant Heritages in America*. New York: Macmillan.

Dumont, Louis. 1982. "A Modified View of Our Origins: The Christian Beginnings of Individualism." *Religion* 12: 1–27.

Durkheim, Emile. [1912] 1995. *The Elementary Forms of Religious Life*. Translated by Karen E. Fields. New York: Free Press.

Edelstein, Alan. 1994, August 31. "Jews Who Choose Jesus." *Moment*, 30.

Edelstein, Moshe. 2005. "Al Ha Derekh: On the Path." New York: United Synagogue of Conservative Judaism. http://uscj.org/congservices/forms/USCJPublications/alhaderekh.pdf. Accessed April 12, 2013.

Endelman, Todd M. 1990. *Radical Assimilation in English Jewish History, 1656–1945*. Bloomington: Indiana University Press.

_____. 1997. "Making Jews Modern: Some Jewish and Gentile Misunderstandings in the Age of Emancipation." In *What Is Modern about the Modern Jewish Experience?*, edited by Marc Lee Raphael, 18–32. Williamsburg, Va.: College of William and Mary, Department of Religion.

Evangelical Presbyterian Church. n.d. *Westminster Confession of Faith.* Livonia, Mich.: Evangelical Presbyterian Church. http://www.epc.org/about-the-epc/beliefs/westminster-confession/. Accessed March 19, 2010.

"FAQs." 2012. Interfaithfamily.com. http://www.interfaithfamily.com/about_us_advocacy/for_press/FAQs.shtml. Accessed May 9, 2013.

Fishberg, Maurice. [1911] 2006. *Jews, Race, and Environment.* New Brunswick, N.J.: Transaction Publishers.

Fishkoff, Sue. 2005, December 8. "At Convention, Conservative Jews Wrestle with Movement's Identity." Jewish Telegraphic Agency. http://archive.jta.org/article/2005/12/08/2929534/at-convention-conservative-jews-wrestle-with-movements-identity. Accessed April 12, 2013.

Fishman, Sylvia Barack. 2004. *Double or Nothing? Jewish Families and Mixed Marriage.* Lebanon, N.H.: Brandeis University Press.

Frank, Shirley. 1978, January 31. "The Population Panic: Why Jewish Leaders Want Jewish Women to be Fruitful and Multiply." *Lilith*, 12.

Friedman, Daniel. 2002. *Jews without Judaism: Conversations with an Unconventional Rabbi.* Amherst, N.Y.: Prometheus.

Gallob, Ben. 1979, May 27. "Reform Rabbi Writes of Temple Serving Mixed Marriage Couples." *New York Jewish Week*, 27.

Gamson, William A. 1999. "Beyond the Science-versus-Advocacy Distinction." *Contemporary Sociology* 28, no. 1: 23–26.

Gan, Katherine N., Patty Jacobson, Gil Preuss, and Barry Shrage. 2008, March. *The 2005 Greater Boston Community Study: Intermarried Families and Their Children.* Boston: Combined Jewish Philanthropies. http://www.cjp.org/local_includes/downloads/24386.pdf. Accessed April 8, 2013.

Gans, Herbert J. 1956a. "American Jewry: Present and Future. Part I: Present." *Commentary* 21: 422–430.

———. 1956b. "American Jewry: Present and Future. Part II: Future." *Commentary* 21: 555–563.

———. 1979. "Symbolic Ethnicity: The Future of Ethnic Groups and Cultures in America." In *On the Making of Americans: Essays in Honor of David Riesman*, edited by Herbert J. Gans, Nathan Glazer, Joseph R. Gusfield, and Christopher Jencks. Philadelphia: University of Pennsylvania Press.

Geffen, Rela Mintz. 2009, March 1. "Intermarriage and Conversion in the United States." *Jewish Women: A Comprehensive Historical Encyclopedia.* Brookline, Mass.: Jewish Women's Archive. http://jwa.org/encyclopedia/article/intermarriage-and-conversion-in-united-states. Accessed April 8, 2013.

Glenn, Susan A. 2010. "'Funny, You Don't Look Jewish': Visual Stereotypes and the Making of Modern Jewish Identity." In *Boundaries of Jewish Identity*, edited by Susan A. Glenn and Naomi B. Sokoloff, 64–90. Seattle: University of Washington Press.

Goldfarb, Solomon. 1976. "Who Is a Jewish Child?" *Conservative Judaism* 30, no. 4: 3–9.

Goldscheider, Calvin. 2010. "Boundary Maintenance and Jewish Identity: Comparative and Historical Perspectives." In *Boundaries of Jewish Identity*, edited by Susan A. Glenn and Naomi B. Sokoloff, 110–131. Seattle: University of Washington Press.

Goldscheider, Calvin, and Alan Zuckerman. 1986. *The Transformation of the Jews.* Chicago: University of Chicago Press.

Goldstein, Eric L. 2006. *The Price of Whiteness: Jews, Race, and American Identity.* Princeton, N.J.: Princeton University Press.

Gordis, Daniel. 1994. "The End of Survivalist Judaism? American Jews in Search of Direction." *Sh'ma* 24, no. 466: 5–7.

Gordis, Robert. 1978. "Intermarriage and the Jewish Future." In *The Threat of Mixed Marriage: A Response*, edited by Sheldon Zimmerman and Barbara Trainin, 114–147. New York: Federation of Jewish Philanthropies.

Gordon, Milton. 1964. *Assimilation in American Life: The Role of Race, Religion, and National Origins.* Oxford: Oxford University Press.

Greenberg, Blu. 1981. *On Women and Judaism: A View from Tradition.* Philadelphia: Jewish Publication Society.

Greenberg, Steve. 2001. "Between Intermarriage and Conversion: Finding a Middle Way." *Spirit and Story.* http://www.clal.org/ss43.html. Accessed March 19, 2010.

Hadaway, C. Kirk, Penny Long Marler, and Mark Chaves. 1993. "What the Polls Don't Show: A Closer Look at U.S. Church Attendance." *American Sociological Review* 58: 741–752.

———. 1998. "Overreporting Church Attendance in America: Evidence That Demands the Same Verdict." *American Sociological Review* 63: 122–130.

Hart, Mitchell Bryant. 2000. *Social Science and the Politics of Modern Jewish Identity.* Stanford, Calif.: Stanford University Press.

Hatch, Nathan O. 1989. *The Democratization of American Christianity.* New Haven, Conn.: Yale University Press.

Hawxhurst, Joan C. 1998. *The Interfaith Family Guidebook: Practical Advice for Jewish and Christian Partners.* Kalamazoo, Mich.: Dovetail.

Hertz, Deborah. 1991. "Emancipation through Intermarriage in Old Berlin." In *Jewish Women in Historical Perspective*, edited by Judith R. Baskin, 182–201. Detroit: Wayne State University Press.

Hertzberg, Arthur. 1978. "An Historical Overview of Mixed Marriage." In *The Threat of Mixed Marriage: A Response*, edited by Sheldon Zimmerman and Barbara Trainin, 1–15. New York: Federation of Jewish Philanthropies.

———. 1989. *The Jews in America: Four Centuries of an Uneasy Encounter.* New York: Simon and Schuster.

Hochschild, Arlie Russell. [1989] 2003. *The Second Shift.* New York: Penguin.

Holden, Jeremy. 2007. "On CNBC's The Big Idea, Coulter Said That 'We' Christians 'Just Want Jews to Be Perfected.'" Washington, D.C.: Media Matters for America. http://mediamatters.org/items/200710100008. Accessed March 26, 2010.

Hyman, Paula E. 1991. "Gender and the Immigrant Jewish Experience in the United States." In *Jewish Women in Historical Perspective*, edited by Judith R. Baskin, 222–242. Detroit: Wayne State University Press.

———. 1995. *Gender and Assimilation in Modern Jewish History: Roles and Representations of Women.* Seattle: University of Washington Press.

Interfaith Families Project of the Greater Washington, D.C., Area. 1996a. "Interfaith Families Project Coming of Age Program." Rockville, Md.: Interfaith Families Project of the Greater Washington, D.C., Area. http://ww.iffp.net/programs/sundayschool/coa.html. Accessed January 8, 2013.

———. 1996b. "Sunday School." Rockville, Md.: Interfaith Families Project of the Greater Washington, D.C., Area. http://ww.iffp.net/programs/sundayschool/SundaySchool.html. Accessed January 8, 2013.

"Intermarriage Not the Major Threat, Jerusalem Dialogue Scholar Asserts." 1978, August 6. *New York Jewish Week*, 9.

"Intermarriage the Price of Open Society? Scholars, Rabbis Probe Views in 2-Day Seminar." 1977, January 15. *New York Jewish Week*, 23.

Jaffe, Azriela. 2000. *Two Jews Can Still Be a Mixed Marriage: Reconciling Differences over Judaism in Your Marriage.* Franklin Lakes, N.J.: Career.

Jewish Outreach Institute. 2008. "About JOI: Who Are We?" Jewish Outreach Institute. http://joi.org/about/. Accessed March 23, 2010.

Joselit, Jenna Weissman. 1994. *The Wonders of America: Reinventing Jewish Culture, 1880–1950.* New York: Hill and Wang.

Kahn, Susan M. 2010. "Are Genes Jewish? Conceptual Ambiguities in the New Genetic Age." In *Boundaries of Jewish Identity*, edited by Susan A. Glenn and Naomi B. Sokoloff, 12–26. Seattle: University of Washington Press.

Kaplan, Dana Evan. 2009. *Contemporary American Judaism: Transformation and Renewal.* New York: Columbia University Press.

Kaplan, Marion A. 1991. "Tradition and Transition: Jewish Women in Imperial Germany." In *Jewish Women in Historical Perspective*, edited by Judith R. Baskin, 202–221. Detroit: Wayne State University Press.

Katz, Jacob. [1973] 1998. *Out of the Ghetto: The Social Background of Jewish Emancipation, 1770–1870.* Syracuse, N.Y.: Syracuse University Press.

Kaufman, Debra Renee. 1991. *Rachel's Daughters: Newly Orthodox Jewish Women.* New Brunswick, N.J.: Rutgers University Press.

———. 2005. "Measuring Jewishness in America: Some Feminist Concerns." *Nashim* 10: 84–98.

Kitov, Eliyahu. 2000. *The Jew and His Home: A Guide to Jewish Family Life.* Jerusalem: Feldheim.

Kleinman, Arthur. 1997. "'Everything That Really Matters': Social Suffering, Subjectivity, and the Remaking of Human Experience in a Disordering World." *Harvard Theological Review* 90: 315–335.

Kosmin, Barry A., Sidney Goldstein, Joseph Waksberg, Nava Lerer, Ariella Keysar, and Jeffrey Scheckner. 1991. *Highlights of the CJS 1990 National Jewish Population Survey.* New York: Council of Jewish Federations.

Kosmin, Barry A., and Ariela Keysar, with Ryan Cragun and Juhem Navarro-Rivera. 2009. *American Nones: The Profile of the No Religion Population.* Hartford, Conn.: Institute for the Study of Secularism in Society and Culture. http://commons.trincoll.edu/aris/publications/american-nones-the-profile-of-the-no-religion-population/. Accessed April 8, 2013.

Kugel, James. 1990. *On Being a Jew.* New York: HarperCollins.

Lamm, Maurice. [1980] 1991. *The Jewish Way in Love and Marriage.* Middle Village, N.Y.: Jonathan David.

Lamm, Norman. 1966, August. "The State of Jewish Belief: A Symposium." *Commentary*, 110–112.

Lester, Elenore. 1978, December 3. "Shalosh Seudot: 'Threat of Mixed Marriage' Brings Out Many Different Views on Growing Problem." *New York Jewish Week*, 41.

Levenson, Alan. 1989. "Reform Attitudes, in the Past, toward Intermarriage." *Judaism* 38: 320–332.

Levi, Shonie B., and Sylvia R. Kaplan. [1959] 1964. *Guide for the Jewish Homemaker.* New York: Schocken.

Lévi-Strauss, Claude. 1968. *The Savage Mind.* Chicago: University of Chicago Press.

Liebman, Charles S. 1973. *The Ambivalent American Jew: Politics, Religion, and Family in American Jewish Life.* Philadelphia: Jewish Publication Society of America.

Lippmann, Walter. [1922] 1997. *Public Opinion.* New York: Free Press.

"Losses from Intermarriage Replaced, Analyst Reports." 1977, December 11. *New York Jewish Week*, 6.

Lowenstein, Steven M. 2005. "Jewish Intermarriage and Conversion in Germany and Austria." *Modern Judaism* 25: 23–61.

Luxner, Larry. 1999, November 30. "Orthodox Conversion Opening Up?" Jewish Telegraphic Agency. http://pdfs.jta.org/2006/2006_04_13.pdf. Accessed May 30, 2013.

Madsen, Richard. 2009. "The Archipelago of Faith: Religious Individualism and Faith Community in America Today." *American Journal of Sociology* 114: 1263–1301.

Maitland, Frederic William. 1898. "The Deacon and the Jewess." In *Roman Canon Law in the Church of England: Six Essays*, 158–179. London: Methuen.

Mark, Jonathan. 2008, June 11. "Rabbi Lookstein Remembers It Well." *New York Jewish Week.* http://www.thejewishweek.com/news/new_york/rabbi_lookstein_remembers_it_ well. Accessed May 30, 2013.

Mayer, Egon. 1994, April 30. "Will the Grandchildren of Intermarrieds Be Jews? The Chances Are Greater Than You Think." *Moment.*

McClain, Ellen Jaffe. 1995. *Embracing the Stranger: Intermarriage and the Future of the American Jewish Community.* New York: Basic Books.

McGinity, Keren R. 2009. *Still Jewish: A History of Women and Intermarriage in America.* New York: New York University Press.

_____. Forthcoming. *Strangers in the Fold: Jewish Men, Intermarriage, and Fatherhood.* Bloomington: Indiana University Press.

Mead, Margaret. [1942] 1975. *And Keep Your Powder Dry: An Anthropologist Looks at America.* New York: William Morrow.

Meyer, John W. 1987. "Self and Life Course: Institutionalization and Its Effects." In *Institutional Structure: Constituting State, Society, and the Individual*, edited by George M. Thomas, John W. Meyer, Francisco O. Ramirez, and John Boli, 242–260. Newbury Park, Calif.: Sage.

Meyer, John W., John Boli, and George M. Thomas. 1987. "Ontology and Rationalization in the Western Cultural Account." In *Institutional Structure: Constituting State, Society, and the Individual*, edited by George M. Thomas, John W. Meyer, Francisco O. Ramirez, and John Boli, 12–37. Newbury Park, Calif.: Sage.

Miller, Jason. 2011, January 13. "The Question of Giffords' Jewishness." *Huffington Post.* http://www.huffingtonpost.com/rabbi-jason-miller/gabby-giffords-jewish_b_808246. html. Accessed April 1, 2011.

Moline, Jack. 2006, June. "The Mitzvah Child." *Philadelphia Jewish Voice.* http://www.pjvoice .com/v12/12701child.html. Accessed March 23, 2010.

Moore, Deborah Dash. 1981. "Jewish Geography." In *At Home in America: Second Generation New York Jews*, 19–58. New York: Columbia University Press.

_____. 1994. *To the Golden Cities: Pursuing the American Jewish Dream in Miami and L.A.* Cambridge, Mass.: Harvard University Press.

Myerhoff, Barbara. 1978. *Number Our Days.* New York: Touchstone.

Niebuhr, Gustav. 1999, November 9. "Coalition of Jews Protests Southern Baptist Conversion Tactics." *New York Times.* http://www.nytimes.com/1999/11/09/us/coalition-of-jews-protests-southern-baptist-conversion-tactics.html?pagewanted=all&src=pm. Accessed April 8, 2013.

Olitzky, Kerry M., with Joan Peterson Littman. 2003. *Making a Successful Jewish Interfaith Marriage: The Jewish Outreach Institute Guide to Opportunities, Challenges, and Resources.* Woodstock, Vt.: Jewish Lights.

Olsen, Polina. n.d. "Mah Jongg—Tiles that Bind." *Jewish Review.* http://www.jewishreview .org/node/8654. Accessed April 8, 2013.

Packouz, Kalman. 2008. *How to Prevent an Intermarriage.* http://preventintermarriage.com/. Accessed April 8, 2013.

A Passover Haggadah. 1993. With commentary by Elie Wiesel. New York: Touchstone.

"Perfecting U.S. Jews." 2007, October 19. *Jewish Advocate*, 10.

Pew Forum on Religion and Public Life. 2009a. "Not All Nonbelievers Call Themselves Atheists." Washington, D.C.: Pew Forum on Religion and Public Life. http://pewforum.org/Not-All-Nonbelievers-Call-Themselves-Atheists.aspx. Accessed March 26, 2010.

———. 2009b. "The Stronger Sex—Spiritually Speaking." Washington, D.C.: Pew Forum on Religion and Public Life. http://www.pewforum.org/The-Stronger-Sex----Spiritually-Speaking.aspx. Accessed April 12, 2013.

Phillips, Bruce. 1997. *Re-examining Intermarriage: Trends, Textures and Strategies*. New York: American Jewish Committee. http://www.ajcarchives.org/AJC_DATA/Files/808.pdf. Accessed April 12, 2013.

———. 2005. "Assimilation, Transformation, and the Long Range Impact of Intermarriage." *Contemporary Jewry* 25, no. 1: 50–84.

———. n.d. "A Typology of Intermarriage." Unpublished manuscript.

Polland, Annie. 2007. "'May a Freethinker Help a Pious Man?' The Shared World of the 'Religious' and the 'Secular' among Eastern European Jewish Immigrants to America." *American Jewish History* 93: 375–407.

Porton, Gary. 1994. *The Stranger within Your Gates: Converts and Conversion in Rabbinic Literature*. Chicago: University of Chicago Press.

Prell, Riv-Ellen. 2000. "Developmental Judaism: Challenging the Study of American Jewish Identity in the Social Sciences." *Contemporary Jewry* 21: 33–54.

———. 2003. "Rage and Representation: Jewish Gender Stereotypes in American Culture." In *American Jewish Women's History*, edited by Pamela S. Nadell, 238–255. New York: New York University Press.

Putnam, Robert D. 2000. *Bowling Alone: The Collapse and Revival of American Community*. New York: Simon and Schuster.

Putnam, Robert D., and David E. Campbell. 2010. *American Grace: How Religion Divides and Unites Us*. New York: Simon and Schuster.

Radcliffe, Sarah Chana. 1991. *Akeres Habayis: Realizing Your Potential as a Jewish Homemaker*. Southfield, Mich.: Targum.

Rawidowicz, Simon. 1986. *Israel, the Ever-Dying People, and Other Essays*, edited by Benjamin C. I. Ravid. Rutherford, N.J.: Fairleigh Dickinson University Press.

"Reform Rabbis Unanimously Back Israel Assault on PLO in Lebanon: Defer Decision on 'Jewish Fatherhood.'" 1982, July 11. *New York Jewish Week*, 3.

"Report Studies Intermarriage." 1979, January 26. *Omaha Jewish Press*, 11.

Reuben, Steven Carr. 1992. *Raising Jewish Children in a Contemporary World: The Modern Parent's Guide to Creating a Jewish Home*. Rocklin, Calif.: Prima.

Roof, Wade Clark. 1993. *A Generation of Seekers: The Spiritual Journeys of the Baby Boom Generation*. New York: HarperCollins.

Rose, Anne C. 2001. *Beloved Strangers: Interfaith Families in Nineteenth Century America*. Cambridge, Mass.: Harvard University Press.

Rosenbaum, Mary Heléne, and Stanley Ned Rosenbaum. [1994] 1999. *Celebrating Our Differences: Living Two Faiths in One Marriage*. Boston, Ky.: Ragged Edge.

Rosenblatt, Gary. 1973, December 8. "False 'Rabbis' May Face Criminal Charges: Sharp Practices Are Uncovered in Inter-faith Wedding Rites." *New York Jewish Week*, 6.

Rosenfeld, Michael J., and Byung-Soo Kim. 2005. "The Independence of Young Adults and the Rise of Interracial and Same Sex Unions." *American Sociological Review* 70, no. 4: 541–562.

Rutten, Tim. 2007, October 13. "Regarding Media: Comment Too Perilous to Ignore." *Los Angeles Times*, E1.

Sarna, Jonathan. 1993. "Marshall Sklare: In Memory." *Contemporary Jewry* 14: 3–7.

———. 1994, October. "The Secret of Jewish Continuity." *Commentary*, 55–58.

———. 2004. *American Judaism: A History*. New Haven, Conn.: Yale University Press.

Saxe, Leonard, Charles Kadushin, and Benjamin Phillips. 2006, November 21. "Boston's Good News on Intermarriage." *The Jewish Week*. bir.brandeis.edu/handle/10192/23003./. Accessed April 12, 2013.

Scheindlin, Raymond P. 1998. *A Short History of the Jewish People: From Legendary Times to Modern Statehood*. New York: Oxford University Press.

Schneider, David M. [1968] 1980. *American Kinship: A Cultural Account*. Chicago: University of Chicago Press.

Schnoor, Randal. 2006. "Being Gay and Jewish: Negotiating Intersecting Identities." *Sociology of Religion* 67, no. 1: 43–60.

Schwarzschild, Steven S., Saul Berman, and Menachem Elon. 2007. "Noachide Laws." In *Encyclopaedia Judaica*, edited by Michael Berenbaum and Fred Skolnik, 2nd ed., 15:284–287. Detroit: Macmillan Reference.

Seeman, Don. 2004. "Otherwise Than Meaning: On the Generosity of Ritual." *Social Analysis* 48, no. 2: 55–71.

Sered, Susan Starr. 1992. *Women as Ritual Experts: The Religious Lives of Elderly Jewish Women in Jerusalem*. New York: Oxford University Press.

Shokeid, Moshe. 2002. *A Gay Synagogue in New York*. Philadelphia: University of Pennsylvania Press.

Shore, Bradd. 2005. "American Middle-Class Families: Class, Social Reproduction, and Ritual." In *Family Transformed: Religion, Values, and Society in American Life*, edited by Steven M. Tipton and John Witte, Jr., 185–207. Washington, D.C.: Georgetown University Press.

Silverstein, Alan. 1995a. *It All Begins with a Date: Jewish Concerns about Intermarriage*. Northvale, N.J.: Aronson.

———. 1995b. *Preserving Jewishness in Your Family after Intermarriage Has Occurred*. Northvale, N.J.: Aronson.

Singer, David. 1979, July. "Living with Intermarriage." *Commentary*, 48–53.

Sklare, Marshall. 1964, April. "Intermarriage and the Jewish Future. *Commentary*, 51–58.

———. 1970, March. "Intermarriage and Jewish Survival." *Commentary*, 46–52.

Sollors, Werner. 1987. *Beyond Ethnicity: Consent and Descent in American Culture*. New York: Oxford University Press.

Soloveitchik, Joseph B. 1965. "The Lonely Man of Faith." *Tradition* 7: 5–67.

Sowell, Thomas. 1981. *Ethnic America*. New York: Basic Books.

Staub, Michael E. 2002. *Torn at the Roots: The Crisis of Jewish Liberalism in Postwar America*. New York: Columbia University Press.

Tenenbaum, Shelly, and Lynn Davidman. 2007. "It's in My Genes: Biological Discourse and Essentialist Views of Identity among Contemporary American Jews." *Sociological Quarterly* 48: 435–450.

Thompson, Jennifer. 2010. "Because Their Children Are Jewish." Interfaithfamily.com. Accessed May 16, 2013.

———. 2013. "'He Wouldn't Know Anything': Rethinking Women's Leadership." *Journal of the American Academy of Religion*. http://jaar.oxfordjournals.org/content/early/2013/04/24/jaarel.lft015.full. Accessed May 30, 2013.

Tigay, Chanan. 2006, January 5. "As Conservatives Question Halachah, Some Predict an Exodus to the Right." Jewish Telegraphic Agency. http://archive.jta.org/article/2006/01/05/2929928/as-conservatives-question-halachah-some-predict-an-exodus-to-the-right. Accessed April 12, 2013.

"Tips for Talking to Your Children about Interdating." 2013. Interfaithfamily.com. http://www.interfaithfamily.com/relationships/interdating/Tips_for_Talking_to_Your_Children_About_Interdating.shtml. Accessed April 12, 2013.

Tobin, Gary A. 1999. *Opening the Gates: How Proactive Conversion Can Revitalize the Jewish Community.* San Francisco: Jossey-Bass.

Tobin, Gary A., and Katherine G. Simon. 1999. *Rabbis Talk about Intermarriage.* San Francisco: Institute for Jewish and Community Research.

Troeltsch, Ernst. [1931] 1992. *The Social Teaching of the Christian Churches.* Translated by Olive Wyon. Louisville, Ky.: Westminster John Knox.

Tugend, Tom. 2003, April 14. "A Unified Conversion Process in L.A." Jewish Telegraphic Agency. http://www.jta.org/news/article/2003/04/14/10157/InLApromiseto. Accessed April 13, 2013.

"2-Day Conference to Explore Threat to Jewish Survival." 1976, December 4. *New York Jewish Week,* 9.

Ukeles Associates. 2007. *Jewish Community Centennial Study of Greater Atlanta 2006: Final Report.* Atlanta: Jewish Federation of Greater Atlanta.

Union for Reform Judaism. 2005. "Inviting Conversion: A Biennial Initiative." New York: Union for Reform Judaism. http://urj.org/cong/outreach/conversion/inviting/. Accessed March 26, 2010.

Verbit, Mervin. 1978. "Alternatives for a Viable Jewish Community." In *The Threat of Mixed Marriage: A Response,* edited by Sheldon Zimmerman and Barbara Trainin, 96–113. New York: Federation of Jewish Philanthropies.

Walzer, Michael. 1994. *Thick and Thin: Moral Argument at Home and Abroad.* Notre Dame, Ind.: University of Notre Dame Press.

Waters, Mary. 1998. "The Costs of a Costless Community." In *New Tribalisms: The Resurgence of Race and Ethnicity,* edited by Michael Hughey, 273–295. New York: New York University Press.

Weiss, Vikki, and Jennifer A. Block. 2000. *What to Do When You're Dating a Jew: Everything You Need to Know From Matzah Balls to Marriage.* New York: Random House.

Welter, Barbara. 1966. "The Cult of True Womanhood, 1820–1860." *American Quarterly* 18: 151–174.

Wertheimer, Jack. 1993. *A People Divided: Judaism in Contemporary America.* New York: Basic Books.

_____. 1994, January. "Family Values and the Jews." *Commentary,* 30–34.

_____. 2001, March. "Surrendering to Intermarriage." *Commentary,* 25–32.

_____. 2009, September 23. "Time for Straight-Talk about Assimilation." *Jewish Daily Forward.* http://forward.com/articles/114911/time-for-straight-talk-about-assimilation/. Accessed April 8, 2013.

Wertheimer, Jack, and Adam Bronfman. 2009, October 21. "Straight-Talk about Assimilation: An Exchange." *Jewish Daily Forward.* http://forward.com/articles/117307/straight-talk-about-assimilation-an-exchange/. Accessed April 8, 2013.

Wiener, Julie. 2001, November 14. "Jewish Identity a Top Priority." Jewish Telegraphic Agency. http://www.jta.org/news/article/2001/11/14/8173/DespitenewneedsJ. Accessed April 12, 2013.

Wiener, Robert. 2007, October 18. "Coulter Shock." *Jewish News.* http://www.njjewishnews.com/njjn.com/101807/njCoulterShock.html. Accessed April 12, 2013.

WIN–Gallup International. 2012, July 27. Global Index of Religiosity and Atheism. Zurich: *WIN-Gallup International.* http://www.wingia.com/web/files/news/14/file/14.pdf. Accessed April 8, 2013.

Witchel, Alex. 2001, January 14. "Counterintelligence: What's So Funny about the 'Coffee Talk' Lady." *New York Times*. www.nytimes.com/2001/01/04/style/counterintellegence-what-s-so-funny-about-the-coffee-talk-lady.html. Accessed May 16, 2013.

Wuthnow, Robert. 1998. *Loose Connections: Joining Together in America's Fragmented Communities*. Cambridge, Mass.: Harvard University Press.

Yaffe, Richard. 1977, January 15. "Equality for Fathers? Russian Mixed Multitude and Ruth's Conversion Cited in Halacha Issue." *New York Jewish Week*, 27.

Yamane, David. 1997. "Secularization on Trial: In Defense of a Neosecularization Paradigm." *Journal for the Scientific Study of Religion* 36: 109–122.

INDEX

195

ABOUT THE AUTHOR

JENNIFER A. THOMPSON is the Maurice Amado Assistant Professor of Applied Jewish Ethics and Civic Engagement at California State University, Northridge. She previously taught at Drake University in Des Moines, Iowa. She earned her Ph.D. in 2010 from the Ethics and Society Program of the Graduate Division of Religion at Emory University in Atlanta.